Northern Lights

Northern Lights

A Poet's Sources

GEORGE MACKAY BROWN

Edited by Archie Bevan and Brian Murray

JOHN MURRAY
Albemarle Street, London

A catalogue record for this book is available from the British Library

ISBN 0–7195–5949 9

Typeset in 11/13pt Monotype Ehrhardt by Servis Filmsetting Ltd

Printed and bound in Great Britain by the University Press Cambridge

CONTENTS

Contents

Contents

Contents

As I came home from Sandwick
 A star was in the sky
The northern lights above the hill
 Were streaming broad and high.
The tinkers lit their glimmering fires,
 Their tents were pitched close by.
But the city of the vanished race
Lay dark and silent in that place.
 As I came home from Sandwick
 A star was in the sky.

(From 'The Road Home', 1946.
The city of the vanished race is Skara Brae.)

The Arctic girl is out tonight.
(Come to the doors.)
She dances
In a coat of yellow and green patches.
She bends
Over the gate of the stars.

What is she, a tinker lass?
Does she carry flashing cans
From the quarry fires?

I think
She's a princess in a silk gown.
She holds (turning)
A bowl of green cut crystal.

Come to the doors!
She is walking about in the north, the winter witch.

(From 'Seal Island Anthology, 1875'
in Selected Poems, 1954–1992, 1996)

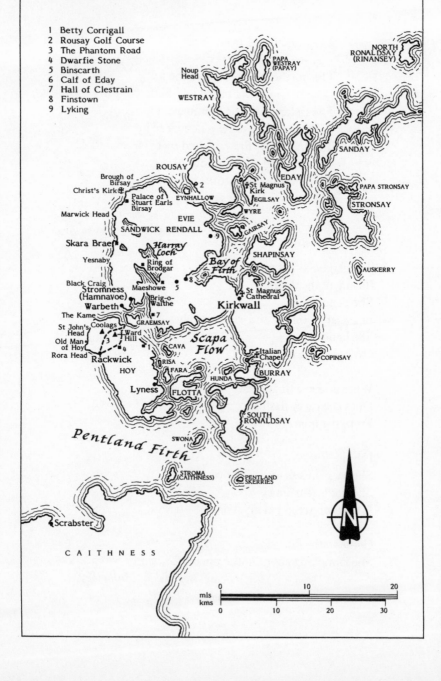

ORKNEY

1 Betty Corrigall
2 Rousay Golf Course
3 The Phantom Road
4 Dwarfie Stone
5 Binscarth
6 Calf of Eday
7 Hall of Clestrain
8 Finstown
9 Lyking

NORTH RONALDSAY (RINANSEY)

PAPA WESTRAY (PAPAY)

Noup Head

WESTRAY

SANDAY

ROUSAY

Brough of Birsay

Christ's Kirk

St Magnus Kirk

EGILSAY

PAPA STRONSAY

EDAY

STRONSAY

Palace of Stuart Earls Birsay

EYNHALLOW

WYRE

Marwick Head

EVIE

RENDALL

GAIRSAY

SANDWICK

Skara Brae

Harray Loch

AUSKERRY

SHAPINSAY

Yesnaby

Ring of Brodgar

Bay of Firth

Maeshowe 5

Black Craig

Stromness (Hamnavoe)

Brig-o-Walthe

St Magnus Cathedral

Warbeth

The Kame

GRAEMSAY

Kirkwall

St John's Head

Coolags

Ward Hill

Old Man of Hoy

Rackwick

CAVA

Scapa Flow

Rora Head

RISA

Italian Chapel

COPINSAY

HOY

FARA

HUNDA

BURRAY

Lyness

FLOTTA

SOUTH RONALDSAY

Pentland Firth

SWONA

STROMA (CAITHNESS)

PENTLAND SKERRIES

Scrabster

N

CAITHNESS

mls
kms

0   10   20
0   10   20   30

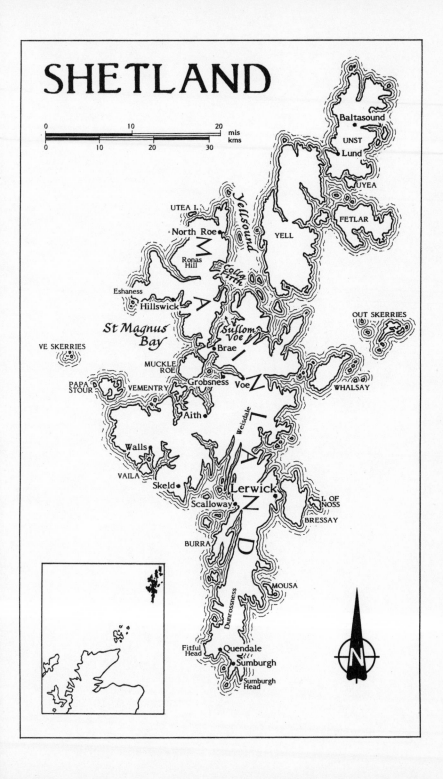

SHETLAND

0   10   20   mls
                             kms
0   10   20   30

Baltasound
UNST
Lund
UYEA
FETLAR
YELL
UTEA I.
North Roe
Yellsound
M
Ronas
Hill
Colla
firth
Eshaness
Hillswick
Sullom
Voe
OUT SKERRIES
St Magnus
Bay
Brae
A
VE SKERRIES
MUCKLE
ROE
PAPA
STOUR
VEMENTRY
Grobsness
Voe
WHALSAY
I
Aith
N
Weisdale
Walls
VAILA
Skeld
Lerwick
L OF
NOSS
A
Scalloway
BRESSAY
BURRA
D
MOUSA
Dunrossness
Fitful
Head
Quendale
Sumburgh
Sumburgh
Head
N

Enchantment of Islands:
A Poet's Sources

A POET COULD not choose a better place to be born than a group of islands, like Orkney.

I know there are city poets, but their craft must be difficult, and will be ever more difficult as time passes. Is it possible to write good verse about unceasing streams of traffic, AIDS, proliferating pollution, tower blocks? Even in the distant past, London poets like Shakespeare, Chaucer, Keats, had to turn to the countryside for refreshment and fulfilment.

Islands have always been enchanted places. In Orkney, since the retreat of the Ice Age, little boats have gone out to catch haddock and lobster. The same men, at plough-time and harvest, have had to turn their backs on the dangerous provident sea to consider the urgencies of hunger and bread. Women kept fires going, drew water from the wells, spun wool, made butter and cheese, reared families. Among the hills, shepherds dug ewes from the lambing snows.

Such people, such ritual, generation by generation, are the stuff of poetry. The places where the folk come together – smithy, inn, kirk, cattle market – become little theatres of poetry. Foreign ships anchor in the bays – ships, cargo-laden, are wrecked in winter storm. A wild stir of excitement goes through the community. There are lanterns, at midnight, along the tide mark.

Young men go to sea, to the Greenland whaling or the American colonies. Sometimes they are never heard of again; sometimes they come home with fortunes, and buy farms or big houses. They have stories of faraway places to add to a legend that had its beginnings in the Stone Age (whose megaliths and tombs and sand-buried villages are everywhere in Orkney).

A poet is wealthy indeed who has such a store of symbols to draw upon. (If I had been born in Birmingham, for example, I would know that any creativity in me would be impoverished from the start, perhaps fatally.)

But, even so, the time is running out. The culture of the cities is everywhere taking root in Orkney. Cars have become a nuisance, even here. The air is polluted with mindless berserker pop music from

3

transistors, as well as with exhaust fumes. Instead of listening to the stories on winter nights, people read the *Sun*. The horses of Edwin Muir's poetry have all but vanished. The sea is emptying of fish. An old man dies, and a store of unique experience is lost for ever.

Sometimes I see my task, as poet and storyteller, to rescue the centuries' treasure before it is too late. It is as though the past is a great ship that has gone ashore, and archivist and writer must gather as much of the rich squandered cargo as they can.

The ethos and outlook of the islanders have changed greatly since I was a child. People are more prosperous, but the community spirit has everywhere slackened, and the language becomes increasingly impoverished. But sea and islands and hills are still there, and I am thankful that I saw those everlasting things with a child's eye, and the vivid people who lived among them, and their ancient benign rituals.

My poetry is a memory and a celebration of such things.

July–October 1993

Under Brinkie's Brae: Wheel of the Year

JANUARY

The Pirate and his Sweetheart

Mrs Gordon was to give a reception to the master of *The George*, the fine ship anchored in front of the Holms two days now.

It was not that Mr and Mrs Gordon gave a dinner to all the ships' masters who called at Hamnavoe – that would have been too much – but the master of *The George* had exchanged respects with one or two of the village's leading merchants at the water-front, and – lo and behold! – the man had turned out to be a son of William Gow, lately (until his death) a respectable merchant in the town; the ship-master had gone away to sea, like many another Orkney boy, twelve years before, and nothing had been heard of him since . . . This was no uncommon thing, though: young men were lost in foreign seas, or they were carried off with scurvy or typhoid, or it may be that they settled down in Leith or Liverpool or London with a wife and saw no chance of getting back to Orkney again. Write a letter? Few sailors in those days could read or write. The only chance of communicating would be if they saw some ship Orkney-bound in a harbour some-where, and could get word with any Orkneyman who happened to be on board.

But this was a bit strange – young John Gow had had as good an education as his father could afford. He had sat in the same classroom as some of the sons of the Orkney gentry – James Fea of Eday, for example . . . There was no reason why John Gow couldn't have written home to tell his father how fortune was dealing with him on the great oceans of the world.

But let that be, meantime. Over the dinner table in the evening Captain Gow would have many exciting things to impart to them, no doubt.

Mrs Gordon's servants were polishing the silver. A large plump salmon was being prepared in the kitchen, and a joint of best lamb. Mr James Gordon had gone to visit a fellow merchant along the muddy street – for it was deep winter, January, and sleet and flung spindrift during the recent storm had made the street a quagmire – the merchant Mr Gordon was calling on had the best stock in Orkney of French brandies and wines, and Hollands-gin (all lately smuggled).

There was a young daughter of the house, but her parents considered her too fine a girl to soil her hands with kitchen work. Thora Gordon sat in her room and sometimes tinkled on the clavichord and sometimes worked at her embroidery frame. In due course, sooner rather than later, a husband would have to be found for the girl, the hard-working son of some local merchant, or one of the better-off farmers from round about.

There would be no question of marrying her off to a Kirkwall man – at that time relations between Kirkwall and Hamnavoe were not at all harmonious. It all came down to the question of Kirkwall's commercial authority over Stromness. There would be hard inter-town battles to be fought in the law-courts soon.

Now, the lamps being lit, everything was ready to receive Captain Gow.

There was a knock at the door.

Host and guest greeted each other cordially. Mrs Gordon glimpsed for the first time a dark handsome face. She saw at once that he was charming and courteous – and yet there was something about him that she didn't altogether take to: a hidden furtive dangerous desperate quality. How could this be?

Meantime there was a flutter on the stair. Miss Thora was descending in her fine blue satin gown.

When she saw the sailor she gasped in wonderment.

*

And this is the beginning of the tragic tale of John Gow the pirate and his sweetheart Miss Gordon, in that fatal year of 1726.*

30 January 1992

---

* When Gow's pirate ship stranded on the Calf of Eday, he was taken prisoner by James Fea, handed over to the authorities, and tried and hanged at Wapping in 1726.

A Ballad of Gow the Pirate

One tree in the garden, Mister
William Gow, merchant in Hamnavoe.
Water the apple-tree, John.
The boy hides among summer leaves.

One tree in the school, Mister
Clouston, dominie: his desk.
'Navis' – ship – decline that, boy.
Ocean branched, many streams, through Gow.

One tree off Sicily, Monsieur
Ferneau, master: his keel.
The arms-chest key, keep it, John.
Smoke, flame, a ball in the Frenchman's skull.

One tree in the Bailey, Mister
Justice Bigwig there: his bench.
Gallows, chains, tar at Wapping.
Night, tree of stars, over Marshalsea.

A bare tree at Thames-side, Mister
Jack Ketch, gallowsman.
Fiddles, broadsheets, bottles of gin.
The boy bites on the salt apple.

14 June 1989

A January Day: Burns

They've blown our coats about, those wandering
Westerlies, since Hogmanay; now and then
   Gesturing to the Pole, and then
   Small artilleries of hail

Stotter on the skylight, and once
North-seeking still, the noon darkened
    With a broken snow-cloud,
    A too deep dazzlement, then.

Masques of the January moon –
Ice sliver, silver gondola, crystal
    Cygnet, till the queen
    Holds the complete orb.

The pauper sun ventures a few steps
Further, east and west, at day's
    Rising and setting – another masquer
    With a gold coin in his rags.

Ancient bard, I too went a few steps
From flames and books to find again
    Under that clatter-tongue of weathers
    The lovely task of winter.

There, under a skeleton sycamore
– above the sea – a cluster of snowdrops,
    Children of snow and sun
    Who must die before the lark sings.

I thought of the immortal
January makar, created (it seems)
    To hammer out winter's worst
    For hansel of delight to a dour folk.
                              24 January 1995

January the Twenty-fifth

I

The old men said the name Robbie Burns
    As if he'd farmed
Very recently, in Cairston or Stenness or Hoy.

What a man, what a man! they said
    Shaking their heads, smiling.
    What a man for the drink!
What a man for the lasses!

It was of utmost importance
    That Robbie was a poor man
Like themselves: a toil-bent farmer.

There might be a Barleycorn pause
    Between a quote and a stave of song.
The women, they never seemed
    To give a moment's thought to that poet.

II

The Hamnavoe kids groaned inwardly. There
    On their open books
Was a new poem nailed to the page
    To A Mouse:
    'To be learned by heart,' said the teacher.

Words like thistles and thorns
They ploughed through the winter language
    And pity ran for cover
    This way and this, and entered
A few small cold wondering hearts.

III

They moved in the schoolroom
    Among heroic images,

The Bruce at Bannockburn under the shouting castles

Mary Queen of Scots
   Inside that English castle
   First in her black gown, then the red,
   Then block and axe and blood.

Bonny Prince Charlie at Holyrood, dancing –
   On the rainlashed moor
   Turning a horse's head into the west –
   An old broken king at the brandy bottle
   In a foreign castle.

Now this ploughman shaken with song and love
   Among stones and furrows.

IV

There was another hero, more marvellous even
   Than Bruce or Burns.

He too died in the glory of the field
   Young and beautiful
   John Thomson, goalkeeper of Celtic.
For the boys of Hamnavoe
Football was war, was magic and chant.
A star glittered and went out.

V

At last, into one council house
   A wonder was brought:
   A wireless set, with wet battery and dry battery.

Better than Henry Hall's dance-band
Better than *Murder in the Red Barn*
Better than Toytown and Larry the lamb
   Was that January torrent of sound, teatime to bedtime.
   'Bonny Mary o' Argyle', 'Tam o'Shanter'

A heuch of pipes,
A trenching of haggis, reek of whisky,
The lass in the cornrigs, the lady
In the Potter-row.
In Dumfries, a debt-ridden deathbed,
The Allowa cottage with snowflakes seeking in.

VI

Not one of the fishermen
Not a single sailor, or farmer
   With sea-light in his eyes

Thought it strange, on 25 January,
   That Burns hardly mentions the sea.
'The wan moon sets beyond the white wave
And time is setting with me – Oh' . . . Only that

All was forgiven the great lover
   Of lasses, cornstalks, liberty
   In the Hamnavoe doorways of herringscales
      And salt fish.

VII

A tinker leaned on the Smithfield bar,
In Dounby (Hamnavoe
   Had no pubs in the time of the kids of fable).

Is Burns still alive? said the tinker.
The tavern was shaken with mockery and mirth
And maybe the tinker went back,
   Ashamed, to the fire in the quarry.

There was no need, wanderer.
   Stand a moment
   There, on the brae: under the white star.
               27 January 1990

FEBRUARY

Stromness and the Nor'Wast

It was a great time when the whalers returned from Davis Straits and other points nor'wast in the nineteenth century.

I have just been dipping into Sir Walter Scott's journal of his trip round the northern and western isles in 1814, in the lighthouse yacht.

The yacht was anchored off Lerwick when the whaling ships were home after their perilous whale-hunt that summer. The whale-men had plenty of money. They hadn't seen drink or girls or green hills for long months among the ice floes and the threshing whales. So they went wild in Lerwick, and the Sheriff of Zetland (one of Sir Walter's shipmates on the trip) had a few of the whalers to deal with – so interrupting what was, after all, a kind of holiday for the sheriffs who were also *ipso facto*, lighthouse commissioners.

Roughly the same boisterous on-goings happened when the whaling ships arrived in Stromness. I have read somewhere that respectable citizens were issued with truncheons to defend themselves and their property from the wild men from the whaling grounds. All those pubs and ale-houses in Stromness – think how the proprietors must have unlocked their doors in trepidation on the morning when the whale-men were rowed ashore – in trepidation mingled with keen anticipation, because the harpoonists and flensers had plenty of silver to splash around, and the barrels of ale from Stromness brewery were in fine late-summer ripeness.

The names of most of those vanished ale-houses are lost. But many of them must have had signs over the door. I remember the fisherman John Folster, a contemporary of my father, telling me that he had seen some of those painted signs, some with scenes on them. I expect they were put into the ash–cart or broken up for firewood. Imagine, if the signs all existed, what a display they would have made in the Pier Arts

14

Centre! In a story, I called one of those pubs 'The Arctic Whaler', but that was a pure invention.

In a strange mood – a mingling of dread and greed – the proprietor of the Arctic Whaler unlocked his door on the morning that the whaling fleet was sighted sailing through Hoy Sound. And a stir of excitement went through the young men and girls of Hamnavoe. And the merchants put their truncheons in a niche under the counter, where they could easily be reached. (There were no policemen in those days – every householder was his own 'keeper of the peace'.) The fleet had anchored. There was a barbarous shouting from the ships!

*

But it wasn't always so. There is the terrible story of the whaling ship *Dee* of Aberdeen, locked up the whole winter in the Arctic ice. When finally she broke through, next spring, most of her crew were dead or dying.

Among them was a young Harrayman from the croft of Handest, Adam Flett. Among the suffering and death among the ice that winter, Adam Flett had the mother-wit to keep himself fit by running in that white world every day. He was one of the few survivors to be brought to the improvised hospital in Alfred Place; spectral mariners like those in the 'Ancient Mariner' . . . Adam Flett went home to Harray and lived to be an old man.

*

Such tragic whale-hunts were rare – such terrible landfalls in Stromness. It was mostly broken staves in ale-barrels – respectable ladies keeping their doors locked for a day or two – a flirtation or two – Bessie Millie waiting for the skippers to come up Brinkie's Brae with their sixpences.*

15 July 1993

---

*Bessie Millie sold favourable winds to sea captains from her hovel on Brinkie's Brae.

John Rae and Sir John Franklin

Sir John Franklin's two ships, *Erebus* and *Terror*, left Stromness in 1845 on Arctic exploration, and were never seen again . . .

John Rae was in every way a remarkable man. He had been born in 1813 at the Hall of Clestrain, near Stromness. In his boyhood, as he lingered at the corners of the Stromness piers and heard the yarns of the old sailor men, his imagination had been quickened by stories of the great white spaces of the north-west. As soon as he became a doctor in Edinburgh he signed on as ship surgeon aboard the Hudson's Bay Company vessel *Prince of Wales*, sailing to Moose Factory. Thereafter his fate was bound up for ever with the unexplored regions of Canada's frozen north.

The highlight of his career was when he discovered the fate of Sir John Franklin's lost expedition. It was then that Rae's name, for a few weeks, was on the lips of all Britishers. The people of Stromness were the last folk in Europe to see Franklin's ships sailing west. It is a rather curious coincidence that John Rae, a man born within sight of Stromness, should be the man to discover from the native Indians and Esquimaux how Franklin and his men died.

c. 1950

Ships in the Ice

I

'The purpose of which voyage shall be: to discover a north-west passage by sea betwixt the oceans, for the furtherance of trade and the enhancement of her majesty's empire'

South-east wind, overcast, out of Gravesend. Bearing north, between dawn and the Longstone light.

The Forth. Two men committed to the courts for drunkenness. A seaman missing. Another taken from the stews.

Our mother the sea, receive us. Who bears, nourishes, chastises. The cold gray mother.

The Orkneys. A pilot: fierce whiskers, rum, pipe-spittle. Upthrust of Hoy, blue shoulders. Herring boats. Cairston, a wide bay. Hamnavoe and 38 howffs.

'Dear one, the only comfort I have in this bare place is to write to you and so I comfort myself and long for you. I carry your dear gift of linen in my sea-chest.'

The White Horse Inn. A whale-man turned away from our questions.

And north and west. Congregation of waters, a lamentation and a gossiping, unfathomed endless utterances, sisterhood of the sea. The North Atlantic.

The green heart of icebergs. Green and black undersea fires. The ice roared. Gray shuffling packs, the ice moved in behind us.

Here a man is as nature intended. Naked he goes among mirrors of ice. Furled to the eyes, but naked, among prisms and mirrors. He walks on a solid sea. Ice is everything. – A man eats ice.

'Gentlemen, nothing remains for us, in these unfortunate unlooked-for circumstances, but to leave the ship and trek south. There are communities of Esquimaux all down the coast. Take your guns and powder. Be of a good heart . . .'

Spalding died. Gregor can walk no further. (Leave him now.) Trewick saw a piece of Cornwall in the snow: a spire, rosebushes. We left Simpson to the bears. One knelt, a flash in the hand, turned away: had white and red stuff in his mouth afterwards.

Alone, on wrapped feet. Emerald, onyx, garnet burn. This is an enchanted city. I go through the street of the jewellers. A diamond blazes.

September 1972

II

John Rae and his Orkneymen discover the fate of the Franklin
Expedition, 1850

West and north. No people for six days,
Then a Russian.
He spoke with eyes and hands.
The great captain had found a way through. No doubt
The captain sat in high honour
Either at the court of the Mongols, or in Siam.
He chewed an offered cut of tobacco.
There was nothing to the east (he said) –
A broken green river, an ice-mill.
A wild goose that night
Rained down fat into the flames.

One morning the snow lay, a knife
Across Folster's face.
Head blanketed, he stumbled after.
A gun, north or west,
Shattered the huge crystal. Feathers, blood
Drifted on snow.
An Eskimo boy, a shadow
Passed the fire. And returned, closer,
Then left. At midnight
The sky was blue and green fountains of crystal.

The Eskimo boy was suddenly there, smiling.
He had something to show.
In his own time, after a hundred smiles.
Bread-eaters? Two ships, ice-bound?
He had no knowledge (smiling).
Had heard of the 'gray troop of ghosts'.
Then from his wolf-coat offered
A blue ribbon (Order of Hanover)
Coins, a silver fork crested 'J.F.'

In the village, no information.
We must first sit at a fish-board
Lit with smiles.
All left, smiling, soon, but an old one.
In the House of Ice (he said)
Iron and oak are frail flowers, bone
Is subtle and lasting.
Our elements came kindly about the strangers.
Birds, fish offered help.
They could not understand. The greeting
Withered in the air.
They could not reply, *Come goose.*
Come, caribou. Come, wolf. Come snow-bird.
They were ghosts before death,
One after another, drifting
In bright and dark circles, untrysted.
We watched, just under the horizon.

They smiled. We faced south.
(I had put a knife in sea boils,
Drawn twelve teeth,
Given hot whisky for belly-ache and cough.)
Down the white ringing map
We strode on to trees and trains,
To ordered stones
Where is no pure tryst of the creatures.
The same Indian woman
In Mackenzie's store, chewing tobacco,
Asked, stone-faced, had we found the heroes?

Guns, here and there, before hunger,
Shattered the crystal.
Birds, twitching, thudded on snow.
Corrigal said at the last fire,
'In Hamnavoe, tonight
Oatmeal and whisky in the White Horse.
I see a fisherman's wife

Waiting at a draughty close-end.
She is taken with bitter sea-thoughts.'

1979

Snow: From a Hospital

Best leave the paper blank.
If you must write,
Imitate old smiling Chinamen.
They scribbled on silk,
Three arrows in a corner (trees),
A broken diagonal
And February's dyke is full.

This is the snow for me –
My bronchial tree loaded and loud
With the white birds of winter.

They come from Venus, Orion, Betelgeuse,
Such unearthly cargoes!
Now wrecked here,
The innumerable shining bales are too much.
What can we do with such delicacy?
Our coarse eyes long for grass, stone, puddle.

Winds like the hands of Penelope
Forever weave
Web after web of snow.
When will Odysseus come, the golden hero?
After the ploughman, sower, harvester.

This snow is like time in its youth.
Against that light
Tinkers are blacker and fiercer,
Birds hungrier,

What so bright as apples and stars and children!
But the swan is jealous.
She pushes her dingy breast over the loch
To find some blue.

How clumsy and endearing he is,
The snowman,
A flocculent teddy bear.
But I tell you, friends,
He's not what he seems to be.
This February
His claws tore my chest open.

1968

MARCH

Bombs at the Brig-o-Waithe

There was one March evening – a Saturday – fifty-four years ago, when we were treated to a Wagnerian drama in the skies over Orkney.

The women of Stromness were doing their shopping along the street. In the Town Hall, now the Youth Hostel in Hellihole Road, the usual crowd were watching a film. There must have been a few golfers at Ness in the fading light. I was sitting at home in Well Park, probably reading a book.

The air-raid sirens began their banshee wailing . . . We didn't pay much attention. There had been air-raid warnings before, and nothing happened. But this Saturday night the dogs of war were suddenly in full cry. The hunt was up.

The sky over Orkney, in the first twilight, was in pandemonium. Guns flashed and thundered from all around Scapa Flow. Every bursting shell left a little puff of smoke. From end to end of Orkney, it seemed, searchlights raked the sky, shifting here and there, probing for the German bombers. We did not see the attackers, but we could hear them; their engines made a peculiar noise, an undulating moan, quite different from the steady drone of the RAF fighters.

Of course we ought all to have gone at once to the air-raid shelters. There was one twenty yards from our door. The air-raid wardens were generally there to make sure you followed the rules. We were certainly not meant to watch all this tumult and fury in the skies from our back doors. But I remember standing watching the unfolding drama over Scapa Flow. The noise of the anti-aircraft guns intensified, the sky was full of clusters of puff-balls. As darkness fell, the searchlights criss-crossed ever more brightly. Among it all came the sinister undulating drone of the German bombers.

I don't know how long it lasted – an hour maybe. It was all intense thrilling drama to us young people. Finally, the guns fell silent. The searchlights ceased their scything of the stars. We heard no more from the German bombers. The biggest air raid we had experienced thus far in the war was over.

Later that night we heard rumours that bombs had been dropped at Brig-o-Waithe in Stenness.

The following day, Sunday, was a good spring day. A group of us boys walked over Cairston to Brig-o-Waithe. Now we knew for sure that a man from that hamlet, John Isbister, had been killed, and another, the well-known character Willie Farquhar, had been wounded. Here and there we found the tail-fins of incendiary bombs. We concluded that a German plane, hurrying to escape from that net of searchlights and shells, had jettisoned its load before hastening home over the North Sea.

But, possibly next evening, William Joyce ('Lord Haw-Haw') announced over the German propaganda radio – aimed at British listeners – that the Luftwaffe had successfully bombed an aerodrome in the Orkneys.

Could it be that one of the fields of Howe, in the immediate vicinity of Brig-o-Waithe, that had been a landing place for planes (civil) some years before, was still marked on German maps as an airport?

There were a few more raids until 1941, but the raid of March, 1940 was by far the most spectacular.

31 March 1994

The First Daffodil: A Tinker Wife

Dead grass whispers under my feet.
I am going from croft to farm
    With my pack – needles, cotton reels,
    Tin mugs, cheap hankies.

I am going past dog-barkings,
Mockery of a bairn, a tree
    Of starlings shaken like a bell.
    Sometimes a farm lass

Buys a trinket, often enough
I'm given the hard door, but
    A kind one here and there
    Pours me a mug of tea.

(I can tell their fortunes too. A few
Suffer a heartfall when I frown.)
    Dead dry grass between the crofts
    Of Quoy and Seatter,

But last month my boots squelched mud
Along that track. On Greenay side
    Boys are lighting fires
    – the muirburn – to clean the hill

Of winter's dregs. Sit in the ditch,
Old woman, sit in the ditch.
    Strike match into pipe. Another flame
    In the wind, over there, a March daffodil.

December 1995

The Harrowing of Hell

He went down the first step.
His lantern shone like the morning star.
Down and round he went
Clothed in his five wounds.

Solomon whose coat was like daffodils
Came out of the shadows.
He kissed Wisdom there, on the second step.

The boy whose mouth had been filled with harp–songs,
The shepherd king
Gave, on the third step, his purest cry.

At the root of the Tree of Man, an urn
With dust of apple-blossom

Joseph, harvest-dreamer, counsellor of pharaohs
Stood on the fourth step.
He blessed the lingering Bread of Life.

He who had wrestled with an angel,
The third of the chosen,
Hailed the King of Angels on the fifth step.

Abel with his flute and fleeces
Who bore the first wound
Came to the sixth step with his pastorals.

On the seventh step down
The tall primal dust
Turned with a cry from digging and delving.

Tomorrow the Son of Man will walk in a garden
Through drifts of apple-blossom.

April 1996

APRIL

St Magnus Day

Today, 16 April, is St Magnus Day.

In these 'enlightened times' St Magnus Day means nothing. For our ancestors, it was a day of feast and rejoicing (even though it involved a very dark plot and a cold-blooded murder).

Did Earl Magnus know he was sailing to his death that Easter Day, on Egilsay? Nine centuries ago, particular attention was paid to omens. Sailing to Egilsay – from Shetland, future researchers may show – a wave rose out of a calm sea and drenched Magnus and his men.

Once the two peace ships of Magnus got to Egilsay, it wasn't long before the men knew they had walked into a trap. For his cousin Earl Hakon arrived with a fleet of eight ships, and Hakon's men weren't singing psalms when they waded ashore and spread out over the island. I imagine the Egilsay folk retired indoors and barred and shuttered their houses.

A man is walking alone under the first star, among the rockpools of Egilsay.

On the other side of the island, Earl Hakon's men are enjoying a good supper of beef and fish, bread and ale. But their lord, Earl Hakon, eats little. He can't join in the songs and laughter. He is almost as lonely as his cousin Earl Magnus.

Lifolf the cook has a busy time of it. The revellers are still wanting their plates and ale-horns filled at midnight.

Meantime, the Egilsay priest, looking into his church to see that all is well, notices a solitary figure up near the altar. The priest can't tell, by the light of his lantern, who or what the kneeling man is. Between midnight and dawn is the coldest time. The priest closes the door and leaves the church. It is now 16 April. Easter Monday.

The sleep of the island is soon broken. Earl Hakon's men are searching everywhere for Earl Magnus. They hear he has been seen walking on the tide-mark the previous sunset. 'Come up,' they shout. 'Come out of the cave, coward! Show yourself' . . . They are a bold swaggering crew, having broken their fasts with beer and leftovers.

Nowhere – Magnus is nowhere to be seen in Egilsay . . .

Then they know that he is in the sanctuary of the church, where no man may be touched or harmed or taken. So they take their taunts to the open church door. And there he is indeed, inside.

And he rises to meet them.

'What's all the brawling and noise about?' Earl Magnus says; and even those rioters whom even their lord, Earl Hakon, couldn't control that morning, are struck by the cheerfulness of his voice and bearing.

'No need for all this rowdiness,' says Earl Magnus. 'We're all here in Egilsay for a peace conference. Is Hakon there? Tell him I'll be out at once for the peace meeting.'

By now he is in the door of the church. He looks to where the strong man, Earl Hakon Paulson his cousin, is standing at the edge of the crowd of armed men. And Hakon turns away; he dare not look him in the eye.

Everyone in Orkney – at least it is to be hoped so, for nowadays the great legends of the world are being forgotten – knows the rest of the story. The loaded negotiations there, in the barren centre of the island – the decision that only by the death of Magnus can peace come to Orkney – the refusal of Ofeig the standard-bearer to do the deed – the summoning of Lifolf, the harmless cook, away from his fire and stewpots to be the executioner. The cheerfulness of the condemned man, 'he was blithe as though he were bidden to a feast' – Magnus' blessing on his unwilling weeping executioner – Earl Hakon's ride to Paplay in Holm to tell (weeping himself, that strong man) the news to Earl Magnus' mother.

What did they think, the Egilsay folk, when the sound and the fury had died away and they could open their doors at last?

Before seed-time that spring, the news was known in the fishing hamlet of Hamnavoe. Another year or two, and the story was known and celebrated all over Western Europe.

16 April 1992

St Magnus

What road did you come, traveller
To this place?

At the first station
I had a white coat put on me, a silver ring.

I went with a psalter
Through the rage of a sea battle.

I ruled in turbulent islands,
Hakon my cousin and I.
We smoked pirates out of caves in Shetland.

There was this chessboard between
Red earl and black earl –
   Ruined crofts, breached boats,
   A people with gaunt faces.

Between Magnus and Hakon
How should dove wings fly out
And a hawk furl on a mailed fist?

I passed last night
In the kirk here in Egilsay.
   At dawn, an old priest said mass.

Now I have come to the last station,
This stone seems better to me
   Than my carved chair in Birsay.

A red martyr coat?
   Domine, non sum dignus

The butcher, Lifolf
Has come up, weeping, from the stewpots.

His axe is the key
For the unlocking of the door into light.

1995

Song for St Magnus: 16 April

I

Keeper of the red stone, remember well
   Sufferers today, those
   Who are to cross the dark firth,
   People in hospitals,
   In hospices, eventide lingerers,
Children who look at daffodils
   (Both with the dew on) each
   To break today in spring tempest.

II

Consider, Magnus, the fishermen
   From Noup Head to Rora,
   Those with a hundred creels,
The old man with two creels behind the Holms,
   Consider a stranger at the shore
Who is in need of ferrying.

III

An Icelander wrote on his skin
   Death is darkness
   Death is the cold skull
   Death is the bitter journey all men take
   Into silence, nothingness . . .
The skald wrote. Music
   Moved across the parchment.

The dancer fared on to the stone.

29

IV

What you suffer at the stone, it has all
Been fore-suffered.
    We sit in an assize of shadows. Evil
Must be atoned for.
Whispers, beyond ear-reach
    Load us with shame and terror.

Heroic one, comfort us, you
    Who have uncovered your head.

V

Magnus, friend, have a keeping
    Of the shepherd on the hill
    Whose ewes are having difficult birth
In the last snow.
Bestow peace to ploughmen in stony fields.

Be present at the fires
    Of women in Bosnia and Somalia
    Kneading dough smaller than fists.

Remember the Easter feast
    Your mother prepared in Holm
    You could not come to,
    Being finished with shadows.

The murderer came. He drank ale there, in Holm. He wept.

VI

Magnus, pray for priests
    In this time of hate
    (Never such hate and anger over the earth)

May they light candles at their altars
This day and all days
    Till history is steeped in light.

It was a cold night, your vigil
  In the kirk in Egilsay.

At dawn an old priest lit the paschal candle:
  Introibo ad altare Dei

VII

Never so many strangers at Orkney's doors
  'We need peace' . . .
  'We are sent here about the business of government' . . .
  'Our quest: silence and healing' . . .

The old ways are worn out
We turn our hands to work on other looms.

Our ancestors
  Beat down the doors of Pict and Celt,
The people of Magnus
  Broke the first curraghs,
  Choked sacred wells,
  Filled barn and byre with flames.

Magnus, give welcome to strangers.
  Their children
  Will sing with new voices, in April,
  The words from the Iceland parchment.

16 April 1993

William and Mareon Clark

There ought to be a big party, open-air at Graham Place or the pier-head, some time this year, because – if a date for the birth of Stromness has to be placed in some year – our town is 400 years old. Actually, in all fairness, the celebration ought to have been last year, 1995. But, better late than never.

In 1580 a feu charter was granted by Earl Robert Stewart to William Clark and his wife Mareon Chalmer, 'With power of brewing and selling, keiping of ostelrie and bying of al thingis appertening thairto for furnissing of the commounes and utheris resorting thair-away . . .' In the Bishopric Rental of 1595 appears the entry, 'William Clairkis house now bigged'.

And so, the town of Stromness might be said to have begun, with William Clark's inn, at the end of the blue tongue of sea that is Stromness harbour. There is not a stone of the inn left. It stood probably near where the new school is.

An inn is not built for a few fishing families and crofting families. They would have baked their own bread and brewed their own beer, and kept their own pigs and poultry. Who, then, were going to eat at the Clarks' table and sit round their fine new peat fire? Sailors, we must presume. And not only Scottish sailors, but the crews of French and Scandinavian and Dutch and Spanish ships seeking shelter from westerly gales. America had been discovered. Bigger ships with wider spreads of sail were abroad on the oceans of the world. Merchants and skippers reckoned on cargoes and fortunes their fathers had never dreamed of. Yes, it must have been common knowledge on the high seas that 'the shoreside of Stromness' was a good watering place.

And it was possible to get fresh fish and vegetables, beef and eggs and ale. But it took time to scour the countryside for those commodities, so welcome to men who had been at sea for weeks. Much more convenient to buy those provisions at an inn, a central gathering place. And oh! the joy of sitting at an open fire drinking good ale, and eating steaks and new-baked bread, to sailors weary of the heave and toss of the sea . . .

We must think that William and Mareon Clark's venture was a great success. The nearby farms, Garson and Hemmigar and Howe, would have been only too willing to stock the larders and cupboards of the new inn. And the fishermen of the growing hamlet of Hamnavoe would have brought their haddocks and lobsters. At the time of the lighting of the lamps with the ale barrel flowing well, Clarks' inn with all the foreign sailors would have been like a room in Babel . . . Let's hope they all got on with one another – though, alas, there must have been a brawl or two.

Little did the good host William Clark imagine that, two and a half centuries later, there would be about forty drinking places in the flourishing town of Stromness . . .

4 April 1996

William's Account Book

Johnsmas
    Mason, joiner, lawyer,
    Palms open and seeking.
    Then silver I have from dangered and dangerous shipmen.

Olaftide
    First horsemen, haymen, shepherds.
    Flame of summer
    Draws dry throats barrelward.

Lammas
    Sun-ember, black and yellow bee
    Your broken comb
    Tempers the lambent rum cask.

Hairst
    Ox-darg, ox-drag, ox-dower
    Furls of gold on the shaven hill.
    Toom jar, spume jar, toom jar.

All Hallows
    Whisper through panel,
    'Will, if you will, seven casks brandy (unbonded).
    Dark o' next moon.' A Hollander. Five sovereigns.

Martinmas
    And the Lord Robert in Birsay
    Has sent an urgent taxman. The same
    Poked, pried. I bought peace
    With French circles, new-minted.

33

Yule
> Sat about our crisp and hollow pig, platter-fast,
> Hemmigar, Howe, Garth, a Swedish skipper.
> Red faces, ready purse, greasy gristled jaws.

New Year
> Fishermen at the door – 'Rum on account',
> 'A poor haddock moon.' 'Drowning.'
>> 'Gale, net-rot.' . . .
> A score of lobsters scrawled their blue receipt.

Candlemas
> Mareon burned a batch of pies!
> Has bottled a sour brew!
> I put the black bell of my mouth on Mareon.

Voar
> The mason paid. Carpenters contented at last.
> Pledge, seal, promise. A westerly
> Strewed the bay with hunger and drouth of hulls.

Magnustide
> Has come at last, Sandwick pulpit thunders
> Against my merry vats.
> (*Note:* To his reverence, one flagon usquagh.)

Beltane
> It does well. The twelve-month sun
> Bred a sovereign swarm in my purse.
> The taxman from Birsay contented.
> Is now such clamour for keeping,
> The full plate and cup my Mareon brings,
> I have bid the mason
> Build of Bewan stone a new chamber eastward
> With six hidden embrasures.

1983

MAY

The First of May

The Orkney girls never do it now – that old beautiful rite – because of all those 'beauty preparations' on television and in the shops, I expect. But on the first of May, in their great-grandmothers' time, the lasses of Orkney were astir early, no matter if there was a blue-gray crackle of frost in the air or the wind was blowing snell and south-easterly.

Down on the piers the fishermen's daughters stirred and kneaded the sleep from their eyes, and dressed quickly and turned their faces from the sea tangle to the steep closes. And the shopkeepers' lasses – it was the same with them. Maybe they didn't even take time to brush their hair or put their shoes on. Their doors opened on to the street. They turned their faces to the clouds and patches of blue in the west, with maybe a last star in it, high above the chimneys. Even the skippers' and merchants' daughters who lived in the grander houses at the back of the town were getting ready, while their fathers still slept and dreamed about bills of lading and a possible smuggled cargo of rum and tobacco from the Low Countries.

Upwards they moved in troops, the girls of Stromness, up the steep stepped closes, gay as the first birds. The pretty ones and the plain-looking ones were there, and those in between who looked pretty when they were happy about something and plain when something sombre had happened – they had lost a silver ring, perhaps, or their little fish-eating cat was sick.

But on this morning hope was bright on all their faces. Upwards they climbed, past the little high crofts, and the network of stone walls built by Peninsular veterans, and the ruin of Bessie Millie's hut. They were quite suddenly there, all of them, clustered about the summit of Brinkie's Brae.

Then all the Stromness lasses bent down and splashed their fingers in the dew and spread the brightness and coldness of the dew over their faces. The early larks were up – the sun over Orphir was brightening sea and land – a fishing boat spread its sail in the first brimmings of Hoy Sound. The sun rose higher, and drank the last of the dew.

So the Stromness girls believed themselves to be made comely and sweet by the May dew. The radiance of summer was theirs, not to be taken away. Down they trooped then, the pretty ones and the plain ones and the ones in between, for breakfast and the day's tasks.

30 April 1981

The First of May: A Vanished Hamnavoe Merchant

So he, turning the pages of the lost man's
    Ledgers, hoping to catch in some phrase
    The flawed fated thread
        That ruined a whole fabric

Found nothing, in notebook and notebook
    But cargoes sent out and received,
    Seamen's wages, price of cord,
        List of shipwright's repairs

And how a southwesterly had wrenched
    Copestones from his pier – what Sabbath
    Coins he had put in the plate,
        How this spring the rheumatics

Had set a clamp on one knee,
    How the merchants had relinquished a Dutch
    Cargo of rum and tobacco,
        The word going from counter to cabin

36

That excise officers, an entire posse
   Lay crouched by midnight rocks . . .
   (The eyes of the seeker, sore now
     With scrolled Hanoverian

'*f*' and 's'). No word of threatened
   Bankruptcy, law's lour, blackmail, the blacker
   Root nourished at some
     Ancestral foetid source,

To show how a sober Hamnavoe merchant
   Suddenly slipped mooring, shook off
   Store, kirk, council chamber,
     This well-kept desk and diary.

Then this: 'Girls passed my door in troops
   For the Ward, at sunrise, for to touch
   May dew to their faces
     That by such beguilement

They might get them good husbands,
   And amongst them one . . .' Pen faltered
   In mid-sentence, but resumed
     Next morning: 'Three baskets

Duck eggs received from Hoy, one shilling
   And fourpence halfpenny . . .' He thought,
   Turning the last blank pages
     How a dry stick

Must have quickened that May morning
   And dared not disclose the madness
   But launched out secretly, at sunrise
     Under a star, to bury the rose
     In salt chasms beyond Hoy.

               1 May 1987

JUNE

The First Houses in Hamnavoe

A very very long time ago, and they weren't stone houses either, they were wooden huts with fishing gear outside. And they were built by stubborn people.

The first longships of families from Norway, who intended to settle on the Pictish fields and pastures at Stromness parish – though it was called by an altogether different, ancient Celtic name then – came ashore about Breckness, on that headland facing the Atlantic.

The chief – the skipper – after the first stormy winter, decided that they ought to have a stone-built farm. Their temporary timber dwelling had been battered and salt-eaten and roof timbers brought down by the ocean gales. So the sailors became gatherers of stone from the shore, and afterwards they yoked the Pictish oxen and made their first furrows.

There was much hunger. A few Norwegians put the Pictish curraghs on the sea and set out to fish, as far as Yesnaby. They were unacquainted with these waters. One or two curraghs were upset and the men drowned. But at last they came home with skate, cod, haddocks.

And the chief nodded in a kind of curt way, but he was not interested in the fishermen. What took all his attention was the plough land and the pasture land. Already the first green shoots were coming up. Secondly, the chief was interested in the building of his house, barn, byres and stable. Slowly it grew all that summer. The women humped stones from a quarry at Innertoon.

At night a guard had to be kept on the long-house, the curraghs and the fields. The Picts came out of the darkness sometimes and put flaming torches in at the eaves. (Those Pictish remnants lived in the hinterland, in the wet places, the Loons.)

The fishermen were learning to read the coast and the tides. Twice or thrice a week they brought their catches to the beach of Breckness.

The chief only said, 'I am beginning to grow tired of fish.'

The oldest fisherman said, 'I'm beginning to grow tired of that self-important upstart whose face is green with looking at the barley field.'

There came to be differences and quarrels between the fishermen and the farm workers.

It came to a climax on the night of the great midwinter feast when all the community gathered in the new stone-built hall to celebrate the first harvest and the new steading.

The ale-cup went round. The brewers were pleased with their first ale. There was a good deal of boasting that night by the ploughmen, the shepherds, the harvesters. The ale-cup was passed to a fisherman called Bui. (Nobody had praised the enormous halibut he had caught that week.) Bui took a mouthful of the ale and spat it out. 'Disgusting filth!' he said.

The fighting went on inside Breckness till beyond midnight.

In the morning the fishermen set off with their curraghs and baskets and lines to the shore with the granite hill behind and the two little islands guarding the harbour from the east. 'This will be our place,' said the old fisherman. 'We will have nothing more to do with the farmers.' They called the place Hamnavoe, 'the haven inside the bay'.

19 May 1994

Hamnavoe: The First Village

The settlers' farm at Breckness built, the builders
Are summoned to the ale-drinking in the long hall.
   Arn tells one, *You are to be shepherd*
   One, *You must see to the horses . . .*

All behaved well on the voyage, says Arn.
Now we must wait till winter to discover
   If bread and cheese are good on this glebe,
   If turf of Orkney will warm like our mountain logs.

Tonight the best barrel is to be broached,
Sea-brought ale, I bid you then
   Wash salt from your throats,
   Rid your teeth of sawdust.

They tilt horns, fire-fast, fleece their mouths.
A few call for stories. The farmer,
   You, Lief, will see to the sty . . .
   Your task, Sven, to drain that field for the plough.

Girls come in with buckets of ale
Slurping on flagstones (wet star-splashes!)
   And Arn to Rudi (oarsman)
   Get shore stones tomorrow for a winter byre.

Now Nord, that had held helm on shipboard
Will sing, but Rann the grieve
   Stills the harp, till each seafarer
   Is fitted with his ox-coat.

A sheet of ale hangs in the air, it lingers
Across faces of ploughman and goosegirl.
   Not long then to fierce kin-combing,
   Flung fists, blood, bench-breaking,

Girls screaming, women stone-faced.
Then Arn to Nord, *Brawlers, ale-berserkers*
   Will not yoke here in Breckness.
   Go, Nord, take your slut and your song with you.

Ten Norskies follow Nord through the mussel-blue night,
Lovers of song and sea, three miles over the ridge
   To the voe with two islets
   And a granite hill behind,

A good place for boat-furl and curing of fish.
Women come also, with pot and lamp and loom,
   One girl – I know this – most beautiful,
   Her hair in the morning broken honeycombs.

They have three boats, *Skarf, Gannet, Skua*
Fishing west, beyond Breckness, at plough-time.
   Fishermen call to hill-combers
   Bondmen! Dung-spreaders! Dumb oxen!

Look, the free fishermen of Hamnavoe
Strike your mud eyes with dazzle of herring.
   We sail through the Sound. Soon
   Beyond Hoy, we are to dredge up pearls.

30 December 1986

The Johnsmas Fires

A hundred and fifty years ago, about this time of year, the young men and women of Orkney would have been engaged in out-of-the-ordinary activities.

They would have been going back and fore between the highest hill in every district and island with caisies on their backs, full of combustible materials – old broken oars and creels, worn-out ploughs and cribs, flotsam and jetsam, as much peat as could be spared. And there, on top of the hill, a pyre was built.

Secretly, the bone of an animal was inserted into the heart of the pyre. Maybe some whale tallow was added. Maybe some old wife poured over all a jar of rancid butter – anything to get a flame going. The thing was, to have a good fire burning on the night of 23 June (Johnsmas) – a magnificent fire to shame the many fires burning in the neighbouring parishes.

The excitement grew as the great day approached.

The women of 'the toonship' were busy for days beforehand getting food and ale ready for transporting to the hill. The parish fiddler took down his fiddle that may have been hanging on the wall, in the peat-reek since the last days of Christmas. The people kept looking anxiously at the sky. If only it didn't rain! . . . A rainstorm on the night of the 23rd would have washed out everything.

And finally, the great day arrived. Everyone in the parish who could walk, run or hobble to the hilltop was there in good time.

The weather had kept faith. The sun had shone all day, with one or two random showers only, and it was still there, a glow buried under the north-west horizon.

In the midsummer grimlings, people moved like shadows here and there on the hilltop. Somebody must have been the master of ceremonies, and ordered the torch to be lit and thrust into the pyre.

Soon the whole hilltop was ablaze! What cheers went up then from the parish folk!

As the flames leapt higher, the young men showed off their daring by jumping through the flames, again and again. The fiddler plied his bow as though he had half a dozen elbows. Then the hampers of food and the stone jars of best ale were opened.

All round, as far as eye could see, the Johnsmas fires burned on all the hilltops of Orkney.

*

Before the big fire burned out, a crofter would light a private torch from the glow and carry it to his own house and steading and fields, as if he was performing a kind of cleansing ritual for the growing crops, and the harvest to come; and for the beasts beyond the dyke.

That is a communal ceremonial beauty that has vanished for ever.

15 June 1995

The Wandering Fiddler

In the island of tall corn
A spit of rain in my face,
A rabbit for my pot.

Down at the shore
Lobster boat, cod boat.
They hung a crooked fish on my finger.

A thick red wife
Stood in the open door
Between me and the apples, the tobacco and the jam.

The farmer set his dogs on me,
A black-and-white storm!
But his lass broke an oatcake, butter and drops of honey.

I shared a roof
With one old sheep,
A bird, spiders, a rat, a broken plough.

I unsheathe my fiddle
At the August Fair.
I strike the islanders to the heart.

My cap rings –
Copper and silver and one gold piece.
They take their wounds home under the stars.

Myself and a sailor
Drank whisky in the tent.
That man told me a hundred lies.

Spring 1985

JULY

A Stone Age Pub Crawl

Did I read about it, or did I dream that one or other of our ancient monuments is to get a drink licence?

Five thousand years ago, there were three young Sandwick men who thought they might as well go for a drink to Skara Brae. It was sheep-shearing time; they had had a long day of it. So off Prem and Prad and Poke set from the hill Kierfiold to the village.

When they got to Skara Brae they found that the village was busy. The fishermen were in with a good catch and the women were cleaning haddocks down at the rockpools, and the salty-throated fishermen were kicking the stone door of the Limpet Arms, demanding a drink. At last the landlord, who had been brewing all day and was a bit awkward and tired, let the fishermen in.

Prem and Prad and Poke thought it best to seek another tavern. The hill-men and the boat-men never got on at the best of times.

The landlord of the Hole o' Rowe was just sliding back the stone bar across his stone door. He was a very merry man called Malik. 'Come on in, lads!' cried he. 'I always like to see the shepherds. No trouble with the shepherds. Now, what would you be wanting to drink?' Prem and Prad and Poke thought for a while, then they ordered three stone mugs of tangle ale . . . It was a rough drink but it quenched their thirst . . . The landlord wrote down their debt on a square stone: he would be paid with a sheep's head on the next killing day.

'Let's move on,' said Prem to Prad and Poke. 'No more tangle ale for me.'

A great noise of singing and laughter was coming from the Limpet Arms. The thirsty fishermen were getting into their stride.

The three shepherds went into the Partan, that was kept by a fierce old lady called Ona. Ona kept only root beer, on her stone gantry.

Prem ordered three mugs. The root beer tasted of ditches and bogs but the three shepherds downed it in a few gulps. 'You're drinking too fast,' said the landlady. 'Watch yourself. I want no trouble in here, mind.' She marked them down for sheep's liver and lights on the next killing day.

'Coorse stuff,' said Prad to Poke as they left the Partan. The noise inside the Limpet Arms was louder than ever, and here and there it had an edge to it.

'What about the Hether Blether,' said Prem. 'Good stuff, the heather ale they sell there . . . It's a bit dearer, of course.'

By the time they had downed their mugs of heather ale, they began to think that no men anywhere in Orkney could be so happy as their three selves. They laughed. They sang a song or two. They even mentioned going to the Limpet Arms. So they heaved themselves from the stone bench to their feet.

'Aren't you forgetting something?' said the wily keeper of the Hether Blether. They promised him three legs of lamb, come killing time.

'It mightn't be a good idea,' said Prad, 'going to the Limpet Arms.' Sounds of raised voices and splintering stone issued from that tavern.

The three shepherds were too happy to fight. Instead, they lurched merrily rather than walked into the Selkie, where all the wise old men went to tell stories and discuss deep matters. Only mead was sold in the Selkie. The landlord lost no time in telling Prem and Prad and Poke that they would not be served. Shepherds from the hill were too poor to afford the ale with honey in it, called mead.

Prem promised most solemnly that the Selkie would have two of the best fleeces now the shearing was done. Stone mugs of foaming heather ale were set before them. The old village men – aged about thirty-five or forty – smiled from every corner. A few shook their heads.

Prem and Prad and Poke remembered nothing after that until they woke up next morning in their bothy. Prem had a black eye. Prad had lost two teeth. Poke said he was sure his nose was broken.

They concluded that they must have gone to the Limpet Arms in the end, to have a word with the fishermen.

11 February 1993

45

Skara Brae: a Time of Drought

The stones hot. Sere grass. The dead ewe
   A bag of stinking bones.
      Big salt round,
Where have you hidden the black clouds?

Girls went to the secret place
   Every girl with a jar
      Their hands clean.
A string of shells at each wrist.

How long till the word came back?
   A month the girls were gone, then all
      Water-changed.
We knew them by their shell signs.

A hawk sat, fierce and gray, on the rock,
   Furled, sun-fallen,
      The cloud cleaver.
The curl of a claw on a limpet.

One was a swan, the white bird,
   Shaking sea from webs, burying
      Her neck deep.
She trod the sand, oyster-beaked.

Nervous deer, hill dweller
   Do you remember your snow?
      Hesitant,
One hoof gentle on a scallop, lifted?

Butterfly, flower of the wind,
   Drinker of dew and nectar,
      Lights on the lip
Of a grottie, flower of the ocean.

The sow came, wisest of creatures
   Snortling, it scraped in a midden
      Orts and roots,
It turned a shell like a great thunder-drop.

A horn cried. The girls tore the masks.
   They danced. They brought the elders.
      To a bruised rock,
Five jars filling with gray blood from the rock.

March 1987

An Old Man in July

I

Images grow slower on the worn loom.

   Lucent rain-bubbles
   Burst on the pools of his balcony
   And a sparrow
   Eyes from the rusted railing
   Bits of bread an old man scatters.

A blue sky patch – a scoured
   Silver coin eastward –
   A golden stone at noon.

No need for other pictures.

II

A burden: weaver, quarryman, poet.

   His house is crammed with books and manuscripts,
   Pictures, jars, music,
   One stone hollow heavy with coins.

47

Better a bare cell in Eynhallow
And a heart at peace.

III

Bairn-coat to shroud, the journey

Near the end of the road
The wind of before and after

Begins to shake the tatters of a man's life.

IV

'If only I was this sunset
Dear friend
Beside your fire, talking, proving
    The depth of your ale-mug . . .'

The quern of too many autumns
    Sifts dust of April into the urn.

All things indeed come from the hand of God
    But the random stone
    Is not thrid with our pain.

V

Think rather: the stone
Ruins in sun and rain –
    Not ruins, it runs out
    Centuries long, fruitful or barren dust.

A wild stalk in a dry place
    Lifts into light.

A thousand winters on, somewhere
    A pilgrim mouth
    Will taste, thankfully or brutishly, the bread.

VI

This is true. Not wisdom or wealth can redeem
The green coat, childhood.

Truth is, an old man comes
Led by a cold hand
To a hovel without a hearth-stone
    Empty cup, bare board.

On a wet morning, in an island
    An old man breaks a crust
    For a sparrow on a rusted railing.

VII

In the white theatre, autumn by autumn
A masquer takes needles to a torn coat

And the man must go out again
    Into deepening winter.

There is no skill or enchantment
    To make the old coat green.
There can be at best, now
A flung or fated pattern of patches.

Stars pierce like nails, after harvest.

Near a hallowed stone
The sparrow also builds her nest
    Introibo ad altare Dei

    Who giveth joy to my youth.

                                                      July 1994

AUGUST

The Tender Tables

Last Tuesday summer came, the first real summer day of 1993 – 3 August – with the sun bright and warm all day. So at last I could shed some of my winter clothes . . .

Was there ever such a summer as this! Now the tourists were out in their light summer wear, instead of drifting past Mayburn into the museum, buckets of rain splashing on to their coloured brollies. Outside, I spoke to a young mother on her way to 'the Tender Tables' with her two bairns.

The Tender Tables – what happy memories the name brings back, of summer afternoons at the West Shore in the 1920s and 30s. But very few children, I think, visit the West Shore and Tender Tables nowadays . . . Cars can quickly transport kids to Warbeth, Skaill and Birsay.

It is a curious name: Tender Tables. The 'tables' part is easily explained – it consists of two great slabs of sloping flat natural stone, set one above the other, with easy access up a broken natural stair. (I will have to visit the place soon, to refresh my memory.) One of those parallel rocks was called the Pulpit – probably because from that vantage one could seem to dominate those on the sand below. But where the adjective 'tender' comes in will have to be left to Norn scholars to decide (it is not in Hugh Marwick's dictionary).[*]

The area round the Tender Tables was a wonderful summer playground for children. Several narrow strips of sand sloped down from the cliff-face into Hoy Sound, and every strip of sand was divided by barriers of natural sloping rock. When the tide was out, the interstices of the rock were dotted with little triangular pools in which tiny almost transparent crabs could be found lurking among the tassels of

---

[*] *The Orkney Norn*, a dictionary of the Orcadian dialect.

seaweed . . . We were well warned by our elders not to paddle or swim too far out in those cold waters, or the fast-flowing ebb of Hoy Sound might carry us off. It was children's territory, the West Shore.

From above, we could hear from the golf course the occasional thwack of a brassie on a golf ball (a Warwick or a Spalding) and sometimes a golfer would slice his drive at the 13th hole and plop would go his ball (costing one shilling and sixpence) into the sea.

We warmed our feet in the rockpools before plunging into the Sound, which was so cold it drove the air out of our lungs with audible gasps.

There was a natural break in the cliffs in which a witch, it was said, had lived who had murdered children, long ago. It took some courage to take a few steps into that cave.

Memory plays tricks. It seems to me mainly boys who built the sand-castles and got stung by jellyfish . . . The few adults who looked after us when we were very young sat on the rocks above and set out the sandwiches, the 'rich tea' biscuits and the Abernethy biscuits, and poured the bottles of Gowans' lemonade. Girls – sisters and neighbours – sat on the greensward above and made daisy-chains.

Of course when we were a few years older we wanted nothing to do with adults or girls, round the Tender Tables . . . By that time, too, we preferred to stretch our legs as far as Warbeth beach. The West Shore was a place of early childhood.

And oh, the flood tide came in and lapped our feet, and fairly hurled trawlers between here and Graemsay, beyond 'the Beacon' and Ness into the hidden harbour. Conversely, in a strong ebb tide those trawlers could be caught, engines pounding, like flies in honey.

And the sun shone every day and the sky was blue with a few white clouds, and the sea was deliciously shriekingly cold, all those long summer afternoons that went on and on.

12 August 1993

The Joiners' Yard: *1886*

The yard above the sea
Is a well of light
This August afternoon, filled with mint
And stars of ox-eye.

Here the joiners worked
A century ago,
The journeymen and apprentices.
And the foreman
Stood at the gate, thumbing
The pages of an order-book.
A yell! A boy
Has hit his thumb with a hammer.
The apprentices titter.
The foreman trances the yard with a black glower.

All week
They've made tables, chairs, a cradle.
The stone floor
Is thick with blond shavings.
Planes whisper, hammers thud.
A dinghy drifts to the slipway.
A fisherman calls,
'She needs a new starboard plank,
Soon, before the winter.'

The edge of the pier is lined with gulls.
A bee
Blunders about with its bag of gold.

Then a woman, black-shawled, whispering.
The foreman is solemn.
'I must go and measure a bairn for a coffin.'

The sun flashes off the blue silk of the harbour.

Two journeymen
Begin to cut the boards for a small voyager.
She waits under a garret window, cold,
For sunset
For the one star of voyaging.

Now the foreman's gone
Apprentices
Shower the stone-girt yard with nails and shavings.
They shout.
The gulls rise in swirls about the yard.

All lie now under a green wave in the west.

9 August 1986

Sunday in Selskay Isle

I

The anvil doesn't ring today.
   The black creels are stacked high.
The village shop is shuttered.
Selskay the island
Floats on a blue Sabbath silence.

There: the kirk door is open.
   The solemn beadle, Tammo
   Looks along the two roads.
There: the solemn bell
   Gives a first cry.

II

The horse gallops in the Glebe field
   As if the sixth day
Had not been uttered yet.
   Beadle pulls rope,
   Bell summons.

The elders in black suits
Put horse and sheep behind them
   Making for the kirk.
Girls droop like flowers, following.
Gravely they dance into the seventh day.

III

Across the Sabbath of peace
  The third bell psalms.

In the Manse the minister's wife
Brushes crumbs and hairs
  From the minister's collar.
Reverend Hector MacSween
  Gathers up the leaves of his sermon.

IV

Laird breakfasts late. Laird
– James Traill esquire of Selskay –
Has sipped port, he has
  Played whist beyond midnight
With the Kirkwall magistrate
  And the excise officer
And with the young Mrs Traill.

The hall chapel is locked.
The Episcopal rector
  Can't cross for matins every Sunday.

What will he have with his toast,
Honey or marmalade?
  The fourth bell stroke
Floats like the tongue of a small angel
  Over the loch to the hall.

V

'Think shame!' cries Lizzie Ann
  To the swine-snores under the blanket.
'All the hen-money
  Poured down your drunken throat' . . .
'High time,' she cries
  'The shutters were up at that inn.'

Lizzie Ann passed the innkeeper
   (Mr Archibald Fettes)
Tying flies to fluent rods. Her fire-words
Die on the fifth bell-tremble.

VI

Mr Frame, schoolmaster
   Drinks coffee in the schoolhouse.
   He will go for a walk, later, through the empty island.

No, Mr Frame is not an atheist
   (He tells this farmer, that fisherman)
But, 'the divine is everywhere
In Nature, in books and music.
   I worship in Greenfields Kirk.'

The sixth bell-song
   Is no more to Mr Frame
(How long will they be able to keep
A clever young man like Mr Frame
   In a primitive island like Selskay?)
Than the chime of his spoon
   Against his empty coffee cup.

VII

Now the road is solemn with folk
Moving out of the death-ending darg of a week
   To Sabbath and resurrection
Drawn by the seventh summons
   In the small stone steeple.

14 March 1993

SEPTEMBER

Lammas Market

I wonder how many Stromnessians remembered that yesterday (Tuesday, 5 September) was Stromness Lammas Market Day?

I myself only remembered in time. But anyway, it didn't matter, because not a vestige of it remains, except (fleetingly) in the memories of a few aged townsfolk. And this is a great pity, because the Lammas Market was a magical day – as wonderful in its way as Christmas – almost as lyrical as the first day of the summer holidays.

It began with the neighbours giving you a fairing, some a sixpence that shone like a star. Talk about people winning the National Lottery! We had been saving up for a few weeks: we might have as much as three or four or five shillings in our pockets – we felt as rich as Rockefeller or Croesus!

It was a holiday from the school, of course.

As I drifted north from the quietude of Melvin Place, the crowds on the street thickened, and near the pierhead I thought all of Orkney must be there! The buses from Birsay and Orphir were bringing in the country folk, and the folk from the South Isles had landed from the *Hoy Head*, or smaller boats . . . It was hard for a small boy to wend his way through.

And there, suddenly, was the fair in all its breath-taking delight! First, at the Custom-house wall, the sellers of fruit and sweeties. Pitched, perilously, on the seaward side, were the shooting booths, offering gaudy prizes. Against the North of Scotland Shipping office, the 'roll-the-penny' stalls – the strength machine where you struck a wedge with a wooden mallet and if it was struck powerfully enough, a bell rang at the top of a column . . . Also, there was the Prince of the Congo who licked a red-hot poker and said in a deep rich voice, 'Sugar!' . . . But dominating this section of the market was a stout red-faced angry-voiced man who whirled a roulette wheel and was forever barking 'Last card! . . . Last card!'

Under the Warehouse wall was the coconut shy . . . A veiled mysterious lady read fortunes, if you first crossed her hand with silver. Girls came and went, giggling, from her booth.

Poised above the inner harbour were the swing-boats, twopence a ride. Most boys delighted in those airy ups-and-downs. But the one and only time I tried, I felt frightened and sick, and was never so glad to step on solid land again!

Further on, at the North Pier, was the spectaculars, which might be a travelling boxing booth, or else the Wall of Death, with Smoky Joe speeding round and round the perpendicular wooden wall on his motorbike. 'A mile-a-minute!' cried the booth man . . . How could any mortal hurtle along sideways at a mile a minute? It was a marvel to us boys.

Along the South Pier was a line of Indians selling silks from open suitcases. Round Graham's fountain a cheap-john dazzled the crowd with cascades of beguiling verbiage. Through it all walked Giulio Fuggacia, with his hound and his ice-cream barrow, intoning 'Cheap today, free tomorrow.' There was also a little photographer who darted here and there taking instant photographs.

Most mysterious and poignant of all was the blind fiddler, who took another route through the crowds.

All this took place, for small boys, in a storm of sweeties, fruit, ice-cream, lemonade, apples, chocolate. Going home for dinner (1 p.m.) and tea (5 p.m.) were resented necessities. We wanted back to the place of magic.

The early autumn darkness came down; and then, yet another enchantment, Naphtha flares were lit here and there at the fairground! Weary, penniless, surfeited with sensual luxuries, we dragged home to bed. No home lessons done, and the prison-house of school to be faced in the morning.

We did not know – innocents that we were – that we had been participants in one of the great feasts of the year – Hlaf(loaf)mas, a time of rejoicing that our winter bread had been secured, after harvest.

14 September 1995

57

The Tinker Wife

Three things have worked her that indignity,
Travelling the roads with her ferocious man,
Until she seems a moving wind-warped tree –
Rope's end, and heather rut, and porter can.

Yet old men swear that when her budded breasts
Flowered from her maidenhood, her glances shed
On market, wayside weddings, harvest feasts,
A grace that might have driven the preacher mad.

And year by year after her breasts were dry
That tinker wife would call for whisky and pipe
And bid old Ezra fiddle a gay snatch,
And dream she offered him again her ripe
Virginal flesh in some predestined ditch
Where youth ended in a cold desolate cry.

Summer 1956

Earl Rognvald's Commission

The most intriguing character in *The Orkneyinga Saga*, I think, is
Rognvald Kolson, Earl of Orkney. He was a man of many talents, as
he tells us (not boastfully) in one of his poems: 'Chessboard, tilt-yard,
trout stream, ski slopes, I'm a master at those. I can sail a boat and
play the harp. I'm a blacksmith too, not at all afraid of hard work . . .'

He took pride in all that he undertook, including labour with
hammer and anvils, and fishing with his fishermen. Earl Rognvald's
two great undertakings were the building of the Cathedral in honour
of his uncle, St Magnus, and the crusade with fifteen ships to
Jerusalem in 1151–54.

A marvellous book could be written about this greatest of
Orcadians; but it will have to wait for a younger writer than me, and
one with knowledge of ships and architecture and the complex politics of the Mediterranean lands in the twelfth century. Until that his-
torian comes along, I sometimes imagine Rognvald Kolson writing a

letter to a master mason in England, inviting him to make the hazard-
ous voyage north to Orkney, him and all his workmen in stone.

Who were those church builders? A great number of magnificent
churches were being built all over England and Scotland in the
twelfth century. Were there teams of travelling masons who went
from bishopric to bishopric building only churches?

Earl Rognvald probably reckoned that not many church builders
would want to travel so far; so he would have used golden words in
his letter. Such as: 'You build great poems in stone, and your fame
has travelled into our northern seas. I am telling you this, for I am a
poet myself, only I deal in harp-strokes that die on the air almost as
soon as they are uttered . . . Renowned builder of churches, it is not
among savages you will be coming, but among civilised and hospitable men. You and your subordinate poets-in-stone will be well
looked after while the work is in progress, and you will be paid regularly golden crown pieces . . . This kirk in Orkney is no mere whim
on my part, or the bishop's, but I know that in England you have
heard of the blessed martyr Magnus of Orkney. The kirk is in honour
of Magnus, and "to the greater glory of God . . ." It is time. You and
your masons will have a few more gray hairs by the time the choir is
built, but builders in generations to come will follow your master-
plan (making due allowance for changing modes and fashions). Sir,
we have here quarries of the best stone, including the fine red sandstone of Eday island, which is the colour of fire and blood, the hue of
martyrdom. If you and your workmen were to come in carts to the
shore of Leith in Scotland, with ladders, scaffolding, plumblines,
squares, compasses, planes, nails, chisels, hammers, a fine ship will be
there on Easter Monday St Magnus Day – to carry you across the
North Sea to Orkney . . . As soon as the foundation is laid I intend to
sail to Jerusalem, with fifteen ships, for a blessing on this undertak-
ing of ours. For this venture also, charts will have to be made. Word
has come to me that you have lately been working on a magnificent
minster in Durham. Your fame has gone before you.

'I have entrusted this letter to a reliable skipper. A horseman will
meet him at Lindisfarne, and bear this plea and invitation the rest of
the way to Durham . . .'

28 September 1995

The Kirk and the Ship

The master mason said
'Sail to the island of Eday
And quarry blocks of yellow stone.'

Others drove oxen to the Head of Holland
Where sandstone is red.
The lark's skein
About and about the April hill was thrown.

They did that work, the labouring Orkneymen.

Masons from Durham, strange speakers,
Squared the blocks rough-hewn.
They chiselled their marks, setting stone on stone.

And the Kirkwall villagers
Paused, and shook wondering heads, and went on.

And the kirk grew, like a lovely ship
Freighted with psalm and ceremony, blissward blown.

*

He that ordered the minster
Fluttered in a frailer ship
Across the Mediterranean
With pauses for dalliance, siege, piracy
But always, Jerusalem-drawn.

*

Pillars soared up, red as fire or blood.
And in one they laid
Their martyr, Magnus: his breached bellchambered bone.

March 1988

OCTOBER

Weather Lore

The 'peedie summer' arrived on Monday (10 October) and it is going on still. Long may it last.

We have (or, at least, the old Orcadians used to have) the weather map throughout the year in the marrow of our bones.

There was 'the gab o' May' – a period of churlish weather before spring began in earnest. There were 'the borrowing days of March', when – it may be – February with its slush and snell winds trespassed into March. And the old folk would say after New Year, 'As the day lengthens, the cowld strengthens.'

They knew the vagaries and chances of the weather at all seasons. The farmers knew well, but I think the fishermen knew even better, because their livelihoods and their very lives depended on a good reading of the weather. Many things had to be taken into consideration: the phase of the moon, the ebb and flow of the tides, the prevailing wind – plus a hundred intangibles the layman knew nothing about.

I seem to remember a beautiful summer morning long, long ago. And I said as much to a neighbour who had lived many years in lighthouses the length and breadth of Scotland. 'A fine day,' said I. There was not a cloud in the sky. The harbour sparkled with a thousand points of light. It was perfect weather.

'Ah,' said the lighthouse keeper's wife, 'I don't like the look o' it at aal. There's a storm brewing. There'll be bad weather, mark me words.'

How could any storm break the crystal and sapphire of such a perfect day? I laughed secretly at such superstitious weather lore.

But she was right. A storm was breeding under the horizon. Before that day was done, we were struggling with the wind, we were drenched with rain. Ever since that day, I have respected the secret weather knowledge of the old folk.

Are there any of them left? Nowadays we don't have to depend so absolutely on that primitive weather instinct. Perhaps it has totally withered away.

We can hear the scientific forecasts on radio and TV. But are they as accurate as all that? I think we Orcadians – according to the TV chart last night – were promised gloomy weather today, with fairly strong wind. And behold, as I sit writing this at my kitchen table, the sun is streaming through the window at near noon, and there is no rattle in the window frames. Of course, the west wind might be strong enough on the braes above Stromness . . . And the sun might muffle itself in clouds by mid-afternoon. There's no telling.

'A green Yule maks the kirkyard full,' was another saying. But, over a century maybe, the broad weather pattern has changed; and there have been no healthy Christmas snowfalls. And, as far as I know, the death-graph has ceased to depend on the absence or abundance of snow.

I think children now don't enjoy the abundant snowfalls of my childhood. (May it not be a result of global warming! – for if it is, Orkney might sink slowly under the water from the melted ice-caps.) But the farmers too wanted a good snowfall every winter, for the earth was warmed by that enormous white overcoat. And the buried seeds were all the more robust when they broke from the furrows, seeking the sun.

*

The weather lady on TV was right last night, after all. For I had no sooner written the above than the cloud-rack covered the sun, and there came 'a slaiver' (thin dispersed rain) on the wind.

20 October 1994

Weather Forecasts

Seven old fishermen
Sit on the sea wall in the sun.
A storm, a week away,
Frets their blood.
They smoke pipes. They reckon
A few baskets of cod between now
And the purple chasms westward.

I sit in my rocker
Watching 'the fronts' on a glimmering screen.

April 1994

Lights Out!

Suddenly, reading a book late at night, there is darkness . . . The 60-watt bulb in the Anglepoise lamp has died the death, without any preliminary sign of ailing – with what Thomas Hardy called 'an eyelid's soundless blink' the lamp is extinguished.

Fortunately, most responsible citizens have a small supply of spare bulbs, and it's no trouble to fit a new one.

*

I'm trying to remember how we fared in the days before electricity, pre-1947. (I was actually present at the switching on of electricity, officially, in Banks' café in Alfred Street: but it was a very quiet affair, and I was present in my capacity as Stromness correspondent of the *Orkney Herald*.)

We had, of course, gas. You had to have a plentiful supply of pennies (the big old round heavy ones) to put in the gas meter. Gaslight was diffused through a mantle, which was very fragile and had to be renewed fairly often. But then one might get some warning. The mantle might begin to look ragged, and in the end collapse in a silent shower of fragments, soft and white as snowflakes . . . Time to fix a new mantle – it was stiffened with wax and the wax had to be burned off with a lighted match, first of all.

Another step back in time, and we are in the age of the paraffin lamp.

There it stood on the dresser or in the middle of the table, crowning the winter with its soft radiance. There we did our homework or played games of Ludo or read the *Wizard* . . . The paraffin lamp needed more attention than electricity or gas. The wick had to be trimmed from time to time with a red-hot poker. The bowl had to be filled with paraffin which was kept in a gallon can in the closet. Forby the lamp, paraffin was used to help light the fire in the morning. A dollop of paraffin was poured over the paper and sticks – then with a swoosh a towering flame poured up the lum, and the housework could begin.

Before the paraffin lamp? Now we venture into unknown territory. My father liked to collect old things and so there were a few crusie-lamps in the house . . . What a meagre glow-worm flame they must have given – impossible for our great-great-grandfathers to have read by them. More light came from the peat fires, probably, than from those glimmerings on the wall.

No wonder the old legends flowered from the lips on winter nights, for many generations. No wonder it was a good era for fiddlers. Both spoken stories and music may well have sounded magical by those muted lights.

And further back than the crusie lamp even. How did they pass the long winter nights in Skara Brae? I expect, once the sun went down, they went to their stone beds.

18 March 1993

Lamp

The lamp is needful in spring, still,
Though the jar of daffodils
Outsplendours lamplight and hearthflames.

In summer, only near midnight
Is match struck to wick.
A moth, maybe, troubles the rag of flame.

Harvest. The lamp in the window
Summons the scythe-men.
A school-book lies on the sill, two yellow halves.

In December the lamp's a jewel,
The hearth ingots and incense.
A cold star travels across the pane.

December 1985

NOVEMBER

All Saints' Day

The first of November, as I sit writing this. Outside, a brisk cold wind, and blue sky, but every now and then a cloud drops rain.

All Saints' Day, today. And that doesn't mean only the canonised saints, like Magnus and King Olaf, and Columba of Iona, but a numberless host of unknown men and women who have led good lives and left the world a little better and sweeter for having lived their lives in it.

We all know a few people, at least, whom we would include in the roll-call. Some of them are almost forgotten now – their names faded in the registrar's book, or becoming ever less distinct on kirkyard stones as sun and wind and rain erode them. But they had something imperishable in their keeping while they lived, and that can never be lost. Most of them were poor and had no interest in making names for themselves – rather, any kind of publicity they shrank from.

Millions of such good people there must have been, all over the world, since humanity took root, and apart from that certainty we know nothing about them. They too, an innumerable nameless host, are celebrated today, on All Saints' Day.

*

Last night, under the street lamps, little groups were going here and there with pokes of flour and jars of treacle, beautifying the shop windows along the street. It was Hallowe'en, the night of witches and cats and candles. Indoors, I wonder if many children were dooking for apples in a wooden tub, or cracking walnuts and brazil nuts in brass nutcrackers?

So we prepare for winter, though autumn has still a month to go.

And tomorrow – 2 November – is All Souls' Day.

It is, I'm sure, natural to remember the dead as the nights grow ever darker, and especially as oneself gets older. Another October past, another winter looming. It is indeed a sure mark of the increasing years, that the dead seem to outnumber the living in an old man's mind.

The town, as always, swarms with young folk – a delightful promise and seal of the future. Those young people have been in Stromness, generation after generation, a perpetual spring; it is impossible to imagine that the fountain will ever dry up.

The disconcerting thing is that I know the names of only a few of them. As one gets older, one lives in a town of strangers, increasingly. You only know your contemporaries, and those slightly younger and slightly older.

I remember my father saying, more than sixty years ago as we walked along the Innertoon road, with the kirkyard down below, fronting the Atlantic: 'There are more Stromness folk lying there than there are living noo in the toon.'

I was touched to awe at the thought.

All Souls' Day – How many Stromnessians are buried at Warbeth? Maybe 50,000, maybe more. Impossible, in early November, not to think of them, especially those we knew. Some we cared for; some we were indifferent to; some we may have feared or disliked.

But of the true worth of each of them we know nothing; and that is something else to wonder at.

10 November 1994

All Souls

'There are more Hamnavoe
    folk in the kirkyard
Than there are walking the
    Hamnavoe street' –
My father used to say that,
    and I a child.

Death was a door
  that never had opened,
I had no dread of the skull
  beyond
Nor of ghosts that troubled
  some of the living.

Today a throng of good
  ghosts visit me,
Coming at the bellstroke of
  the prayer *de mortuis*
A host so numerous I
  can't name them all.
Name seven, as the
  second sun of November
  comes cold in at the
  window
And a November cloud
Rattles first hailstones on
  bereft gardens.
Name Peter Esson, tailor,
  presiding from his bench
Over sailors' nightly anthologies,
  stories
Rooted in Shanghai,
  Rio, all ports between,
And Peter stitching a
  Sabbath suit for some
  farmer.
Name Attie Campbell, whose
  every utterance
Brimmed the ears of beermen
  with joy
As his mug brimmed with
  tawny Barleycorn fleeces.
Bring Edwin Muir:
  he in age with the chalice of childlight still.

Bring John Folster, fisherman
  who gathered haddocks
  and lobsters
From the thunder-bruised
  Atlantic
Into his frail boat, then
  read his books by
  lamplight,
A lonely gentle pier-dweller.
Summon John Shearer, teacher,
  kinder to his stumbling
  pupils
Than to those who moved
  dextrously
Through the labyrinth of his
  little lab.
Come Peter Leith, farmer,
  turning the leaves of
  books
As familiarly as furrows
In a farm, generations-old, above a loch.
Sing an unknown brother,
  whose bead of light went out
Before the first star.

How many crowd today
  at the kirkyard gate!
Such fragrances filled Hamnavoe's
  closes and piers!
Seventy-year-old tongue
  of dust
Say a blessing now, once more
  in early November.

Mary Jane Mackay, died 3
  November 1967.
At her name's telling,

a light breaks
   still
On older Hamnavoe
   faces.
In this year's flower-time
She'd have garnered
   a hundred summers.

2 November 1991

DECEMBER

The Shortest Day

Today is the shortest day of the year – winter solstice – and it must have been a time of great worry for the first Orcadians, those who came after the retreat of the ice.

Ever since midsummer – a time they had greeted with dancing and fires – the sun had begun to dwindle. True, the grass patches were long and lush, and the new lambs were growing, and there was abundance of fish and birds. But the sun was making an ever-narrowing circle through the sky. Instead of going down to the north-west of Birsay, its setting time was drawing closer to Hoy, as the summer passed and the shadows clustered.

In its shortest passage, the sun made a red and gold pyre on the Coolag of Hoy.

True, every winter hitherto the sun, after the time of bright stars and snow, had begun to revive, making wider arcs through the sky; and though the days were cold and stormy (the very worst weather of the year) there was no doubt that the sun was renewing itself. It would, as every year, keep tryst with the new grass and the lambs and the shoals of fish and the wild flowers. Even the people who were older by a year felt the new resurgence of life within themselves; old men sipped once more from the cup of springtime and youth.

And yet the thinking men of the tribe – those with imagination, who looked before and after, and pondered the mystery of things – reasoned that this cycle of the sun might not necessarily last for ever. Nothing lasted for ever. Children became shepherds and fishermen and mothers, then they began to droop slowly deathwards. At last they lay silent and cold, among witherings and scant white hairs, and it was time for the ceremony of death to begin to be enacted.

For the dead islander, there was no new beginning, other than in his children and grandchildren . . . He himself was, if anything, a thin ghost in the cold and dank of death.

So it might happen with the sun.

There might come a winter in which there would be no miracle of renewing. No, the winter fire of the sun would cool to a glowing cinder and then go out, finally and for ever. And the tribe would perish in that last ice.

So they reasoned.

And to show that they had the welfare of the life-giving sun at heart (as well as, incidentally, their own welfare) they consulted with the quarry-men and the hewers of stones and the mightiest mason among them sketched plans on a sheepskin with a charmed stick.

They built, over a generation, a stone hymn to the sun on the moor between two lochs.

Then they attempted what seemed impossible: the building of a great sun-temple six or seven fields away. It was no easy task. Maybe two generations lavished their skill and strength on it. They made niches in the walls where dead chiefs and young dead princesses were laid.

There, along the corridor of Orkahowe, the sun entered at the solstice, and touched, with a golden finger, a tomb with the dead jewelled bones in it.

We must imagine, perhaps, a great cry of lamentation changing to a chorus of joy. The sun would not die. And even the dead would taste the chalice of immortality (who knows how?).

21 December 1995

Two Maeshowe Poems

Circle of light and darkness, be our sign.
We move in shadows.
Brodgar* has burned on the moor a dance of sun.

Ring of quern and plough, contain
Our tumults of blood.
The stars' chaos is caught in a strict rein.

*Brodgar – a Neolithic stone circle comparable to Stonehenge.

72

Wheel of life and death, remove
The sweet warm breath.
Ingibiorg flowers in stone, all beauty and love.

Round of sun and snow and seed,
Out of those skulls
Breaks the first green shoot, the full ear, then the bread.

Summer 1978

*

The first island poems
Cuttings in stone
Among the tombs of very ancient dead,
Young men's lyrics
Struck with chisels among thronging ghosts
INGIBIORG IS THE LOVELIEST GIRL
HERMUND WITH A HARD AXE CARVED RUNES
A GREAT TREASURE IS BURIED NEARBY
JERUSALEM-FARERS BROKE IN HERE
DRAGON, GUARD THE BONES AND THE VERSES

The young seamen climbed out of Maeshowe,
Their nostrils wide to the salt wind.

1995

Carol

First, the making of sun and moon and stars.
Then: sea girdling the seven continents.
A green fountain, a tree, shaken with wind
 and sun and rain – and green
 seas, prairies.
The lion burns, the lark is a sweetness
 lost in light, lamb and horse

73

converse at ease with ant and elephant, a
salmon climbs the loud ladder of
a mountain torrent. They go
their separate ways in a wind of morning.
At last, a garden in the wilderness, well
watered, a house of branches:
there stand in the door a man
and a girl and a child, under
the apple blossom.

History has cancelled that music. History
has brought these ruins,
confusion in the elements, disaster
to the blood and dust of man.
In the darkest time, we bring
candle and carol to the door of
a byre.

1995

Hogmanay

Hogmanay came in the early 1930s and it was nothing much for small
boys. Nothing happened in our house in Melvin Place except that a
few neighbours and friends dropped by on New Year's Day, usually
after dinnertime (roast beef, the only roast beef of the year).

Some years there was quite a crowd in the living-room. My father
liked to sing Edwardian music-hall ballads, when he had drunk two
or three small glasses with that yellow stuff in them. 'I'll stick to the
ship, lads,' he sang, and 'A Beautiful Picture in a Beautiful Golden
Frame', and 'Sweethearts and Wives'.

Jimmy Bruce the postman was forever urging my father to sing
'The Bible at Home', a very sentimental piece of religiosity. And
Jimmy Bruce would say, sipping the mysterious yellow liquid in his
glass, 'I think that's the bonniest song that was ever written . . .'

Once, when my father was on his feet singing maybe 'Brighton,

Brighton, I'll never go there any more', I decided to enquire deeper into the mystery of this yellow drink that impelled men to sing and tell extravagant stories, and behave in uncharacteristic ways, such as kissing ladies, laughing uproariously at nothing, or wiping a tear from their eyes . . .

So, I took a tiny sip out of my father's glass. Hellfire and brimstone! Poison and burning acid! Ah, surely my tongue was burned in my mouth beyond mending. Surely my throat was so corroded I would never be able to speak again. There and then I took a vow that never, should I live to be a hundred, would that dreadful drink called whisky pass my lips! Never.

I was glad to wash my palate out with my mother's home-made Crestona ginger wine.

Since then, I have to confess that I must have, over four or five decades, drunk a hogshead of whisky at least, and much trouble and distress it has caused me and my friends. But also it has given me hours of great joy, in which the world and all its tedium and grief were caught up in a wild Scottish reel. Life was worth living, after all. But I always went to bed with a bottle of Alka-Seltzer and a glass of water on the table.

28 December 1995

New Year's Day: 1920s

On New Year's Day
My father took us to visit the Museum
Just across from the derelict
'Old Orkney' distillery.

There Mrs Lyon, curator, received us.

And we had our Sunday suits on.
And we had just eaten
The one and only roast beef dinner of the year.

75

And, there, among the furled birds in glass cases
The Golden Eagle stared out.

Then there was the world-famous fossil, 'Homosteus Milleri',
Hugh Miller, geologist,
Had found in his west-shore wanderings.
My father said his name with reverence:
'A self-taught man, Hugh Miller,
A stonemason.
A whole book he wrote about this fossil,
The Asterolapis of Stromness.'
To me it was just a black mark on a stone.

And there, tall in a corner, the first clock in Hamnavoe,
The brass face beaten like a boxer's.

And there, the model ships,
Their wings yearning towards Diemen's Land or Boston,
Their masters boys
From pierhead and close and croft.

And there, a congress of stone smiling Buddhas.

The chief thing we wanted to see
Was the wooden idol from Borneo, hideously
Carved and dyed, a dancer.

December 1990

Island Epiphanies

the
Arctic Whale

BINSCARTH WOOD

The parish of Rendall, as seen from the bus, is not remarkable for beauty. It is a bleak dreary road that connects Evie with Finstown. But when you approach Finstown from the rear, an element of sweetness and charm enters the scene.

I always think of Finstown as a place of contradictions. At the lower end of the village, next Kirkwall, I always feel depression, especially at ebb tide. But looking at it from the school, or from the upper end of the road, one feels the unique charm of the place. Whence comes this special Finstown charm? From the gentle green hills that enclose it from the west; from the mild pastoral slopes under Binscarth full of contented sheep; from the inquisitive arm of blue sea that runs in almost to the edge of the Binscarth plantation; from the plantation itself, the most memorable element in the entire landscape.

We got out of the bus into the evening sunlight streaming benignly from the west over Binscarth, and descended over the sloping field towards the entrance of the wood.

Immediately a new world of green gloom received us, different to anything else in the islands. We were moving now through an intimate sylvan world, and the sense of space and light felt elsewhere in Orkney, was lost. But this new green world was not hostile. Rather the contrary. The brutality of Nature, the vast forces of energy and ruthlessness which can be felt even on a peaceful afternoon at the top of a sea crag, were in this woodland muted and softened to a delicate gentle beauty. One felt that no evil could touch anyone under the spell of this wood. It was a world of silence and soft whisperings. The same kind of sacred gloom pervades the interior of St Magnus Cathedral. One feels that merely by speaking one may taint the rare atmosphere.

The birds, however, did not think so. Suddenly, to the right, an invisible blackbird burst into rapturous song, and the green silence was deliciously shattered. Again and again, for two long amazing minutes, he turned over on his tongue the exquisite cadences. One

79

could feel the throbbing, the passionate throbbing, of his glossy black throat. Then the sun must have burst out of a cloud. The silver light was shaken in long spangles through the branches. It was as if a precious fluid were being poured without stint through the crystalline atmosphere. A little breeze sent the leaves whispering earnestly together, conspiring with each other to catch as much of the sunlight as possible. What reached our grateful human eyes was the precious remnant of the light, strained and purified by the lofty whispering leaves. As suddenly as he had begun the blackbird stopped singing. Silence surged back: the bird's song was now only a precious memory. The sunlight remained, but it, too, soon disappeared.

We walked on. The path was wet. Little tinkling rivulets of water flowed in and out of small light-reflecting pools. It had been a rainy morning, and the woods bear memories of the morning's weather long after the outside world of nature has clean forgotten. We had to watch where we set our feet.

There must be fairies in Binscarth plantation. It is unthinkable for such an exquisite place to lack them. At sunset they peer shyly from behind the backs of the trees, and seeing that no mortal defiles the place with blood and flesh foot, they come out and dance gravely to the music of pipes on the woodland paths. Normally I am a scoffer at the supernatural, but on evenings like this I am convinced deep in my heart that the fairies exist, just as you and I know on solemn winter midnights that the eyes of forlorn spirits are watching us with uncanny interest. The old people in Orkney believed in fairies: they often saw them on summer evenings and even spoke with them. Dark superstition, you think? But consider that such a brilliant enlightened scientist as our Hugh Miller believed in them too, with a deep unquestioning faith.

Even as we left the enchanted wood of Binscarth, out of the corner of my eye I saw the bright eyes of the peedie folk watching us depart. As I turned to investigate, the eyes winked, flashed, and melted into the gloom. Then I saw that it was only the last evening light on the rivulets of the wet woodland path. The light gleamed on the water, but moved and darkened when I moved. We left Binscarth in Sabbath twilight behind us, and the peedie folk to their unearthly revels.

August 1946

YESNABY IN SPRING

It was a chance encounter with Willie, an old school friend. He was standing at the North End, outside the garage, stowing a tin of petrol into the side-car of his shining new motorbike.

'Would you care,' he said, 'for a run through the country?'

It was the first day of spring. The wind swayed the budding branches of the trees. The black mould was aflame with tiny crocuses, the wide sky had great gaps of blue torn in it. Swift gleams of sunshine and shadow chased each other over the housetops, over the fields, over the distant hills and islands, and were gone. All Nature was alive and dancing.

I left Willie in no doubt as to my answer. Silently he helped me into his side-car. He strapped the helmet about his ears. Then he turned the machine round, and we were racing for the open countryside.

O, but it was glorious to be alive! We were splashed with sunlight; the wind tore at us and whipped our faces and spread the hair over our eyes. The fields flashed past, green and black. Here a ploughman turned the sodden furrows, and a cloud of seagulls hovered and dipped behind him. A black dog tore after us, but tired after half a mile, and turned aside, tongue lolling, into a ditch.

Then we got clear of the twisting highway, and the road gleamed before us, straight as a die for two miles. We hurtled along it, and the wind was a roaring tornado in our ears . . . The loch beneath us echoed the blue of the sky. There, where a small brown-clad hill stands guardian, we turned up a side road, with a few small crofts on either hand. A tractor trundled down the road towards us, and the driver gave us a cheery wave of his hand.

The roar of the sea grew louder. Against the skyline stood the crumbling remains of a naval encampment. We edged cautiously up the incline. The paddock-shaped peninsula of the Broch came into view. The ocean was in a sombre mood, and growled resentfully. The motorbike stopped between two ruined wartime towers. We got off, lit cigarettes, and looked down on Yesnaby.

As always, in that delightful place, special things were happening. The sea and the land are hopelessly entangled here. Strong-based headlands jut capriciously out into the Atlantic, which pokes long fingers far inland. Rock and ocean are at perpetual warfare, or else celebrating together in a kind of wild joy. For whatever activity they pursue, there is nothing tame or mild in it. Nature has the primitive ecstasy here, as she has nowhere else in Orkney.

The great waves came in, flush from the west. Green and gleaming, they poised to strike. But the steadfast rocks withstood them, and those proud columns of water crashed in white ruins among the pebbles. Then the wet rocks exulted, the sea roared another challenge; and another ponderous wave rose from mid-ocean and came on, quivering and shining and surging higher . . .

When men fight, they splash their battlefields with red blood. But there is no guilt in the war that land and sea fight eternally – for the foam engendered of the struggle is whiter than snow, pure and immaculate as bride's lace. The lighter spume was whirled up on the wind and blown inland over the cliffs.

The gray waves came on; the brown rocks shouted defiance. Where they met in the shock of battle, an acre of white foam surged, the ultimate purity of colour. Out of such perfection, the ancients imagined that all beauty was born.

We watched the sensational conflict for a few minutes, and walked downwards over the wet turf. In the Noust the sounds of battle were hushed. The foundations of two fishermen's huts were all that remained as evidence of man's participation in the fight. Heroes, that the paintings of Stanley Cursiter* made of them, they were – and heroes they must have been to seek precarious livelihood between those gnashing jaws of ocean and rock. Cannily, and with a wry Orkney humour launching their slim boats, they little dreamed that they were figures out of ageless legend, old before the Vikings reached our shores.

---

*Orkney artist (1887–1976). Former Director of the National Gallery of Scotland, and Queen's Painter and Limner.

Now Linklater and Greig are dead, and there are few like them left in Orkney. It was melancholy to see, above the Noust at Yesnaby, the few stones that remain of their dwellings; especially for Willie, who is Linklater's grandson, and Yesnaby holds associations for him which I could never guess at.

Along the cliff's edge we went, until a sudden turning brought us in sight of the Castle of Yesnaby, one of the land's great outposts in its perpetual war with the ocean. Dimly, southwards, we saw, etched against the late afternoon sky, an even more spectacular outpost – the Old Man of Hoy.

The sea explodes against their bases, and wears them away, carrying away a few fragments of stone every century or so. Even now, though Yesnaby Castle's turrets are proud and rugged, its base is slim and impossibly fragile. Some morning when we have been sleeping for centuries in Orkney earth, what tumultuous exultation there will be in the waves when the Castle of Yesnaby totters on its base!

Over Yesnaby all was gloomy, for the sun had run into battlements of cloud. But, as the motorbike sped southwards, the sun burst out again, till all the earth looked new and bright. The sap of springtime rose in my own veins, and I was happy. Dogs barked. The ploughman strode after his patient team, and the new-turned furrows gleamed with wetness. The sky was a changing patchwork of blue and white. The sun stooped low over Hoy.

Presently we turned on to the main road, and hurtled for home. The eternal roar of the sea held our ears no longer.

April 1949

CROSSING THE PENTLAND

The sea was as calm as a millpond, and a slight haze lay over the islands, as the *St Ola* cleared Stromness harbour and passed through Hoy Sound. It was almost the last day of March, and the passengers lingered on deck, though there was still a winter nip in the air. They smoked and sucked sweets, or loitered aimlessly from side to side of the boat, or prepared miserably to be sick.

It was not a beautiful day by any means. The sky was obscured, and island and cliff were softened by the all-pervading haze. Only the sea, calm though it was, assumed a more deadly menace, and it made a sound like a sinister chuckle as it washed against the sides of the ship.

We edged round Hoy, and the island turned its great rugged cliff-face towards us. The cliffs are inscrutable and vast. It is impossible to realise just how terrifying and massive they are, until one sees the minute wings of the seabirds flickering against the red pillars.

Then we came to the crowned head of all that superb coastline, St John's Head. It stands aloof, and separate from the other cliffs, as if conscious of a nobler destiny. And the great waves thundering against its base pay it resounding homage.

Now the Old Man of Hoy watched our approach, turning his several faces to us as we edged round him. At first he was like a stately gentleman with a pigeon breast and a top hat, and he watched the insignificant mortals below him with pompous annoyance . . . When we looked again, he was a long, inscrutable rectangle of rock, without feature or individuality . . . Finally, as we left him behind us there was something infinitely touching and reassuring in the sight of the Old Man. There is a comical and lonely aspect to him, but also an enormously powerful one. He is the gateway to Orkney. He is Orkney's Statue of Liberty, carved seemingly by the hands of the Norse gods themselves.

Now the Firth took us and rocked us gently in its breast . . . There

are vague and unresolved stories, all over the world, of an unbeliev-
ably savage piece of water which is the dread of the hardiest traveller
by sea. One trawler skipper called it the Gate of Hell, but it is more
commonly known as the Pentland Firth. Men never speak of it
without a shudder. Great tides thunder across it, from east to west,
from west to east, four times daily. Twice daily the Atlantic pours
itself through this narrow channel into the North Sea; and twice daily
the North Sea by the Pentland's gateway empties foaming cataracts
into the Atlantic Ocean.

Through this incredible disturbance of the sea, the *St Ola* is
whirled like a piece of derelict wood. On some days the wind, a boisterous Fury, sets itself maliciously to oppose the outpouring of the
tides. Then one sees such heroic conflict as only people of clear and
innocent conscience are able to behold. The clear rhythm of the
waves is broken, they lurch and surge in wild pandemonium, like a
million drunkards at a berserk feast. The gale, clear and cold, whips
the scum from their wavering crests through the yelling air . . . But
always one is conscious, on board this tiny ship, of a set course and
controlling hand. For nigh on sixty years this little mail steamer has
sailed to and fro across the Pentland, and become acquainted with all
her moods. It is impossible not to believe that there exists a strange
sympathy between the untamed element and the little ship that rides
it twice a day, six days a week in calm and storm. And certainly no
man living knows the Pentland Firth as well as Captain Banks.

There was no anger on the Pentland Firth the day we sailed across
it. The Orkneys passed from sight. The gentle rounded hills of home
dissolved in the mist: the outlines of the vast cliffs softened and
blurred, and presently disappeared. We looked ahead, but there was
no land to be seen. Then we realised, with a start of pleasure, that we
were in the middle of the dreaded Pentland Firth, and that it was
treating us as amicably as a millpond treats a paper boat or a piece of
straw. The passengers, waiting miserably to be sick, stirred themselves, and actually began to enjoy the gentle motion of the ship.

I stood right in the bow, and watched the *Ola* cleaving its way
across the Viking path to Caithness. Gently she would lift, easing
herself upwards; and then, as she fell forward in a long and dizzy
swoon, the white foam spurted from her bows, like plumes of vapour

from the nostrils of some proud-stepping horse. For an hour or more the rhythm, fascinating and soporific, was maintained, until one almost wished that it would go on for ever. The short lift of the bows, then the long dizzy lunge forward . . . And always the hiss of the foam, the beat of the engines, the cry of a solitary seabird, the laughter in the cabins, and the leisurely footsteps of the crew on the deck.

Perhaps I fell asleep, or was lulled into a doze, for when I awoke again we had cleared Dunnet Head, and the spires of Thurso appeared through the haze.

The *St Ola* glided towards Scrabster pier. The ropes were thrown and received. Tart Caithness voices shouted from the pier. The gangway was laid, and we stepped blithely ashore.

'If that's the Pentland,' said a cheerful voice, 'I love it.' Four mornings later we were to see the Firth in an altogether different mood.

For the moment, however, we were concerned with the long railway journey before us, with the strange cities and the strange faces we would see; and if we remembered the Pentland Firth at all, it was with a friendly and reassuring emotion.

April 1949

IN SEARCH OF A GREEN VALLEY

There are so many places to choose from on a beautiful Sunday afternoon – Birsay, Aikerness, Waulkmill, Skaill, Warbeth, Orphir. We had no such choice to make, for our Sunday afternoon destination had been decided on a week previously, and our anticipation flew straight as an arrow to one particular and precious place – Rackwick.

It only remained to hope that the day appointed would be a fine one.

The early dawn broke cloudless and clear. The birds woke to a new summer day. Whispers of wind went over the sea and rustled the heavy grasses.

When the people, coolly and doucely dressed, were returning from morning worship, I pulled a comb through my hair, packed some sandwiches in a cardboard box, and set out leisurely through the hot streets of the town. One by one the company gathered at the pier above the waiting motor-boat.

The engine woke to life and the boat made a quiet contented sound as it chugged out of the harbour. White waves spurted from its bows. The town fell away behind. We cleared the point and sailed westward between Graemsay and the Stromness pleasure beach. Smooth and treacherous, the current swirled around, but the plunging bows of the boat spurned it. Familiar landmarks came into view. The Black Crag raised its high and man-hating head, and we saw God's acre, the quiet fields where the dead lie above the sounding breakers and the dangerous reefs.

Then we came where the western lighthouse, white and squat, warns of the brown reefs below, and the immense buttresses of Hoy a mile beyond.

We edged carefully round Graemsay, and great hulks of rust and ruin – the block-ships sunk in the two world wars to seal the treacherous tides – reared starkly out of the water. Seabirds soared over the stricken masts. The ships, which have defied the fury of storm and tide for so many years, await the coming of the great wave which will finally shatter them and mingle their strong iron plates with shells and tangle at the restless sea bottom.

And now Hoy was before us, an island of strange wonderful contrasts, as we viewed it through binoculars passed quickly from hand to hand. Green and wooded, a scene from a tender pastoral comedy, it rises gently from the sea. Old brown farmhouses, stately manorial buildings with burns rushing by the garden walls, humble crofts crumbling to ruin . . . Then there is drama, as sudden and startling as the riot of murder in *Hamlet* after the courteous play of swords, or the cataracts of dreadful and splendid sonority which follow the sweet blowing of flutes in a Beethoven symphony.

For out of the pastoral serenity the hills of Hoy rise sudden, immense, and dramatic. Wave after wave they stretch westwards, until they overlook the Atlantic in a line of superb perpendicular cliffs.

But Nature has worked out a subtle drama here. For it is not the mountains, the high glens and the crags that conquer after all. At the extreme west of this lofty and wild terrain, hemmed in by the hills, a valley lovelier than any other in Orkney slopes down to the sea. Here are white sands and singing larks; here in Rackwick is a patchwork of fields, and a burn where the music is sweeter because of the surrounding hostility and desolation.

More satisfying than the overflowing beauties of Nature in these few acres is to see the old low crofts of Orkney with smoke coming from the chimneys and people moving peacefully about the doors as they have done, unaltered, for generations. The universal curse of concrete has not yet laid its blight on this fair valley. So the symphony has a quiet ending, of ineffable loveliness. The wild drama ends in joy and consolation.

The motor-boat, with engines shut off, drew in at the concrete pier of the island. We piled into the back of the enclosed van that was waiting for us, and moved off, in the pleasant pastoral landscape of woods, cornfields and streams, under the shadow of the Ward Hill.

Then, with that dramatic suddenness that belongs only to Hoy, we were plunged into gloom and desolation. The hills enclosed us. No plough had ever cloven these heathery slopes, no man had ever set up his habitation in this appalling solitude. The Psalmist could have found no better setting for the soul in the valley of the shadow.

It is indeed a place of the dead. Through this black glen the primitive Orcadians carried to burial some mighty chieftain, and placed the warrior reverently in his rock tomb, which we call the Dwarfie Stone. But the tomb has long been rifled, the bones of that exalted chieftain of Hoy have long since crumbled to dust.

By this dread valley the narrow road winds onwards, under a desolate sky, to the western sea. At the end of it there is a sudden blaze of colour and majesty, like unexpected victory after defeat, like resurrection after death. At the end of it all is Rackwick.

July 1949

RACKWICK

Let no voice idly whisper here.
Between those strong red cliffs,
Under that great mild sky
Lies Orkney's last enchantment,
The hidden valley of light.
Sweetness from the clouds pouring,
Songs from the surging sea.
Fenceless fields, fishermen with ploughs
And old heroes, endlessly sleeping
In Rackwick's compassionate hills.

1950

ROUSAY: ISLE OF BEAUTY AND HISTORY

Golf, I suppose, can lead a man into many excesses – into extravagant exaggeration, into neglect of wife and family, into moods of bleak despair. It can also lead him to Rousay.

Now Rousay is not half such a celebrated island as it should be. In parts it is very beautiful, as beautiful as Westray or Hoy. It is one of the classical islands of Orkney's Norse history too. Many fearful and wonderful things happened in 'the island of Hrolf'. Chiefly I remember how the good Earl Paul, out hunting the otter among the rocks below Westness, was kidnapped by the reckless outlaw Sweyn Asleifson, and borne away into oblivion.

At 12.45 p.m. on a hot day in mid-July over twenty Stromness golfers and their supporters crowded into the bus at Ness. Golf clubs were carefully stowed away, jackets taken off, and perspiration wiped from brows. Then the bus started, and a current of cool air circulated.

It looked a good bus, a reliable bus. But suddenly, going up a hill in the parish of Sandwick, the engine gave one disgruntled snort and ceased functioning. The bonnet was lifted, the experts peered inside. There was talk of a 'frozen plug' or some jargon like that. We lounged in ditches, chewing juicy grass stems and swatting the clegs that hovered with silent menace around, until another bus, urgently telephoned for, arrived. We all piled in, and the journey was resumed, through Sandwick, Dounby, Evie . . .

The sun had run into a long reef of white cloud. Orkney, which had been blazing with vivid colour like a fairground when we set out, was now flooded with subdued pearly light. Lovelier perhaps it is, and mellower, but Orkney, scourged with darkness and storm a winter long, thirsts for pure naked untrammelled sunlight. And a summer day that lacks it is somehow a cheat and a disappointment.

In Evie, just above where the slipway runs down, the bus jerked to a halt. We got out and stretched our limbs.

The big motor-boat was waiting for us, and there was no delay in packing aboard. The engine started, foam churned astern, the bow cut through the cold blue water, past Eynhallow, towards the brown hills of Rousay.

The water in the Sound, on such a day, is a beautiful blue. Not the harsh blue that one sees sometimes on an Orkney loch when the wind ruffles it, nor the insipid blue of a languid sky. But this blue is soft and sensuous, vivid and dancing, a blue like violets or a child's lively eyes . . . There are great masses of nebulous white cloud in the sky, the same that goes with early morning and late evening mist. Sometimes the sun breaks out, a great golden trumpeter, and the hills and the rocks respond with a rush of colour to the ardency of his summons. The next minute the sun is among the reefs of misty cloud, and the benison is withdrawn. As if in the orchestra of Nature, after a glad brazen clangour, somewhere a sombre cello has begun to play. But the sea of the Sound eastward is unchanged. The blue waves dance along, bright and lively, under the temperamental sun.

Strange how interested people are nowadays in Nature and its moods. The change came about five generations ago, when a humourless and observant young man called William Wordsworth pointed out that a mountain, far from being a vast ugly excrescence on earth's surface, is part of God's vision, is a mighty being proclaiming the infinite wonder of life. Some of Wordsworth's ecstasy, so pure it was, has filtered through to succeeding generations in a very much diluted form. It is now the done thing, if you see a sunset, to stand and gape at it, though with us it is no more than a slight tickling of the palate. With Wordsworth it was high religious sensation.

I'm sure that when the reckless Sweyn drove his longship through this Sound 800 years ago he never paused to meditate on the sheen of a wave's back, or the dazzling tip of a whitemaa's wing, or the little silvery sound the waves made slapping against the flanks of his boat. The Norsemen were not interested in Nature. If they thought about it at all, they thought of it as a nuisance. The Saga never wonders, for a moment, about the flowers of summer or the deep snows of winter.

The strenuous life of the body – that exclusively was what interested our ancestors. It is probably because they had so few distractions – no gnawings of conscience, no subtleties of thought, no random bewilderment of nature – that they were able to live their lives, their narrow lives, so well.

But enough of this. It fills me with horror to find myself theorising at such a time.

Dazzling spray spurted from the bows of the post-boat. Long delicate feathers of white cloud ruffled the sun's face. Away to the left, beyond Eynhallow, the cliffs of Birsay stood up bright and lofty. Wafts of sea air struck, strong and salty, into our faces.

When we stepped ashore on the Rousay slipway, the sun once more had broken free of the entangling cloud. We jumped over the pebbles and the squelching seaweed towards the road.

Rousay was a happy lyric poem this day. Bees, drunk with excess, rolled heavily among the clover. A burn gossiped and rattled and bubbled through the fields. The grass was teeming and vividly green.

We sat down at the roadside to await the arrival of our transport lorry, on the soft cool grass. Two larks were going up, in ecstatic corkscrew flights of song. You must have noticed how, after a sea crossing, clover smells specially sweet and intoxicating. The senses reel and are tipsy in the delight of it.

*

We had to wait for rather a long time, but we were not restive at all. We realised that country folk have urgent work to do and cannot leave the hayfield to drive a ball round a few acres of turf. Besides, we were not entirely unprovided with comforts as we loitered by the roadside. From every lip drooped a cigarette, purchased from the Post Office a little further into the heart of the island. There was a large cardboard box, discreetly covered with sacking, over which there was much bargaining . . .

Nature, too, spilled everything good from her horn of plenty that afternoon. Up aloft the larks staggering invisible about the blue sky emptied themselves in clear heart-bursts of song. The burn went chirruping and leaping over the rocks. So fragrant the air was too, with clover – a wild intoxicating aroma wafted from the fields. But any island, on a day like this, is a very anthology of smells and scents. Walk but twenty paces down the road to the beach, and it is the sea that assaults the nostrils – the pungent salty smell of the roosts and the decaying tang.

An islander that passed us slowly on his bike looked at us for a moment, goggle-eyed, and his front wheel wobbled a little. Then he recovered his composure and pedalled along with dignity, eyes straight ahead. But no wonder he was surprised. The sight of a score of able-bodied men, lounging about on the grass verge on such a halcyon day, was enough to unnerve any good countryman.

We were a motley crew. Every type of Stromnessian was represented, from Provost Robertson – still a good golfer – at the top, to Islandman at the foot, where with becoming modesty I place myself. We sat on the dyke, or lay in the grass, waiting for the lorry to come. I watched out of the tail of my eye the clegs hovering round. Suddenly one of those gray horrors would come in to land on the back of my hand with every intention of gorging himself on my rich red blood. But for once I was too quick. With the book poised in my free hand I struck smartly and viciously, and the winged abomination fell, a crumpled corpse, into the grass. I can never understand why God made clegs, to share the mild summer air with larksong and the breath of clover.

At last the lorry came, in a flurry of dust. Hearty greetings were exchanged between the Rousay men and the Stromnessians. There was a rapid piling on of golf bags, followed by human bodies inserting themselves into every nook and cranny. Then, with a jerk and a rattle, we were off again, up the gentle incline of the hill road. The air became fresher as the lorry mounted. A cultivated segment of Rousay lay before us, and above stretched the brown hill, climbing up wild and rugged.

After a too-brief journey – for following the lotus languors of the afternoon, the jolting and bone-shaking had been welcome – the laden lorry came to a halt above the golf course. The road here undulates along the sheer hill half-way up. Below are Eynhallow with its roosts and the treacherous foreshore where Earl Paul was seized and bundled into Sweyn the outlaw's ship. Above, over the summits of the hills, lie the Muckle Water and the Peerie Water, which trout fishers speak of with reverence.

What a fantastic stairway leads down from the road to the clubhouse! Rousay, in this region, seems to ascend from the beach to the lofty hilltops in a series of gigantic natural steps, maybe hacked out of the gradient by Cubbie Roo the legendary giant himself.

Just keeping our balance and no more, we eased ourselves down through the heather. At the corrugated-iron clubhouse, Rousay had sent one of her best and most magnanimous hosts to meet us – that jovial man in the red polo-neck jersey, Jas. Robert Lyon. I refuse to write about this welcome: it would require the pen of an angel to treat adequately of it. My stumbling sentences can only falter out a praise too poor.

But when the golfers came back from their loosening-up round there was a royal feast waiting for them. They sat out on the grass, picnic fashion, on the slope of one of those gigantic stairs, and gorged themselves to repletion on jammy cookies where the jam was almost as thick as the cookie; and flaky biscuits plastered with golden butter; on sandwiches with great wedges of cheese between them, like closing your teeth on a dream.

Well, at evening the golf began, when the Rousay players turned up. There was little curiosity about the score; all keen-edged rivalry was lacking from the game; to this day I don't know who won, and I don't care.

One tiny fly had strayed into the golden ointment of the day. With the approach of evening a fringe of cloud covered up the sun. Watching the golfers, as small as puppets far below, toiling up the gigantic natural stairway of the Rousay golf course, I felt an involuntary shiver up and down my spine . . . My scarf of many colours I knotted about my neck, and dreamed of supper. Across the Sound, Costa and Marwick were bathed in the warm light of evening. But over here, in Rousay, the cold shadows were folding.

The quartets of golfers returned. Supper was served, J.R. Lyon presiding. It was a magnificent repeat of tea, in every respect. I wished that night for a dozen stomachs.

Thicker and colder the shadows gathered. The lorry (we were told) was waiting. The Provost, in precise heartfelt phrases, expressed our thanks. Then we were off, going down, down, past Eynhallow and the Pictish Brochs, towards the slipway. Other faces rose out of the summer gloom to meet us – Stromnessians who hadn't been at the golf course, but had picnicked elsewhere (and, I warrant them, not in such luxury).

We sang all the way home in the boat and the bus, and arrived in Stromness on a sleepy midnight, when most of the houses were dark, and here and there a friendly light shone through the grimlings to guide our errant footsteps home.

August 1950

A Sky-scape in March

It was the first real spring day. The sun had been bright all morning, but the wind swirling in from the south-west was cold. Everywhere birds were singing; men were painting their upturned boats in back gardens, and the first spadefuls of earth were being turned . . . The pleasant rituals of springtime were beginning.

When, after dinner, I threw on a light raincoat and set out to take my usual leisurely walk round the Point, a huge black cloud was brooding on the summits of Hoy. There was an oceanful of moisture in it. And sure enough, in a few minutes, the black cloud let down long gray delicate veils of rain over Hoy, until the island appeared sombre and ghostly.

I like to watch the behaviour of clouds. They interest me more than birds or flowers. Soon a great solid-seeming wedge of cloud split off from the main mass, and sped away northwards, driven by the trumpeting wind. Against the cliffs and fields of Sandwick a deluge would burst in fifteen minutes. Meantime the large cloud over Hoy reached up and swallowed the sun. I was looking at the wet Coolags, when the shadow fell over Stromness town and parish. The effect was dramatic and frightening. – Yet over towards Orphir the hills lay in full sunshine, and the waters of Hoy Sound were of an indescribably beautiful blue.

It was only a spring shower. Gradually the curtains of rain lifted from Hoy. First the Kame, then the Coolags, re-emerged into sunshine, looking the fresher from their wetting. Then the Skallowirt cleared up, and the Ward Hill shone out strong and serene.

The vast rampart of rain was tumbled along eastwards by the wind, but not before a ragged tatter of cloud had pelted me and the road I was walking along with a thousand brilliantly gleaming raindrops.

Now over Orphir and the South Isles the shadows were falling. I thought how, in a few minutes' time, the streets of Kirkwall would be gleaming wet. A truncated rainbow sprouted out of Brinkie's Brae. Over the gray harbour water went a flush of blue – a lively sensuous blue to set the pulses racing. The sun came out again, magnificently. It was a wonderful spring day, with only dull bruises in the sky, north and east, to witness to the late downpour.

I arrived at the Shelter, just as the bogie was being lit for the day, and smoked a pipeful, pleased with the best walk I have had this year.

March 1951

OUT ON THE LIFEBOAT

'Keep your head down,' said the lifeboatman, 'and hold on to the rail.' The boat began to move down the slipway. It emerged from the gloom of the shed into the gray light of an April afternoon. Two seconds later it hit the water, engines churning. Immense white billows rose on either side. There was one moment of fierce exaltation, and then the lifeboat was buoyant on the sea and heading merrily out of the harbour.

Even to watch a lifeboat diving down to meet the sea is exciting. Hundreds of times I must have seen it, and always wondered what it was like to be on board the lifeboat that poetical moment. Well, now I knew – there is that one moment of high excitement, and then things quieten down to a more even tempo . . . Unless, of course, one is going to rescue drowning seamen, with mighty seas running and a great gale blowing.

On this occasion, however, the lifeboat was out on a mild practice run. The sea was calm and gray. The air was cold, and grew icier the further out to sea we went. Hoy still wore caps of white on its summits. And, rather to the amusement of the stalwart fishermen who man this lifeboat, there was a reporter on board.

Standing on the deck, we chatted about this and that. They were gloomy over the lobster prospects. Heavy seas out west for the past few days had meant they were unable to visit their creels. They anticipated with the virile fatalism of Orkney fishermen that when they did manage to go out most of the creels would be smashed or missing. And they spoke of the Swedish tanker *Oljaren*, fast on the Pentland Skerries. Just the previous day it had come over the wireless that the crew's private belongings had been pilfered. The lifeboatmen spoke bitterly about that.

One of them said, with a twinkle in his eye: 'Plunder the ship of coorse, if shae's a total wreck. Orkneymen hev done that for centuries. But tae pinch the crew's private possessions – that's hellish.'

Then, to show that lifeboatmen are not exclusively interested in things of the sea, we began to speak about Gilbert Harding and *Twenty Questions*, and of the forthcoming municipal election.

Noticing that I was a bit cold (we were now in the middle of Hoy Sound, which surged and eddied round our powerful little tub of a vessel like a glacial stream) Bob Greig began to make allusions to the vast quantity of rum that was hidden somewhere on board . . . I was quite content, however, to leave the rum to poor shipwrecked mariners. Needless to say, we completed the journey that day without a drop of Nelson's blood.

Meantime the lifeboat, chugging along at a steady nine knots, had rounded the Graemsay east light and was running along the barren coast of Hoy. I allowed myself to be appalled for a moment, seeing the battery at Scad Head. How could men from London or Glasgow have borne to live here for months on end? Miles of moorland, utter dark desolation, closed it in.

On Cava there was no sign of life, but on Rysa Little muirburn was in progress. One would scarcely have believed that a fire could give off so much smoke. Westwards it rolled off the tiny islet, a slow undulating wedge of solid gray. As the lifeboat went through it, visibility suddenly narrowed to a few feet. The smoke of muirburn eddied round us like a dense summer fog. Then hints of brightness appeared. The solid gray atmosphere was prinked with bright bluish tints, and then quite suddenly we were in the free open air again.

Fara, bleak and apparently deserted, lay on the left, and on the right appeared the first hints of the shanty town, Lyness, which was our destination. The only men who were working were Coxswain Sinclair, who steered through fog, tideways and bursts of sunshine with the same rock-like imperturbability; and the engineer, Mr MacLeod, who was speaking to the coastguards at Wick. Back came the answer from Wick, so ear-shattering that the small cabin trembled. The wireless of the *J.J.K.S.W.* was evidently in good repair.

Now Lyness swam into our ken – the immense rounded oil storage tanks, the wooden jetties, the endless huts, the hopeless ugliness and depression everywhere. The lifeboat merely touched at Lyness, to put ashore the engineer inspector; and then we turned for home.

By now the coldness had struck into my very marrow. My hands were of a corpse-like blue colour, and my teeth chattered when I tried to speak. So I lay, with two other members of the crew, in a sheltered apartment in the bow, and we smoked.

They spoke of the new lifeboat, which is expected in a matter of months. The days of this present one, launched by the late Duke of Kent in 1928, are almost over.

On the whole her career has been quiet. She has been called upon to perform no spectacular rescues, unlike her predecessor the *Good Shepherd*. But the crew were always ready. Night or day the summoning rockets might call them from their beds, or from their line-baiting, to hazard and danger. These are words they are inclined to laugh at when they hear spoken; it embarrasses them to be thought of as heroes. And yet it is a simple fact that, for very small remuneration, these men are willing and ready to undertake duties which could lead them into situations we shudder to think of.

As the boat headed once more northwards into Burra Sound, the engines had a solid baritone pulse. We knew that her heart was sound.

We re-entered Stromness harbour and approached the slip. One or two youthful idlers hung about the adjacent piers, watching our return; for anything to do with the lifeboat is news in Stromness. The folk are inordinately proud of the boat. Kirkwall may boast of the Cathedral and the Earl's Palace, but any good Stromness man will think the balance adequately restored if he retorts that Kirkwall has no *Ola* and no lifeboat.

If there is a certain glamour in the launching of the lifeboat – the sheer nosedive into the sea and the dazzle of spray bursting over the bows – there is none whatever about the return to the station. It is a slow protracted business, rather undignified, rather an anti-climax; for the blue jaunty little dancer is hauled, stern-first and by inches, up the wooden slipway down which she careered with such *élan* only two hours previously.

The lifeboat was back in her shed. Stiff and blue-fingered, I climbed down the ladder. The crew were scuttling round everywhere, busy about a hundred little jobs. The engineer was filling the tanks with petrol for the next emergency, which might happen tonight, for aught anyone knew . . . He calculated that 25 gallons had been used in the practice run to Lyness.

I had satisfied another ambition dear to the heart of every Stromness man, but denied to most of them – a trip on the lifeboat. My step, as I went up the street, was jaunty; and who can blame me.

*

I have, in the above account of *J.J.K.S.W.*'s 'quiet' career, quite forgotten about the famous episode in the early morning of 14 February 1929, when the crew of the *Carmenia II* were snatched from death at the Kirk Rocks. The late coxswain Johnston was the man in charge on that memorable occasion.

May 1951

From Brinkie's Brae

The other Sunday night we climbed to the top of Brinkie's Brae, hurriedly, to see the sunset. But we were a quarter of an hour too late. The west showed long parallel reefs of crimson and gold, very beautiful, but the sun was under the horizon. All the same, we thought the effort worth while.

In the lingering twilight of mid-August, everything around us had an evanescent beauty. Sitting at the base of the granite cairn 300 feet up, half of Orkney was spread out below us. Northwards were two silver gleams with a thin line dividing them – the lochs of Stenness and Harray. We looked closer at the thin black dividing line, and there was the circle of Brodgar, very tiny against the silver of the loch. Fortunately, we had binoculars, or half of the night's enchantment would have eluded us. There, in a fold of the hills, was the Binscarth plantation, rich with summer foliage. A little to the right the Hill of Heddle, with Buckle's Tower a dark nodule against the sky. And then the powerful glasses picked out the wind-generating plant on Costa Head. Over to the left was Kitchener's memorial, squat and solid against the flush in the west.

It was as rich and dramatic a landscape as anyone can conceive.

Stromness lay beneath us. The hill cut off the North End, but in the South End the first lights were appearing in the houses. The Holms lay spread out flat as on a map, and so close that you might think one gigantic leap from this granite cairn would land you on them. The sun still flared crimson against the Kame of Hoy, but the hills themselves were changing from purple to black, and the lighthouse on Graemsay shot out long, wavering pathways of light across the quiet Sound.

All behind us was the 'vacant wine-red moor', tough with luxuriant heather, and here and there a green patch starred with daisies, eyebright, tormentil. Across the undulating moorland rolled the sounds of the western sea – a long low sonorous croon that reminds men of the vastness of eternity. At any rate, most of our Orkney kirk-yards are built beside the sea, and one can imagine no fitter resting-place for the vanished generations.

And we saw a kestrel in the gathering darkness, cutting a superb graph of flight against hill and sky – the long downward glide on level wings, the sudden fluttering rise, the incredible hover, pivoted motionless in space – and then that downward glide again, till we lost him in the hollows.

We had one more fine sight as we were coming down by another route. Suddenly a yellow segment swam up, until the harvest moon appeared over the Orphir hills, and stood precariously balanced, like a large improbable orange, on the sheer crest. We turned the binoc-ulars on it, and saw the peculiar map on its surface. Now it was clear, and the sky had a new splendour in addition to the few stars, the red west, the hovering kestrel.

We climbed down into the silent town, all four of us, and thought that, from the point of view of worship, it was almost as good as having been in church.

August 1951

A PHANTOM ROAD

Two ways lead out of Rackwick to North Hoy. One, skirting the east side of the Ward Hill, is beautifully tarmacked and five miles long. It winds through utter desolation, and hills with weird-sounding names like the Knap o' the Trowie Glen, look down on it. A few hundred yards from it is the Dwarfie Stone, lying bearded with lichen among the heather.

The other way girdles the Ward Hill on its west side. About it we knew nothing, except that the path was now little used. Compared to the modern road it was, we were led to believe, rough and craggy, and had only one advantage – it was much shorter.

We decided to adventure home along it.

The sun was going down as we left Rackwick, after a happy day of conversation and good food. The sun slid prematurely behind the high hills, and a great silent shadow moved across the valley, until only the brown hills to the south remained sunlit. The mild wind of afternoon had turned chilly now.

Between the Coolags and the Ward Hill – which we were seeing from the rear – straggled a long line of telegraph poles. The rough road, we had been told, accompanied these all the way. We couldn't possibly go wrong. It was half-past seven by our watches. We had promised the boatman to be at the pier of North Bay by nine o'clock.

I kept looking for the track that was supposed to be there. But, except for a few broken hints, there was nothing. We were not so much walking as precariously scrambling up a long heathery incline, beyond comprehension gloomy and barren. And the light was thickening.

Once, looking back, I could still see the upper houses of Rackwick against the horizon. The sky above and around them was bright; the cliffs glowed red in the horizontal sun; the sea shimmered.

But as for us, we had to turn our backs on Rackwick, and clamber through rough heather into deeper and deeper shadow.

Now a formidable obstacle opposed us. Our way lay across the burn, wide at this point, and all stepping stones had long since been washed away. We lifted great boulders and heaved them down into the stream, but the water flowed and frothed over them. One of my companions, six feet four and a half inches in height, then made a heroic leap and, with an inch to spare, landed safe on the other side.

Somehow we others got across it, and resumed our trek through the heather, which, growing ever more luxurious, clawed harshly at our shins.

It would not have been so bad if the ground had been dry. But a long summer of rains had made this valley full of little streams and runnels. It was impossible to progress in a straight line. One had to zigzag, sometimes violently, to avoid a sudden gurgling pool. Once I stepped up to the ankles in mire, and the thick clay almost sucked my shoe off. But long before the end of that journey my saturated foot was dry again. I walked and clambered it into aridity.

Once more we looked back. Rackwick and its houses had vanished. Nothing was left but the shining sky above it, and the flushed brow of a cliff. Down over the Coolags and the Ward Hill came a clinging mist. I imagined us fog-bound in this horrible place, and quickened my steps.

Now we had left the heather paths and were walking along what appeared to be the dried-up bed of a considerable burn. Sunk deep, like a gully in the heather, it was paved sometimes with sand and sometimes with sharp uneven stones. Progress along it was a kind of hop, skip and jump. One had to be as agile as a goat to preserve one's balance, and it was fatiguing work.

It was only later that I learned that this was the road, or what remained of it. Long neglect and the continuous heavy rains had washed this once-important highway away. What we were walking along was its uneven foundation. For considerable stretches it was under water. Then we had to climb again on to the heather, and trudge through barren scratching luxuriance.

Watching the shadows gathering, and the weird fingers of mist groping down from the hill summits, I couldn't help thinking of Captain Scott on the Antarctic ice-cap, and that one tent in the midst of the howling blizzard.

But, however slowly, we were making progress. The Ward Hill, on our right, kept turning a new now faintly familiar face towards us. I saw, right at the foot of it, the Sandy Loch, a stretch of water I had never seen before. What like it is in sunshine I have no idea, but on a summer night it is as ugsome and horrible a place as you can imagine. It lay in a cup of the valley, under the scarred hill, long and still and black. When Shakespeare wrote that powerful line – 'Nero was a fisher in the lake of darkness' – he must have had a place something like this in mind. I was glad to keep my eyes averted from it. Even to think of it now makes me shudder.

Among the heather we came on fragments of a crashed aeroplane. In that dark place the broken pieces of fuselage gleamed weirdly. Later, we were told that the dead airmen are buried in the hill: but perhaps that is pure imagination.

But now our fantastic walk was almost over. We struggled to an elevated ridge of ground from which the land fell away on both sides. Before us lay North Hoy, benign in the evening light. Houses, crops, the sea, blessed our eyes.

A few hundred yards further on and we were out of wet soggy heather, on the firm metalled road. Never, I think, have my feet walked more sprightly and gay along any highway. Only in a trackless wilderness do you appreciate the blessings of civilisation. The road was all downhill now. We swung briskly past Orgill Lodge and the Post Office, shouting a farewell to our friend, Mr Isaac Moar as we passed. At the small concrete pier Angus Brown was waiting for us in his motor-boat. The tide was full. The time was 9.30.

It was a swift journey back to Stromness. We steered between the block-ships, passing thrillingly close under the stern of one. In the fast-gathering darkness Hoy Low shot its gleam across our bow. Soon we were in Hoy Sound itself, and, securely held in the powerful tide race, went catapulting between the winking Beacon and the steady glare of Hoy High into Stromness harbour. The town was all aglow in the summer darkness. In a flat calm we glided into the nearest pier.

We went ashore up the stone steps and made for home. My legs moved under me, mechanically, like a puppet's blocks of wood. It was only then I realised how tired I was. And how glad, too, because of the extraordinary day we had spent.

August 1952

A VISIT TO THE CATHEDRAL

I went one afternoon last week with my friend Ernest Marwick to visit the Cathedral. When one lives close to it, one is inclined to take it too much for granted, forgetting what a rich and marvellous building it is.

Not in any serious or antiquarian mood we went to visit it, stepping from the large June sunlight into the heavy rich glooms of the kirk.

The first thing that strikes you overpoweringly is its stoniness. I don't mean that it is hard and cold like a stony place in Nature. Behind those great symphonic masses of stone, you can sense the skilled workman and artificer. They expressed their faith in stone, and it wasn't a weak-kneed watery faith – it was strong and virile, and so the kirk they built, being a true reflection of their faith, is strong and virile too. Not for them the graceful feminine contours of some southern minsters. Our Saint Magnus is a masculine cathedral, with a touch of stimulating harshness in it.

We climbed the stone spiral stairway into the triforium, and there, in the spacious 'Sooth Loft', saw many symbols of Kirkwall's history. Up there is the public hangman's ladder, a tall affair of great wide rungs divided into two sections. Up one went the master craftsman, with prospects of a good dinner when the job was finished. Up the other side stumbled the poor devil who would never come down again . . . And there, near it, like a dead iron flower, very big, was an old bell of the Cathedral which had summoned pre-Reformation Kirkwallians to mass.

There were the works of the old town clock, a weird but strongly built complication of wheels and balances, like a piece of very modernistic sculpture. We saw a number of old pew panels where the local gentry and county people had sat to hear the word of God, while the poor squatted in anonymous filth wherever they could get a seat. Many of these pews are beautifully carved.

Preserved under glass is the most valuable relic of all perhaps – the wooden casket which held the bones and the cleft skull of the saint whose life and martyrdom inspired men to build this great kirk.

Stored against the walls are some of the ancient windows with the leaf design. Nowadays light comes richly into the Cathedral through the eighty-three stained-glass windows of the Thoms bequest: comes in blue and red and green and silver, flooding the interior with shifting, changing colour . . . But while Sheriff Thoms was still with us, lost and tangled in wild undergrowths of eccentricity, light entered St Magnus through those plain glass windows with the charming leaf design. Mr Albert Thomson, the well-informed caretaker, showed us two leaf windows that still remain. Compared with the richness and splendour of their stained-glass neighbours, they are not so poor-looking and tawdry as you might think.

The great Thoms Memorial Window itself, at the east end of the kirk, can only be viewed in all its beauty and intricate detail and symbolism from a certain arch in the choir triforium, where we stood with Mr Thomson while he explained it to us. It is a lovely work of art; not to be compared, perhaps, with the sheer magnificence of the glass of Chartres Cathedral, but, all the same, full of grace, sweetness and light. In his will, the only stipulation Sheriff Thoms made about the memorial window was that it must depict the Crucifixion.

Of the remaining 116 windows in St Magnus, 82 are in stained glass, and depict saints, patriarchs, prophets and (rather surprisingly) one or two arrant rogues like Turf-Einar and Norsemen of that ilk. They make a varied and goodly company.

Mr Thomson let us into the strong-room in the south transept, where are stored all the Orkney Presbytery records since the late seventeenth century. We didn't have time to look at any of them, but we knew that in those rows of manuscript volumes must be true stories of great drama, great courage, and probably much that is comic and sordid.

Mr Thomson told us that the strong-room was, once on a time, the courtroom. In it, no doubt, stood many an accused man with hope bright on his brow: to go out, an hour later, with the angel of death shadowing him.

Before we left the Cathedral, Mr Thomson showed us, in one of the side chapels, two enormous old-time collection plates, massive things of beaten brass, as large as cart-wheels, with the Garden of Eden drama quaintly depicted on them. They date from 1636.

We had time to explore only a tithe of the marvellous things that St Magnus contains. Symbols of evil and good, of power and mercy and sacrifice lie in close proximity and rich profusion in those red shadows. We hope to return again fairly soon; to climb to the top of the tower, perhaps, and see all Kirkwall spread out below us, from Scapa to the Peerie Sea, nipping the Mainland in two, and catching all the wealth that flows through Orkney from West to East, and from the North and the South Isles.

June 1954

A Day in Rendall

Last Wednesday afternoon David Fox, senior, and I went to Rendall to see our old friend Jimmy Sinclair of Lyking.

The Evie bus was crammed with folk. At our back visitors from Glasgow were quizzing a young countryman about this, that, and the other thing. And he, not to be outdone, was quizzing them in return – Where did they come from? What were they doing in Orkney? Had they seen the battleships in the Flow?

At Finstown, that delightful village, the bus strikes northwards – all hill on one side, all dreary flatness on the other. Not by any means do you see the best of Rendall from the Finstown–Evie road.

Jimmy Sinclair was there meeting us at the end of his own branch road. It is a lyrical little road to Lyking, with a good deal of winding in it and ups and downs, and that afternoon it was gay with trefoil and buttercups, daisies, cotton and springy heather. There was an invisible lark singing, and a lapwing flying overhead and making sounds like a boy blowing through a split grass.

Coming over a small rise I could see that Rendall has another ace which she rarely shows the public. Lyking lies snugly on a beautiful grassy eminence above Gairsay, which floats like a German bun on the bright water. To the left are the hills of Rousay, and Wyre is a little green strip in front.

When Jimmy Sinclair came to Lyking forty years ago, it was a small stony croft of some 14 acres arable. Today there are more than 50 acres, for Jimmy Sinclair and his family have pitted their strength and skill, aided by all the resources of a machine age against the primeval hill, and gradually tamed it. This has been happening all over the islands. No wonder there is such an air of confidence these days in the Orkney countryside.

We passed masons adding a new wing to Jimmy's living quarters, and then went in to a bountiful meal of sooan scones, rhubarb jam, and good strong tea. The three ladies of the house – Mrs Sinclair, Mrs Harrold and Dora – looked after us well, and there was much pleasant talk and laughter. It is a typical Orkney farmhouse kitchen, with blue flag for a floor, a bright array of tins on the mantelpiece, numerous calendars and pictures of champion horses on the walls, and that delicious all-pervading smell of burning peat.

Afterwards Davie Fox and I walked with Jimmy across his land, every now and then bestriding a fence. The afternoon was bright, with a warm wind blowing. Chiefly Davie Fox was interested to see the hill land that Jimmy had broken out over the years. It was very impressive. The hill round here is tough indestructible stuff: stone and heather densely woven. Jimmy has transformed the dead places into soft green fields, with fine fat beasts strolling through the shimmering grass, and oats beginning to sprout.

The country folk are proud of their achievement, and no wonder. It is more fun, I should think, to see these green fields where once there was bog, than to do something new with the language, like T.S. Eliot or Dylan Thomas. At least the field is actual, animals can feed there and men sow and reap the bread of time; but Eliot may only have provided a field for a few barren intellectuals, with that sowing which poets like to call 'eternal', flattering themselves.

Jimmy pointed out, with great pride, the pool that never dries summer or winter, and the good white cow that has had nine calves ('every dealer wants tae buy her'); and Davie promised to set his ferrets on the rabbits which breed like mad round a little knoll. We saw an old hen tenderly fostering a brood of young turkeys in the back yard, and the milking cows, their udders swollen with plenitude.

The ladies of Lyking must have thought that the country air would make us very hungry, for when we went in there was a really enormous tea spread for us, of roasted chicken and bere bannocks and cakes and Swiss roll . . .

Afterwards we lit our pipes and strolled over the hill shoulder to Orquil, which is farmed by Mr James Skea. Sixteen white and red Ayrshire cows were being electrically milked in the byre.

On to the pigs' house, where four grunters – one yellow, with a dainty white head – romped playfully, while, led by the Skea boys, I picked my way through gilded pools and that strong sweet gorge-raising smell peculiar to pigs, into an inner sanctum, where a really immense porker lay on her side and a dozen week-old piglets with curly tails scampered round her. Two sought her dugs, and used their whole bodies for sucking pumps. The naked pair were quickly joined by half a dozen others, all wallowing in an ecstasy of greed. ('They're gettan nothing,' said the elder boy, Ian. 'The sow'll only let them get milk if she wants. You can tell when they're gettan milk because the sow grunts different then.')

The old sow, a great sausage-shaped hulk of inert filthy sensuality, decided not to gratify her offspring, for she lurched to her feet and the baffled feeders dropped from her flanks.

In a little stall by himself crouched, shivering and asleep, a tiny piglet small as a kitten. There is no room for him at his mother's dugs, so he must be artificially reared. His drinking trough, a small tin, lies beside the sleeper . . .

So ended our trip to Rendall. It had been such a full happy day that, when we were besought and entreated to return soon, we considered that all the beseeching should have come from us.

June 1954

THE MYSTERIOUS HARRAY LOCH

On Thursday afternoon we went for an hour's fishing on Harray Loch.

The countryside wore its lovely June garment as the car took us quickly to the inland parish. Fields were overflowing with buttercups. Here and there in the distance a streak of white told us the cotton was flourishing, the harbinger of a fine sunny summer. As we got into Harray the wild blue lupins raised their tall spires in the fields.

The sun was aloft and untouchable in the afternoon sky, with a few mild white shreds of cloud. Only Hoy, over the flat landscape, was covered with a film of rain.

We left the road, and the brake went clattering down a rural track. We stopped in the yard of an old low farmhouse, almost derelict. But when we looked through the window, the chairs were set out in order and the oilcloth gleamed on the table. Someone was still using it for a summer residence.

Immediately below us was the loch, with an islet off-shore guarded by a swan, and a little green promontory tipped with the ruins of a pre-Reformation chapel. A lovely place to worship in. The ancient generations of Orkneymen had genius when they chose the sites for their kirks and monasteries.

In the field next to where we were standing, the young cows eyed us long and solemnly, and then suddenly, losing interest, went down to the loch to drink. When they raised their heads again their snouts were all white with marginal foam.

The boat was waiting for us, drawn up at its rude landing slip. We untied the heavy mooring rope, and pushed her into the water. A small breeze had sprung up out of nowhere, ruffling the water . . . The great smear of rain over Hoy was reaching after us.

I was surprised at the shallowness of the loch. After we had rowed twenty strokes towards the islet, I looked over, and could almost have touched the bottom with my fingers. What a fantastic floor it has too, this tideless freshwater Loch of Harray – a litter of great flat brown stones, some of them immense, overlaying each other. In those mysterious interstices lurk the famous Loch Harray trout, noted for their strength, intelligence, and the goodness of their flesh.

A strange loch, with a drunken, capricious floor to it, rising into bare reefs and green islets, and sinking into opaque depths.

But meantime we were afloat on the loch, and were casting all round us for trout. The swan rose from beside her small islet with a clap of her wings, and flew away northwards. A field inland, a skylark was singing as if he would burst with joy. Teeacks cried plaintively over the green oats.

It seemed it was not a good day for fishing. Strange-shaped flies hovered and darted over the still surface of the loch. The trout were after them all right, rising in a quick bronze arch and falling back into the water with a plop. They're wise, these trout, and they knew well enough that our gaudy-coloured flies were made to deceive them by some girl in an English factory.

The blue-black rain cloud spread rapidly over the sky. We were fishing beside Kirkquoy, with its ruined chapel all overgrown with buttercups and nettles, when the first heavy drops fell, wetting our hands and spreading frail concentric circles in the water. It was just then that we caught our one and only trout – an innocent young cratur too immature to know the difference between real Harray flies and the flies they make in an English factory. He made a fight for his life, too, darting under the boat and into the rocks. But at last we reeled him in; and, seeing how brave he had been, we returned him to the loch.

Soon it was time to return. We navigated the safe channels that score the Harray Loch, trailing the line behind us. But though fish were jumping here and there, devil a one would bite. The sun was out again, warmer than ever. The surface of the loch was rapidly spreading to a flat calm, and the air was thick with flies – just the worst weather for catching trout.

Merkister, the house Eric Linklater built, lay just across the loch from us, like a white immaculate dice. Eric Linklater has often written beautifully about the loch, and about its variety of moods. We had seen one or two of them in two brief hours that afternoon.

The strangest thing that happened to us was the coating of flies we got when we were beaching the boat – weird flies, cut like modern stratocruisers, and with wings like opaque plastic. They clustered in scores, immobile, on our jackets and trousers. And then, as we left the loch, something utterly unheard of began to happen to them: they disintegrated before our very eyes. They shrank and turned into a white ash, like tiny shreds of burnt paper. Never have I seen death in such an astonishing disguise.

Loch of Harray, you are a mysterious piece of water, with strange creatures alive on you; and sometime soon we must investigate you further.

June 1955

Finished Fragrance

KIRKYARD

A silent conquering army,
The island dead,
Column on column, each with a stone banner
Raised over his head.

A green wave full of fish
Drifted far
In wavering westering ebb-drawn shoals beyond
Sinker or star.

A labyrinth of celled
And waxen pain.
Yet I come to the honeycomb often, to sip the finished
Fragrance of men.

1971
(*Selected Poems, 1954–1992*)

A FORGOTTEN TOMB

I like walking through Orkney churchyards, for reasons not entirely morbid. It is a relief to escape from the world of the present, with all its doubts and difficulties, into the fragrant storied past. Here, in the kirkyard, is the history of our ancestors, with its great stone pages that you turn over with endless fascination. It is an obscure jumbled history, full of hints and guesses, and, unless you bring to it sympathy and imagination, you will only be baffled and repelled.

In the kirkyard that I like best of all, there are thousands of tombstones, dating back to the sixteenth century. There were burials before then, certainly, but in the remoter past tombstones were put up for the wealthy only. The poor people were simply gathered to their fathers, and that was the end of them. They lay patiently in their dust, waiting for the trumpet of resurrection. I can never forget my father saying, 'There are more folk lying dead in this kirkyard than there are living nowadays in the whole of Orkney.' It seemed, to my childish mind, a most powerful illustration of the transitory nature of human life.

*

Somewhere in the seventeenth century, it seems, tombstones became the fashion. Slabs of blue stone, with the beautifully cut inscriptions of the period, were placed horizontally over the dead. A century later, the tombstones, still flat, had decorations of a grim sophistication – a frieze of hour-glasses and scythes and skulls round the border. Death was real and stark to those ancestors, and was not to be hidden away under masses of flowers and soft words.

Then, with the nineteenth century, vulgarity began. Tombstones stood upright, and blossomed with angels and funereal urns. The ugliness of extinction must be hidden under an efflorescence of tawdry beauty.

There was one tombstone in particular that always fascinated us when we were children. It was the memorial of a girl who had died in 1858 when she was only seventeen, and it was the rhyme at the foot of it that troubled us with its wistful ghostly melancholy:

> Stop for a moment, youthful passer-by,
> On this memento cast a serious eye.
> Though now the rose of health may flush your cheek,
> And youthful vigour, health and strength bespeak,
> Yet think how soon, like me, you may become,
> In youth's fair prime, the tenant of the tomb.

Ellen Dunne was the girl's name, and we often wondered about her, what she was like, and whereabouts in town she lived. Someone, her father most likely, had planted a tree on her grave, and put around it a massive iron railing. The tree's branches brushed the face of the tomb, so that we had to draw them aside to read the inscription; and the iron spikes had turned brown and flaky with rust.

*

That she was a girl of some wealth, according to Orkney standards in the mid-nineteenth century, was obvious from the size of the tombstone. Her father was probably an exciseman or a shipowner, and lived in one of the tall houses overlooking the harbour. She went, demurely, in her long skirts, to the school on the side of the hill, and piously, on the Sabbath, to the big new imposing kirk with the wooden gallery in it, and the clock, and the loud summoning bell.

When spring came, gaiety flushed her heart, for the sky was full of returning birds, and the pier in front of her father's house was bright with dandelions and buttercups, and over towards Garson the ploughman was turning, with every slow furrow, the book of April.

Then it was summer, and the bare-legged boys fished for sillocks off the neighbouring piers. There were always foreign boats sailing into the harbour, and the sun shone all day with such brilliance that Ellen thought winter could never come.

The town was full of strange, lovable macabre sights – old shawled women running to the ale-houses with furtive porter cans; evangelists shouting damnation and redemption at the foot of Hellihole; men astray in their wits mouthing and grimacing in dark corners of the street.

And oh, she grew to love it all as the brief years passed – even the tragic story of Gow the Pirate and the sorrowful tales of all the sailors who drowned round the merciless winter coasts of Orkney. And a still more piercing sweetness was distilling in her young breast, for sometimes she would notice the sailors looking at her boldly and eagerly, and she looked back at them with a shy answering gladness.

*

From where does it come, the worm that blights young life? On what dark wind is it carried, and why does it choose for its resting place the brave and the beautiful?

There came a springtime when Ellen Dunne began to droop. The health left her cheek and a grayness settled on it for a few months, to be succeeded by a fierce hectic blossoming. Her feet dragged on the street, and a great weariness filled her young body. The old bearded doctor looked at her, and nodded sagely. 'We can no more stop that decline,' he said to her father, 'than we can stop the wind blowing or the tide ebbing.'

It was all over so quickly for Ellen Dunne. The last scene of all was the open grave beside the kirkyard wall, and the massive Presbyterian ritual of death, and the mourners standing round smelling of mothballs and whisky.

Then, a few weeks later, her father planted the tree on her grave, and put the iron railing round it.

*

Last month I visited the kirkyard, and went to see the grave of Ellen Dunne. I drew aside the branches once more and a bird flew up out of the heart of the tree. The waves thundered on the beach of

Warbeth. The sun was high and hot in the sky. On the other side of the wall, only a few feet from where she lay, the corn was turning yellow for harvest. From the tomb came to me once more that hundred-year-old rhyme, that dim tangle of ghostly loveliness and age-old sorrow.

13 September 1955

MARY JANE MACKAY – 1891–1967 (A MEMOIR)

I think that branch of the Mackay clan was uprooted in the great nineteenth-century clearances and told there was land for them northwards, on the Pentland Firth coast. And there was land, but bare and bleak and stony. *But there is the sea on your doorsteps – you can catch haddock and cod and lobsters.*

Some of them had never seen the sea before. The noise of it may have been a terror to them. They had no skill in boatbuilding or making of creels.

Somewhere along that coast they found a man with knowledge of the curves of a boat, and the fitting together of planks, and how canvas should be sewn for sails.

And another man led them to the one door of life and death, the fish-fraught sea, and tried to tell them of the shifting of the tides, and rocks seen and unseen, and how to discover a storm under a limpid horizon.

And they built their hovels.

And they set wooden ploughs to stony acres.

They had to deal in money instead of in chickens and pigs. The coins, such few as they handled, were hard and alien and cold.

Their Church of Scotland ministers had sided with the alien lords who had uprooted them from their green straths and sweet waters, so that large English sheep could graze there, in the emptiness and silence. Their new pastors were men of a bleak gloomy faith, such as perhaps went better with their new way of life; from which laughter and poetry and Celtic legend were uprooted: a kind of racial mutilation.

But the joy of life could not be held down in the children. Round hearth and table and doorway Gaelic lingered in the mouths of all. In

124

the kirk it was the seventeenth-century English of the Bible. In the classroom it was the heavy moralising Victorian English that their tongues were twisted into speaking; and they felt the sting and fire of the tawse if they dared utter a syllable of Gaelic in the playground even.

This, as far as I can make out, is my mother's early background.

She was one of nine children. She was born in June 1891, in Strathy, Sutherlandshire. Her father was Hugh Mackay, a crofter-fisherman (nicknamed Gow). Her mother was Georgina Mackay. The exiled Mackays were dense in that part of the north coast. By the time she was born, they had two generations of the craft of fishing behind them, and had mastered many of its skills and mysteries. And they had put green corn patches on the bleak moor.

There was a town, Thurso, a few miles along the coast, in Caithness, for buying tea and sugar, newspapers and drapery. They set their shillings and pennies on hard counters. (A few of them entered into the mysteries and skills of money, as will be seen.)

The old harp of Gaelic withered fast on the walls.

North, beyond the stormy Pentland Firth, lay the Orkneys: Hoy, a great blue heraldic shape, and beyond, like hidden whales, Hrossey and Ronaldsay, Rousay and Sanday and Westray and Stronsay and Rinansay. Alien places too, where Gaelic had never sounded; only the harsh saga-uttering harp of the Vikings.

*

She came, aged fifteen or sixteen, to work as a waitress–chambermaid in the fine new hotel in Stromness, Orkney, that had been built and was owned by a Mackay from the same region as herself. This John Mackay had begun as a 'boots' in a hotel in – I think – the town of Wick, and he had risen very quickly in the world of hotel business, in the approved manner of the times, until in the end he owned four hotels – in Stromness, Kirkwall, Stenness (beside the fishing loch, near the famous Ring of Brodgar), and one in Shetland. The Stromness Hotel was built just above the pier in 1900, and cost (it's said) £8,000 – an enormous sum in those days.

It was a hotel built and run mainly for the growing tourist trade.

People with money were beginning to use the railways and steam-ships to explore the unknown places of their own country. Orkney had such attractions as free trout fishing on a cluster of lochs; and also an extraordinary wealth of ancient monuments were being uncovered from year to year: Maeshowe, Skara Brae, early Celtic forts, Viking farm foundations, Stone Age burial chambers.

Because such summer tourists usually had plenty of money to spend – and money was becoming the sign of gentility rather than possession of land or ancient birth – they were called 'toffs'. Even my father called them toffs, but only – I suppose – if they behaved decently in the way of giving him tips.

The way those English tourists spoke seemed grand and superior to the local people, who regarded their own language as of the earth, earthy. So the tourists were said to 'chant'. But, strange to say, the tourists professed themselves charmed by 'the singing speech' of the Orcadians. It must be that every strange way of speaking has an undersong woven through it.

So one imagines them, in their knickerbockers, with box cameras and guns and trout rods, moving with their loud strange speech among the soft-slow-spoken locals, admired and on the whole approved of, because they added a certain exotic tone to the islands each summer. (There are thousands of contemporary photographs, in ancient slides, recording Orkney in the last Victorian decades; those grand romantic aspects that the tourists thought worthy of record: the rockstacks in the west, the ships of the British Navy beginning already to use Scapa Flow as a base, the midsummer mid-night sunglow in the north.)

Still earlier, Orkney had been regarded as a marvellous haven for the mentally retarded children of wealthy families. These unfortu-nates – most of them young men – were boarded out, sometimes for years or even decades, with farmers who had rooms to spare, in this parish or that island. They were called 'feeders' by the Orcadians because they could eat without working: an astonishing state of affairs. They seem to have been harmless eccentrics or 'poor things' – *no witty*, as the local folk used to say . . . Here was a piece of social surrealism.

But it was to attend on this new and growing class of tourists that the hotels were being built: the hotel in Stromness was a grand affair with over forty bedrooms. The like of it had never been known in the islands before.

Hither my mother and other Highland lasses from the same area were summoned by their affluent clansman to tend to the wants of 'the toffs'. Hardly had she got off the boat than she was given to understand that she would have to work every day in the week, including Sunday.

Work on the Sabbath! Work on the Sabbath (excepting only the works of necessity and mercy) had been a thing forbid all over north Sutherlandshire; certainly in the little croft where she had been brought up. It was proscribed in The Book.

My mother spent one or two sleepless nights, her conscience in a turmoil. Ought she, or ought she not, to pack her little case and re-cross the Pentland Firth on the *St Ola*, before the first wrathful Sunday came? Perhaps it was next to impossible – perhaps she didn't have the fare. If old John Mackay could do it – and the other Highland girls who had been brought up in the same strict tradition – perhaps she ought to stick it out for a weekend or two.

She stuck it out, and the heavens did not open to consume her . . . After that she was happy enough in her job, though all the waitresses and chambermaids had to work hard enough, and in a rhythm quite different from the fishing corngrowing rhythms of Strathy.

Mhairi-Sheena as she had been called in Strathy, quickly became Mary Jane. She was a tall pretty blue-eyed girl, with a slightly snub nose and her hair a dark surge of waves. There was in her a fountain of endless cheerfulness that no reverse or disaster could choke for long. Laughter and singing went with her always.

These natural gifts must have made her uncommonly attractive. Even some of the toffs felt drawn to her – and this could always happen in spite of the fact that the hotel servants had strict warning by no means to flirt with the guests.

One thing marred her comeliness, for a short time at least. Her teeth decayed, probably in one quick onrush of rot: was it possibly the sudden transition from the fish and oat-bannocks of home to the cakes and sweeties of Stromness? (She had a sweet tooth all her life.)

Anyway, her teeth were drawn at one session, and soon afterwards she smiled clumsily and unnaturally with the thick heavy false teeth of those days. But, even so, she so enraptured a tourist that he went and had his own apparently sound teeth drawn, so that he could sport false teeth like Mary Jane.

The hotel girls were strictly forbidden to attend local dances: probably because they had to be at their tasks early in the morning, and also because John Mackay and his wife regarded themselves as keepers of the girls' morals, *in loco parentis*. That prohibition became so intolerable that the girls actually went on strike until they got some liberty in the matter. Could the faint stirrings of the Suffragette turmoil have reached those far islands? (It was being spoken about.)

One mid-December, storms kept the ferry-boat *St Ola* harbour-bound. The hotel guests who were eager to be home in England for Christmas had to content themselves in Mackay's Stromness Hotel. They improvised parties and games, and enjoyed themselves as best they could away from their families – all except one old misanthrope who sat forlornly by himself and took no part in the festivities. 'Mary Jane,' said one of the guests, 'I dare you to kiss that poor old gentleman under the mistletoe.'

My mother took a sprig of mistletoe and brought her sweet mouth to the old Scrooge-face beside the fire.

Would he be angry at the impudence of it? Would he complain to the management?

Not a bit of it: he was so delighted that the very next day he gave my mother a big expensive box of chocolates and a fine pair of gloves.

Once, in a room of the hotel, a clergyman made advances to her. She ordered him, coldly, to unlock the door. She never brought a meal to his room again.

Many years later, my sister who was then a teacher in Rousay, one of the north Orkneys, read in some biography or book of reminiscences a page or two about the author's stay in Stromness Hotel, and how much he had been taken by this tall pretty dark curly-headed Highland waitress; and my sister was convinced that Mhairi-Sheena was the girl being described so lyrically. But of course it could have been another girl; many Celtic women answer to this description.

Where and how my mother and father first met, I don't know. It was probably at one of those forbidden dances. She would have been seventeen or eighteen at the time; he was fifteen years older, a rather small witty good-looking man with a waxed moustache. He walked back with her, from whatever function they were at, and at the hotel gate he asked her for a kiss – but he asked with style, like an actor in a melodrama; for all his life long he had a kind of panache and flourish – 'Hold up your mouth, girl.'

My mother didn't hold up her mouth. She turned her back on him and walked into the hotel, thinking (possibly in Gaelic) 'What a cheeky man! – I'm never going out with him again!'

They were married in June 1910 in the Free Presbyterian Church of Strathy – in the Manse, I presume. A tribe of passing tinkers danced and fiddled at their wedding.

As they sailed back to Stromness on the *St Ola*, the masts fluttered with flags, to my mother's delighted astonishment.

My father was well liked in the town. He brought her to a house in Alfred Street, just opposite the pier where, now, the Orkney Fishermen's Society processes crabs and lobsters and scallops.

In that house, ten months later, my sister was born.

*

My mother was the most naturally cheerful woman I have ever known. She went about her household tasks from morning to night, making a cheerful noise. It couldn't be called singing, for she had no musical ear at all; it was more like a low chant, or like the murmuration of a bee among flowers. Whatever her hand found to do – and that was plenty, with six children, five of whom survived – she did it with this invincible joy; in spite of poverty, in spite of poor health.

Life was a gift; she was properly grateful.

Her poor health consisted mainly of prostrating attacks of asthma, that struck her mainly in the summer months when all the pollens are in the air. Then, in her bouts of illness, she could do nothing; she lay in a deep chair, or in bed, while the spasms went through her and she fought for breath. But always, at the end of a few days or a fortnight, she was back at the household round, like a bee in a garden. Looked at with the cold eye of a modern housewife, it must have been boring drudgery, year after year; with, every two years, a new child in the cradle.

Monday should have been called Washing Day for the housewives of Orkney. Morning to night they were at it. On the red-glowing range an oval tin boiler seethed and simmered with its weight of clothes. I would be sent to the grocer's for a cylinder of Reckitt's Blue, or Robin starch. Then, if the day turned out the way the women wanted it, sunny and windy, they hung up the clothes to dry in little gardens up closes – a flutter and dazzle of shapes – and then, in the evening, they were brought in in wicker baskets, with smells of wind and sun in them. I can't remember what happened when the weather was bad. Probably the women just waited, with a patience that is hardly known now, for the next blue bird-flung day. But even so, some articles – sheets and pillow-cases – were hung on a clothes horse, a jointed wooden frame, to get a final draught from the fire. (The old folk had a great dread of dampness – underwear not properly aired could lead to rheumatics or consumption.)

And then, perhaps on the Tuesday, all this array of washing was ironed on the kitchen table. Oh, lovely mingled smell of fire and hot metal and linen and sweet air! The nostrils of children winced with delight.

For years my mother wasn't robust enough to manage the washing by herself. She was helped by a succession of washerwomen – Dinah and Bess and Aggie, who all had their own distinct characters; the only thing they had in common being their affection for my mother. Dinah especially I remember. In my childhood she was an old half-blind woman who had had several illegitimate children, and in spite of a hard life accepted her lot as cheerfully as my mother. She claimed that she had been devoted to one of her lovers, the one from whom she got nothing but rough treatment. So, Dinah would say to my teenage sister, 'Never merry the man thu loves, but merry the man that loves thee . . .' And she had other sayings, pithy and apt and begotten no doubt of bitter experience, that were so true and funny that my father delighted in them.

Kitchen and living-room in the first house I remember were one, with a blue flagstone floor, a scrubbed table, a sideboard with dishes and a lamp, and a sink; and a dry lavatory off it. At night a paraffin lamp was set in the middle of the table. There, in that mild circle of light, the older children did their homework while we younger ones slept above. And my mother would mend and patch by the fire, and my father would be along the street and up and down closes delivering his letters, in all weathers.

I remember the enormous feeling of security that my mother put about my childhood. I woke one night, aged about four or five, and discovered that she wasn't there – she wasn't anywhere in the house. Probably she was out visiting a neighbour, or at a concert or kirk soirée. I was overwhelmed by a feeling of desolation and bereavement: she was gone, she would never never come back again . . . I made the night hideous with my keening.

It was a bad day too, being torn from her to go to the school on the side of Brinkie's Brae for the first time. My mother used to tell how I came home that first dinnertime and threw the little satchel in a corner and said, 'That's that – I'm never gaan back there again!'

It was a joy to go shopping with her on a Saturday night. The shops stayed open till 9 p.m. in the 1920s. The kind old grocer weighed out her messages on his scales, and put the sugar and tea, lentils and flour and oatmeal, in separate strong brown-paper pokes. Last came the great excitement: the poke of sweeties, for in those days I'd have sold my soul for a pandrop or a brandy-ball or a yellow butternut. Home we would go then, under the hissing gaslamps, among the other shopping lingering clucking women. Always the Salvation Army raised a glad brazen sound at the pierhead or at the foot of Kirk Road.

Then it was the wooden bath-tub, with a few drops of Lysol in the warm water to kill germs, and a clean shirt, and a warm bed . . .

Flowers she loved passionately. In the Melvin Place house where we stayed for six years, there was no garden; but the neighbour below (Mary Rendall who was blind) gave my mother free run of her garden up the steep stepped close, full of dew and grass and bluebells; and the neighbour across the way let her use the tattie-patch further up. There my mother spent happy summer hours. If there were no garden flowers, always there was a jam jar in the kitchen window with 'curly doddies' (wild white clover) or marigolds or mayflowers in it.

Finally, in the new council house at Well Park, she had a garden front and back. She put the seeds and roots in indiscriminately and without pattern, just for the joy of the riotous blossom-time. In dry summer spells, how anxiously she tilted the watering can. We younger boys oiled the lawn mower and set it rattling across and across the grass patch, a moving fountain of green.

Gradually, she forgot her native Gaelic; the only one she could speak it with was her sister who lived along the street. But she had a good working mastery of English. Her letters were vivid and fluent, even if she ignored the finer points of punctuation and let her happy little communications flow on unchecked like a burn. She was a much better letter-writer than my father, who uttered only a brief pencilled note at very rare intervals. She had this latent gift of image and rhythm, and I think this came from her purely Celtic blood. (In my own writing, a strong Celtic element is discernible, a mingling of mysticism and intricate image. A month or two ago a cousin of mine from the Mackay area of Sutherlandshire wrote to me about the great eighteenth-century bard of the Mackays, a marvellous poet called Rob Don Mackay. I have still to read his poems in translation. I like to think I may be related, however distantly, to Rob Don.)

Visitors came and went about our house, a constant stream. The neighbours were always dropping in to drink tea with her. One of her gifts was 'reading the tea-leaves', but in this she had a limited and repetitive repertoire: 'expect a dark stranger' . . . 'a change for the better in your life in a few weeks' time' . . . 'an unexpected letter'. The tea-drinkers never tired of it, morning after morning, with the cake crumbs clinging to their eager mouths.

She was a great baker – Friday was cake-baking time, and she shared a fire with Mrs Will next door (the air of Mrs Will's kitchen was a blue hot reek). They baked sponge cakes, cheese cakes, short-bread, cream 'kisses', and a light-as-air confection they called 'melting moments'. (My father called them 'sleepless nights'.) But more often than the cakes, she baked on her own range flour and bere bannocks, and hot pancakes, and thick gritty oatcakes.

The sponge cake – oh joy! – was cut always on Sunday teatime.

Whoever visited, she always thanked them on the doorstep for having come – a ritual that bred satirical asides in my father, especially if he had little liking for the visitor. *Thank you for coming*, he would imitate her, witheringly. But she never saw any failings in anyone, or if the failings were too obvious to be overlooked, she would always mention certain good qualities they had.

It was the same with entertainments: concerts, plays, whist drives, kirk soirées. I have never met anyone with such a capacity for enjoyment. Even if the concert was really bad and was being condemned by everyone, she would say, 'Oh but they were doing their best', and 'Think of all the lines they had to remember.'

The 4th of June, she said, was her birthday. But after she died, I found in a drawer her birth certificate, in which the date of her birth was entered as 2 June 1891. Such small irrelevancies disturbed her not at all. (Of course it may have been the carelessness of the registrar in Strathy: 'what is a day or two here or there, whatever?') One 4 June, I was told that my mother was forty. I remember feeling a sense of desolation – 'Forty! – but she's an old woman now!' She continued to be as carefree at seventy as she had been at forty, as she must have been at ten. In that sense she was ageless.

*

My mother was perhaps a little careless about money. Of course she never had much money to play around with. I have the feeling that if she had been better-off, she would have got now and then, or often, worried calls from bank managers. This carelessness came from a natural generosity; it also sprung perhaps from a naïvety about money (her great-grandparents, perhaps, had never handled coins, nor any of the clan. Money, when it first circulated among them, must have been touched by a kind of dark magic.) But in the thin economy of our household, the thread was occasionally broken; there would be bills from shoemakers and other tradesmen that could not be met, or only by making drastic economies elsewhere in the family budget. There were never any 'scenes', or rows, that ever I witnessed. Still, a child is very sensitive to those tensions in the cloistered atmosphere of a small house. There were turnings-away, seethings, stony silences. I was all the more frightened because the tuneless song in my mother's mouth withered, maybe for a whole morning. The crisis never lasted. By the afternoon she was back among the flowers again . . . Brightness flowed through the house! (But I was always aware that sooner or later the shadow and chill would fall again.)

I have photographs (or, as they were called then, 'snapshots') of her in her thirties and forties. She was a really beautiful woman, tall and slim, her head a cluster of dark curls, blue-eyed, with a slightly snub nose that (though an imperfection perhaps) made more interesting a serene and gentle face.

All round us the housewives knitted and sewed. Strangely, she never stirred to do anything like that. My father made us jackets and trousers in Peter Esson's tailor shop where he worked part-time.

*

The war came. We heard Neville Chamberlain announcing it on our old battery wireless on Sunday, 3 September 1939.

Almost at once Stromness was inundated with khaki: 60,000 soldiers girded and guarded Scapa Flow with anti-aircraft batteries and searchlight batteries. And with them came hordes of construction workers. Local families were expected to take in boarders, though in most houses accommodation was very limited. So, for four and a half years, there was a succession of lodgers, military and civil, in our house. Most of the family had scattered and were living otherwhere at that time, and my father died in 1940. But even so, in the small ugly council house, it was inconvenient having this sequence of strangers coming and going. For one thing, fuel was scarce, so they couldn't have a fire in their room, and had to share fire and board with my mother, my sister (who was a teacher) and myself. Some of them – most of them, I think – were likeable people; others had to be put up with; a few didn't fit in well. The strange thing is, they all – good, bad, indifferent – seemed to like my mother. One family from the south of England invited her, years after, all expenses paid, to stay with them in Dorset; and Mrs Galpin wrote regularly till my mother died. One of our lodgers was the poet and critic Francis Scarfe, then a captain in the Army Education Corps.

The blackout, billeting, gas masks, German air raids, rations – to my mother they were minor nuisances, like midges in August or black frost in winter. The fire burned bright – she kept baking her

Christmas cake and Scotch bun in November – she watered and weeded the chaotic unpatterned garden (that a storm might ruin overnight). The only thing that appalled her was the voice of Hitler that could be heard sometimes on the wireless: the mad screams and rants, the blind acclamation of the mob – that more than anything convinced her that we were fighting against an evil power on earth. The traitorous broadcaster William Joyce made us all laugh.

One lodger she did not greatly care for; or rather, liked less than the others. One day, exasperated, she called him (in Gaelic) 'you devil of an old man'. And she nearly collapsed when he replied, promptly (in Gaelic too), 'What about the devil of an old woman?' The episode ended in laughter. Even he, though he left our house for other lodgings before long – he and my sister openly disliked each other – spoke well and fairly about my mother to the new landlady.

My three brothers got married within a few years. During the war they served in the RAF. I noticed, on those three nuptial occasions, what must be a timeless universal thing: the reluctance of a mother to let her son pass into the keeping of another woman, however good and worthy she might be. With my mother, it was only a kind of token resistance. Once the marriage was an accomplished fact, she got on well enough with her daughters-in-law.

I inherited her breathing trouble, but in the more sinister form of tuberculosis. The disease was confirmed in 1941. Because of some National Health Insurance mix-up I got no benefit for the first three years of my illness, and was therefore destitute. She kept me uncomplainingly (and even bought me cigarettes on a Friday, her shopping day) until the mistake was rectified and I began to be given a weekly pittance. It was in those years of solitude and sickness and poverty – made bearable by my mother's bounty – that I began to absorb from a wide spectrum of reading some of the techniques that I was to use later myself as a writer: the 'shaping spirit', the sense of form, how much a given vessel – sonnet, short story, play – will hold in the way of image and word-pressure without flowing or brimming over.

She never read books herself, only the rather sentimental love stories out of women's magazines. (I think she had too many things to do, to open books under the lamp.) And yet she had an innate feeling for literature, that manifested itself in her fluent vivid letters.

Of my own early published poems and stories, I can remember her saying, 'They're all about pubs and drinking.' She didn't much approve of drinking, and herself indulged in only an occasional glass of sherry. She had never darkened the door of a pub till my friend John Broom brought her into Milne's Bar in Rose Street, Edinburgh, towards the end of her life; and there, it seems, she made a great hit with Sydney Goodsir Smith and some of the other literary folk.

She loved travelling. When her children were young she was housebound, like all working-class women. There was only the rare visit to a farm, or to friends in Kirkwall. She took my brother Norrie and me to have a holiday with her parents at Strathy, when I was about five. I remember my grandfather's gray beard and rather stern expression, and the kind round large-eyed face of my grandmother. They spoke mostly in Gaelic – 'we only speak English to dogs and strangers' – and there were long Gaelic prayers before dinner every day. They tried to keep me from straying too near the cliffs with talk of some kind of monster ('the rone', I think it was called) who lived thereabouts in a cave. And once I fell in the burn. And once I got into trouble for slipping away during one of the family pre-dinner prayer sessions. The loneliness of the peat moor desolated me. (Orkney was a land of milk and honey, in comparison.) We loved the new sweet warm milk from the cow. But on the whole I think I was glad to be home in Orkney again. I did not inherit my mother's wander-longing.

Once in the mid-1930s she flew from Howe aerodrome near Stromness to Thurso; and so on home to Strathy. The word went from croft to croft – 'Mhairi has come by wireless!'

The gray was in her hair, increasingly, as she began to make her long annual journeys to Aberdeen and Edinburgh; and when she went to Dorset. ('Oh what a lovely sight – the lights of London below!') She liked travelling on the city buses, and a huge store like Marks and Spencer's was a cave of pure enchantment to her. 'I think,' she would say, 'I'll take the bus down to Malcolm Spencer's.' (She had a habit of getting names wrong, as well as common expressions: small lingual aberrations possibly stemming from her ancestor-rooted original tongue.) Her three Edinburgh granddaughters, who loved her, would explain gently, 'It isn't Malcolm Spencer's, Granny – it's *Marks and Spencer's*.' 'Oh, is it?' she would say. Then a couple of breakfasts later, she would announce once more, 'I just love that Malcolm Spencer's shop – I think I'll take a ride down to it in the bus before lunch.' Looks of happy exasperation on three girls' faces.

She enjoyed those south holidays enormously. I was concerned when she came back from her last trip to Edinburgh and Aberdeen looking unwell. She had fallen in the corridor of the train, she said, and hurt her head. It seems to me that she may have had a slight stroke, or 'blackout'. If so, it was the first of a succession of small cerebral haemorrhages that, spreading ever more extensive damage, killed her before that year was out.

Once home, her health deteriorated rapidly. What made the sickness specially distressing was that, progressively, it altered her whole personality. From being an open cheerful person she became suspicious and moody. The first hint I had that something was seriously wrong was when, one evening, she began to go through all the drawers in her bedroom, over and over again. 'Are you looking for something?' I asked. 'Have you lost something?' 'Somebody,' said she, 'has been stealing my clothes.' I expostulated. She was adamant. 'But who?' I asked. She said she didn't know, but her clothes were being stolen. This was so extraordinary, coming from her, that I knew at once something was seriously wrong: it was like the touch of a chill finger on the heart. She herself was the one lost in deepening winter.

That was the beginning. There followed a rapid erosion of memory. There were sudden unmotivated outbursts of anger (again, totally out of character). I was the butt of much of this rage – and sometimes I spoke back to her harshly, as if that might bring her to her senses.

It was as if she was learning a part in a frightening play, and a part totally unsuited to her: a Beckett tragedy rather than the pastoral comedy that she had played with such natural grace and gaiety all her days. This 'learning of the new part' was accompanied by increasing physical weakness. More and more time she spent in bed, or (if it was fine weather) on a chair outside in the sun, looking out with a rather hurt baffled expression, like a wayfarer in a hostile land. People came and spoke to her, but she had forgotten who they were. One neighbour in particular was enormously kind to her; no near relative could have tended her better. She seemed to be grateful for that, but in a distraught uncaring way.

In between, there were periods of lucidity, when she laid the dark mask aside, and made flawed attempts to be what she had been. But she grew weaker and more confused; the destruction spread quickly through the cells of her brain.

At last she had to be taken by ambulance to a hospital in Kirkwall. I saw her after the nurses had settled her in her bed, and she seemed in one of her benign (if confused) moods.

My sister-in-law arrived with her car from Edinburgh to be near her. The next day we went to visit her in hospital. It was disturbing to see how distressed and disorientated she was, and unable (of course) to account for her distress; now she was learning the confused mysterious language of the dying; through which we could guess at nameless (and doubtless imaginary) dreads.

She did not know who my sister-in-law was.

I brought three of my books to her and put them in her locker; that seemed to please her, in a vague way.

Towards the end, I was a shadowy vaguely hostile stranger to her too.

She died on 3 November 1967, leaving an estate of £4 and a few pence; aged seventy-five.

There was an oxygen mask over her face when we were summoned to her ward. Six or seven of us stood round the bed. The sister-in-charge held her pulse. Time passed. At last the sister said, 'Now there's no pulse . . .'

*

I have spoken of my mother's lack of 'artistic sensitivity'. She had no interest in art, music, literature. Her garden was a formless changing swirl of colour. She liked the plastic and Formica articles of mass production; our house was as hoarded with those tawdry ornaments as any corporation house in Falkirk or Birmingham. Really fine well-wrought artefacts in wood or stone or bone, for example, she thought relics of a bad time and ripe for the dust-cart. My father had, somehow or other, got hold of an *objet d'art* from one of the sunk

German battleships in Scapa Flow. It was a rough-hewn piece of stone, the size of a bonnet: on it a young German sailor had carved a submarine and the word HELGOLAND, and inset was a photograph of himself, protected with glass – a young handsome humorous sensitive face. My father treasured this ornament enormously: to my mother it was a nuisance. Anyway, dusting it, it must have fallen from the mantelpiece time after time, for it was always getting chipped and cracked. In the end, long after my father's death, I don't know what happened to it . . . I mention these things to show how, in an egalitarian society where worth tends to be equated with knowledge of and sensitivity to the arts and culture, my mother would be considered one of the 'proles'. Yet it seems to me that, in the true scale of human worth, she was at least as valuable as most of the music and art lovers I have met. (I am setting this down as mildly as possible, for consanguinity of course will be reckoned to result in a kind of bias; especially a mother–son relationship.) All the same, I am sure an objective observer would have come to the same conclusion . . . This small detour opens the field into a much larger speculation: that as traditional religion is increasingly neglected all over the world, people turn to other gods. Mammon of course is always with us, a mighty god in the seven continents. The muses have been taken from the waters and woods and fields and set in galleries, concert-halls, museums. Wealthy patrons are reckoned to have done much to enrich the world with works of art; but as soon as the arts are cut off from their primitive pristine sources, they are invested with a kind of unwholesome idolatry. Universal education has taught the people to read, and what do they read? The *Sun* and the *Daily Mirror*. Their illiterate great-grandfathers knew the rich poetry of the King James Bible, and the ballads that changed marvellously from region to region and from generation to generation. We of the 1872 Education Act are not interested in Picasso or Stravinsky or T.S. Eliot. The oneness of culture has been lost; the web riven . . . This is one of the tragedies of our time. And yet, in some important way, the inner core of character remains untouched; those who suffer most are the art idolaters, those for whom concert hall and gallery have come to take the place of the church. I have a feeling that, secretly, however the 'proles' of culture – the readers of the *Sun* and those who watch soap operas on their colour TV sets – are seemingly outside the temple, the ancient streams are in their veins yet, and the roots firmly bedded. In spite of plastic and Formica and newsprint, here and there are still to be found that vividness of speech, that delight in language and in character from which poetry springs. Hands yearn still to make good and useful (and therefore beautiful) objects. Those ancient heart-urgings will take – it may be – many a generation to wither: but perhaps the rot has proceeded too far.

My mother was not that far removed from the great Gaelic bards. The generosity and courtesy of an ancient race was strong in her still. That being so, it was no mark of inferiority in her that she welcomed the mass-produced artefacts of the twentieth century; rather, it was a source of strength; for the person who shuts himself or herself off from the products of the time is also, in a way, 'lost' – 'Time present and time past / Are both perhaps present in time future, / And time future contained in time past. / If all time is eternally present / All time is unredeemable . . .'* Time past and time present were (though she laughed indulgently at the recorded voice of Eliot) alive in my mother. To time future she had given six children and a mellification of grandchildren, and a fragrant memory.

*

I used frequently to see my mother in dreams, in the years following her death; and in nearly every dream she was displeased with me; she looked hurt and angry.

This may have been caused by my memories of her last months, when she was often angry with me, for no good reason.

But in addition, I had a complex of guilts concerning her. I knew that I had often caused her distress, especially through overindulgence in drink. And then, somehow, I was not 'a success'; at least, in the way that success is counted nowadays. For years – but for her protection – I was hardly better than a tramp. I did go to university and get a degree, and at once fell ill again (not wishing to take part in society as a teacher – so strongly do the mind's revulsions crack the

---

* T.S. Eliot, 'Burnt Norton', lines 1–5, from *Four Quartets* (1943).

framework of the body). So there I was again, taking the meagre handouts of National Assistance.

In the midst of all this, I was converted to Roman Catholicism. She offered no overt objection to that; indeed, she greatly relished the visits of the Jesuit priests from Kirkwall. But (though she did not go to the local kirk in her latter years) the Free Presbyterianism of her upbringing must have been worked deep into the early grain of her; one could hardly be more Calvinistic than a Free Presbyterian. To extreme Calvinists, Roman Catholicism is idolatry of the worst kind. 'Some Catholic you are!' she would say when I was trying to recover from a hangover after a pub crawl. Scorn was so little a part of her nature that an expression like that, coming from her, did haunt and shame me . . . But, however badly I behaved, she came to accept over-indulgence in alcohol as a kind of ineradicable strand in me. 'Nothing in it but pubs and drinking,' she said after reading *A Calendar of Love* (which was published eight months before she died). But she said it without surprise.

On the first anniversary of her death, I hired a taxi and put flowers on her grave in the kirkyard beside the Atlantic. She loved flowers; the houses we lived in were splashed with the colours of blossom and plant. My father had a great scorn of the usual paraphernalia of death and funerals: black clothes, wreaths, pious verses in the *Orcadian*. 'Give them their flowers while they're alive,' he would say; and my mother would agree, but only I think symbolically, in the sense that one should be kind and pleasant in all ways while they still drew breath. Anyway, that 3 November of 1968, I thought she might not object to a spray of flowers on her grave.

But that was the last fresh garland she got. And I have thought, superstitiously, that she comes back to censure me in dreams because I have, over the years, neglected the filial duty of flowers. (It is the guilt in my own mind that would not let her rest. For many months now I have not dreamed about her.)

May these few pages in memory of her stand in lieu of flowers. If there is any fragrance in these paragraphs and sentences, it was there, fresh and sweet and natural, in the child born in a poor Sutherlandshire croft on either 2 or 4 June 1891.

I have a deep-rooted belief that what has once existed can never die: not even the frailest things, spindrift or clover-scent or glitter of star on a wet stone. All is gathered into the web of creation, that is apparently established and yet perhaps only a dream in the eternal mind; and yet, too, we work at the making of it with every word and thought and action of our lives.

May she rest in peace.

October 1981–February 1983

JOHN BROWN – TAILOR AND POSTMAN

There have been Browns in Orkney for centuries, it seems. Most of them are rooted in Stromness and Sandwick parishes, in the west. They are incomers from Scotland, surely. They may have come with the bad Stewart earls in the early seventeenth century, retainers of some kind. They were farmers and shopkeepers.

I know nothing of them beyond my grandfather, who was a cobbler. He died before I was born. An old fisherman told me my grandfather had occasional bouts of drinking that lasted for days. For those sprees he dressed in his best clothes. Afterwards he returned quietly to his last and his leather and his resin and twine.

My father was a tailor and a postman. He had apparently no interest in his forebears at all.

He was rather small and stout. He had a moustache that in his youth he waxed. He had cut quite a dash in amateur drama circles, being an excellent mimic and comedian. He had such a gift for it that often his 'victims' forgave him, and laughed too.

He had a good tenor voice but couldn't read music. He liked to sing when he had drunk a glass or two of whisky. His cheeks then were apple-bright. I think he was fond of holding the floor. He liked Victorian and Edwardian music-hall songs, and evangelical hymns, especially 'The Old Rugged Cross'. Perhaps his own favourite was a ballad called 'When Johnston's Ale Was New'.

He smoked black twist tobacco in his pipe. He cut thin slivers of tobacco with a little bright knife. He was a 'wet' smoker, and spat often, athwart clouds of smoke, into a spittoon. He had a quick tongue and a witty turn of phrase. Old women would say, laughing, 'Oh, Jack Brown, it does me good to hear thee!'

Yet he was a melancholy man. When he was alone, he often spoke his worries aloud to himself. Outside the closed door, I used to eaves-drop, a half-frightened child. The man inside was a stranger to me.

He refereed football matches in his young days. He won some-where a draughts competition, and the winner's medal was a proud possession.

He liked books. There were only a dozen or so undistinguished books in the house, but he borrowed copiously from the Public Library. He liked books about the trials and tribulations of poor people – Patrick MacGill's *The Rat Pit* and *Children of the Dead End*, Jack London's *People of the Abyss*. One of the books in our house was *From Log Cabin to White House*, the story of the rise from poverty of an American President. The great heroes of our youth, who were held up to us as models, were 'poor boys who had got on'. My father admired such struggles and achievements, and so did everybody else in Stromness. It was the true religion of Scotland then, perhaps.

First, I remember a little house built sideways on to the only street in Stromness, and with the front door looking obliquely eastwards to a fisherman's pier and slipway, and the harbour with fishing boats, and Orphir and Scapa Flow beyond.

The owner of the house lived further down the pier. In middle age she lost her reason. She had been saved from a bigamous marriage to a naval man during the First World War; that was what had eventu-ally deranged her, the folk said. She turned for no reason against my mother. We had to leave that house. I was six. I was shattered to see my mother in tears one day. For she too was a stranger then.

We moved along the street to a house in a beautiful close called Melvin Place. There was a flower garden at the top of the close, and further up still a vegetable patch was loaned to us. My father never sank a spade. My mother loved the flowers.

Melvin Place was one of the parts of Stromness that had belonged to the Brown family – a branch it called 'the Melvin Browns'. But we were an inferior branch. My ancestors, it seemed, had kept ducks in a pond nearby, and so they were called 'the Duckie Browns' (or Broons, to be correct). Indeed, an ancient virago who terrorised my childhood used to hiss at me in passing, 'the Duckie Broons'.

But this house was not healthy. It was said that there was a drain right under the flagstones of the floor. It was while living there that my father was stricken with rheumatic fever. He lay in the upstairs bed for a long time. He recovered, but the sickness had broken him physically. His hands and feet were twisted with arthritis for the rest of his life. Sometimes he sent us for a bucket of sea water, but not the tame harbour water; the strong tide of Hoy Sound was what he wanted. There he would sit, his feet in that bucket with a piece of the Atlantic Ocean in it. It don't think it helped him.

It was probably not the house that wrecked his health. I think of him on stormy winter nights coming into the house, with his bag of letters and the lantern pinned to the lapel of his coat and the peak of his postman's cap dripping with rain. Then out again he would go into the storm. A few hundred storms like that over the decades, and ice and east wind work themselves into the strongest thews.

Another reason he mentioned as the possible source of his illness was a damp bed he slept in during a holiday in Sutherlandshire.

A doctor suggested that the root of his trouble might be his teeth. He had them all extracted at one go, he and Teddy Tait the dentist consuming a half-bottle of whisky during the operation. He wore his false teeth; but not at the table, to eat with. He put them into a large envelope and ate with his hard gums.

We were very poor when my father was ill. (I was a child, poverty meant nothing to me.) But it preyed on my father's mind. As soon as he could hobble around, in pain all the time, he resumed his letter-carrying. Even I felt a pang of pity for him. In the end he had to give it up. He stayed at home and read. On summer afternoons he played putting with the old men at Ness. Perhaps he managed to do a bit of cutting and sewing in Peter Esson's tailor shop. He felt that he was useless and a burden on the family; it was a bitterness to him. Yet we never lacked for food or clothes.

He had a hobby: collecting coins. He had a case specially made to hold his collection, which was prominently placed in the best room. Whether the collection was valuable or not, I don't know. My father was particularly proud of a little hoard of 'gun-money', so called because one of the Stewart kings – I think – melted down some guns to mint pay for his soldiers. If there were visitors to the house, and my father liked them, he would take them upstairs and show them his coin collection.

He dreaded fire. Anger wasn't part of his daily nature. He never raised a hand against one of his five children. One evening he came in from his postal round and saw one of my brothers trying to revive the gray embers in the stove with paraffin poured from a can. He shouted with rage.

Insincerity he disliked – for example, the old women who went around lamenting if anyone was sick, or dead, or if the weather was bad, or a cat was missing. He would say something scathing to the lament on the threshold, and usually it was so funny that it kindled laughter. It was as if Falstaff had exchanged a few words with a chorus of Trojan women.

On Sunday mornings in my childhood he made the breakfast: that was the only housework I ever remember him doing. He went down the stairs to light the fire. A seven-year-old, I crept into the warm bed beside my mother. Feet on the steep stair: my father came in with a carved wooden tray with tea, toast and boiled eggs on it. I remember the eggs especially, because on Sunday morning my mother and I opened them in a different way; instead of cutting off the tops with a knife we shattered the shell with a teaspoon; this seemed to add to the enjoyment of Sunday morning in bed.

'Getting on in the world' was the unspoken religion that was beaten and branded into us at school. My father half subscribed to it, and half not. It was admirable when it happened; but there were inherent dangers, the principal one being pride. Much better to remain poor and content than to become, out of lowly beginnings, a professional man or a businessman and then give oneself airs. That was insufferable, in his scale of values. We children could stay on at school, so long as we worked. Once, in my adolescence, he caught me playing truant. 'Right,' he said tartly, 'I'll speak to the baker about you in the morning'; that is, he would arrange to have me apprenticed in the baking trade. I must have mended my ways, for nothing came of it.

One young man from a poor family in Stromness had become headmaster in a country school. At prize-giving ceremonies, it was usually someone fairly distinguished in the vicinity who was called upon to hand out the prize books. This young headmaster sent down to Stromness for his mother, a poor hardworking woman, to do the honours. My father couldn't get over it; that the headmaster should have remembered his origins and honoured his mother in that way. This was the way it should be, always: achievement going hand in hand with gratitude and true humility.

We went to the kirk every Sunday, all seven of us. My father was satirical about some of the ministers and elders. 'Hurry on past the Jews,' he would say to us anent the two office-bearers, usually businessmen, who stood beside the collection plate in the vestibule. (And indeed they always looked unctuous and smiling to me.) He would sing the hymns and the psalms, setting one foot on the pew and hitching up his trousers until his long drawers showed. (I was bitterly ashamed about that.) Often he would shake his head over a sermon, as much as to say 'That was pitiable'. But this was the risk that every Presbyterian minister ran. The sermon was the kernel of the service; the sermon was tasted and tested like wine in other cultures. He had a soft spot for the Salvation Army; his elder brother Peter had begun in the Salvation Army and ended as a Congregational minister. William Booth, the champion of the poor and the oppressed, was his hero, if he had a hero at all. The *War Cry* was taken into our house every weekend . . . He contrived not to be at home when the minister came round on his pastoral visitation.

On Sundays and holidays he wore a small ivory crucifix on his watch chain. Where he had got hold of it he never said; perhaps he wore it to disconcert people, a little. An old tinker woman had commented on this adornment with approval; the tinkers being Irish Catholics in origin.

Once he went on holiday by himself to Strathy in Sutherlandshire where my mother came from. Wearing his dark blue suit, with the watch chain from which hung the ivory crucifix, he went to that lonely place and came back with stories. He had gone to the inn and had met no one going or coming back on the long road but a sheep and a tramp. The service in the Free Presbyterian Church was in Gaelic; the sermon seemed unending. The minister 'roared as if he had the toothache' . . . And he would say, referring to my mother, 'She couldn't speak a word of English when first I met her', and 'The heather was growing out of her ears'. At which extravagant lies the neighbours laughed delightedly, and my mother joined in the merriment, at a New Year.

In his own immediate family there were troubles. His younger brother had married a half-crazed woman, the one who used to hiss at me, 'the Duckie Broons' – and had left her – and lived on in quiet gloom and despair. He was reckoned to be a good country-style fiddler. How depressed I was always when that melancholy uncle of mine came for his dinner on Monday afternoons. Even his stories of ghosts and fairies were told in a doom-ridden way, so that I who loved stories even more than sweeties, was dejected by them . . . He went missing, one day in the mid-1930s. His body was taken out of the harbour a few days later.

*

The war came. My father was crippled with arthritis and out of work. He felt himself to be a burden on his family. In the island of Hoy huge oil tanks were being built into a hillside: fuel for the ships of the British Navy in Scapa Flow. Hundreds of workmen were employed. There was such a demand for labour that even my crippled father was taken on as a 'hut-tender' – that is, he had to keep the living quarters of the workmen swept and clean, and make their beds. Occasionally he got a weekend off and came home. At other weekends he sent most of his wages to my mother by the hand of a fellow worker. He enclosed, with the money, a few scrawled words on a lavish quantity of paper.

And sometimes when he did come from Lyness in Hoy to Stromness for the weekend, his mouth was full of strange swear-phrases that we had never heard before; certainly not from him. The diggers into the hill from central Scotland used a colourful language. Good mimic that he was, he absorbed it and vented it unconsciously.

He seemed to like his fellow workers. Sometimes he had to arrange a hut with wooden forms for a religious service, of one denomination or another. Only the Catholic priest, he said, gave him a tip.

*

France was defeated in May 1940. He was pleased, strangely. 'Our boys won't have to go to France now,' he said. The France of 1914–18 had been a nightmare of mud and horror, wounds and gas, barbed-wire and rats and death for the young men of three nations. (He had been just too old for conscription.) There was to be no repeat of those terrible years, but he did not live long enough to see how the pattern of the new war was to develop.

He said once, when he had bought a new suit, 'My next suit'll be a wooden one.'

One morning in July 1940 I was wakened by the sound of weeping downstairs. It was my oldest brother, who had always been particularly attached to my father. I had never seen him in tears before. The police had come to him at his place of work and told him that my father had died suddenly in Lyness that morning. My brother brought the news, first to my mother, then to us who had just woken, clear-eyed, from the gentle daily death of sleep.

He lay in his coffin in the little bedroom downstairs, more remote than a star. 'Touch the forehead,' said someone. There was a belief that you must touch a dead brow, otherwise pictures of the person would linger and disturb you in some way or other. I have never felt a coldness so intense as that touch. He had travelled such a far way from the wells and fires of the blood.

'Coronary thrombosis' was written on the death certificate. He was sixty-four.

I think that, after his illness crippled him, he had no great desire to live. Yet he had, right up to the end, a gusto for life. Certain kinds of people intrigued him always, especially those on the fringes of society – tinkers, eccentrics, tramps, people with unusual skills and trades, fairground men and women: 'all things counter, original, spare, strange'. He sought them out and conversed with them. For the establishment of town he had small regard, unless this shop-keeper or that doctor was distinguished by an endearing quirk. Often he preserved the memory of those people, long after they were dead, by his gift of mimicry. 'I thought,' one woman told me when I was a child, 'I was sure I heard the throaty screech of Joanna Gold in the street. Then round the corner came your father, Jack Brown.' A young teacher came to Stromness; he was coldly hostile when my father offered him a year's subscription card for the local Natural History Museum, price four shillings and sixpence. 'He looked at me like the far end of a fiddle,' said my father ruefully. These funny felicitous phrases were always on his tongue.

He went to see an old sweet kind neighbour woman who was sick. 'Your time's not come yet,' he said. She laughed, and began at once to feel better, and outlived him by many years.

In the last year or two of his life I was discovering poetry. One of my happiest memories is reading poetry aloud to him in the winter gaslight of the new council house: *The Ballad of Reading Gaol* and Ralph Hodgson's *The Bull*. He was not a poetry-reading man himself, but he seemed to like those raw recitals. And I think he read the first crude verses I wrote, and approved of them.

A quintessence of dust, he lies in a field above Hoy Sound among all the rich storied dust of Stromness. The postman had left the last door, he had quenched the flame in his lantern. The tailor had folded the finished coat and laid it aside. He was at rest with fishermen, farmers, merchants, sailors and their women-folk – many generations.

I wish there was a Thomas Hardy in Orkney to report the conversation of those salt and loam tongues in the kirkyard, immortally.

27 January 1980

THE DEATH OF PETER ESSON – TAILOR, TOWN LIBRARIAN, FREE KIRK ELDER

Peter at some immortal cloth, it seemed,
Fashioned and stitched, for so long had he sat
Heraldic on his bench. We never dreamed
It was his shroud that he was busy at.

Well Peter knew, his thousand books would pass
Gray into dust, that still a tinker's tale
As hard as granite and as sweet as grass,
Told over reeking pipes, outlasts them all.

The Free Kirk cleaves gray houses – Peter's ark
Freighted for heaven, galeblown with psalm and prayer.
The predestined needle quivered on the mark.
The wheel spun true. The seventieth rock was near.

Peter, I mourned. Early on Monday last
There came a wave and stood above your mast.

1959
(*Selected Poems, 1954–1992*)

PETER ESSON

Someone has asked me to write a note about Peter Esson, to be included in an anthology of poetical epitaphs over the centuries. Why, readers of the anthology would want to know, write a poem about such a man? Even in Stromness, nowadays, most people don't know who Peter Esson was . . . But, fifty years ago, every Stromnessian knew.

He had a small tailor shop at the foot of the Kirk Road, its door opening on to the street. I visited there from the age of four onwards, because my father worked part-time beside Peter and his brother Willie Esson and his daughter Effie Esson. There I went on urgent feet every Friday to get what those tailors called my 'pension', a halfpenny; immediately translated into sweeties at Janetta Sinclair's sweetie shop on the other side of the street.

In the evening men would drop by and sit on Peter's bench. Most of them were retired seamen. The stories went on for hours. (When those legends were being wrought, I was of course curled up in bed at home.)

Tailoring was a trade in decline in the 1920s and 30s. People were buying their suits ready-made. So Peter had a secondary job. He was the town librarian, issuing books twice a week – I think, Wednesdays and Saturdays – from the library that is still there at the foot of Hellihole Road. Peter and his wife lived in the flat above.

But tailoring and giving out books were, in a sense, secondary mundane activities. The most important place in Peter Esson's life was the Free Kirk that towered over the adjacent buildings, including the tailor shop. It might be said that Peter was acquainted with every stone in that building. He revered it, with a deep devotion. He knew all the ministers who had led worship there. (In fact, I have never known anyone who was so thoroughly acquainted with the highly complex history of Presbyterianism in

Scotland, with all its schisms and branchings and reunions over four centuries.)

Peter was a Kirk elder. The expression on his face on Sundays seemed to be different to the other days. There was a kind of earnestness and veneration.

Towards the end of each week the minister, Revd James Christie, entered the tailor shop carrying a bill concerning the Sunday service for Peter to put in his window. That was always a hushed half-minute in the general tone of genial levity that prevailed, until Mr Christie left again.

24 August 1995

ERNEST MARWICK

I first met Ernest Marwick towards the end of the war. I was then in the habit of making fairly frequent bus trips to Kirkwall, to see if there were any new books in Leonard's, and always I got a friendly greeting from Mr George Leonard. Then suddenly there was a new assistant in the shop, a young man of strong country build wearing spectacles, and we would discuss books together, though at the beginning we didn't know each other's names.

Then one day – it must have been in 1945 or 1946 – Ernest Marwick told me that he was compiling an anthology of island verse. Did I, by any chance – he wanted to know – write poetry? And if so, would I let him see a clutch of poems?

I sent a few of the better ones to Ernest, and in due course got a kind and appreciative letter; which must still exist, somewhere, in the haystack of interesting letters I have hoarded over the decades.

I don't look at those early poems now with any joy at all, but Ernest's praise came at a time when a writer is at his most sensitive stage, not knowing if what he writes has any merit or is a heap of words merely, already beginning to moulder.

From then on our friendship grew. I was invited often to spend a few days at Westermill, and was looked after with great kindness by Janette, Ernest's wife – a truly good and delightful woman. There I saw the work that Ernest was doing on his anthology, and I could only admire the meticulous scholarship and the love of Orkney and of poetry that he was pouring into it. (This was to be no quick impressionistic gathering.)

At Westermill, too, I met one of the most extraordinary Orkneymen of this century, the draper and poet and theologian and conchologist Robert Rendall. Robert's house, Dawnvale, was only a few sylvan steps away from Westermill, across the burn, and the poet frequently dropped by for a chat; often enough it was about some new poem that was working itself out in his imagination; or it could be to talk about Birsay shells, or a haul of cuithes taken from a Birsay sea-rock. (He had a little wooden house in the village.) At this time Robert Rendall was busy at a book too – his first collection of poems, *Country Sonnets*. In spite of his deafness, Robert had the joy and enthusiasm of a boy about any of a half-dozen activities occupying his mind at the time.

Of course the friendship between Ernest and Robert enriched Orkney literature. With generosity but complete frankness they estimated each other's work. There was a kind of merchandise of the imagination, an exchange of fine cargoes and silver.

Those brief holidays at Westermill – the house was like a well that I continually returned to for refreshment and peace . . .

Country Sonnets came out in 1946. Ernest's *Anthology of Orkney Verse* wasn't published till 1949; for no work ever left his hands that wasn't as perfect as he could make it. I sometimes spoke in those early days of publishing a small collection of my own verse. Ernest strongly advised against it, saying that in later years I might not be well pleased with what I'd done. How right he was. In 1953 I published *The Storm and Other Poems* – now I wish I had held my hand for a few years, until the cloud in the liquor had cleared and the vintage was ripe.

*

Ernest Marwick was one of those men not uncommon in Orkney, a natural intellectual. The Education Act of 1872 caused many of those hidden intellects to burgeon and blossom. The roll-call of Orkney professors in the early twentieth century – most of them farmers' and crofters' sons – makes impressive reading. I have no doubt that Ernest would have equalled their academic achievements, if ill health in his boyhood hadn't interrupted his schooling. But that ill health and lack of early instruction in letters and numbers didn't stunt his intellect. His mind was naturally keen and subtle and far-ranging; nor did it have what some good Orkney intellects have, a kind of aridity. Imagination had been gifted to him at his beginning, and it illuminated everything he wrote and did. (He was, as well as writer, an artist and a photographer of some talent.)

Always his mind moved eagerly through a galaxy of artistic and intellectual disciplines: 'a mind . . . Voyaging through strange seas of thought' (to quote his favourite poet, Wordsworth). It was an impressive experience to sit with him in his upstairs study at Westermill. There, carefully filed and indexed in desk and drawer, were (it seemed) a score of projects he was busy at – an account of witch trials, Orkneymen in Canada, fragments of autobiography, essays, legends, lore. I estimate that there must have been at least a dozen books-in-the-making in that quiet study of his. And yet the scholar was so scrupulous that he would allow nothing of the rich hoard to be published until it had reached that degree of perfection that he demanded of himself. (Many readers must remember the series of essays – studies of social life in Orkney in the nineteenth century – written by Ernest, which appeared serially in the *Orcadian* in 1949: a fascinating compilation that took increasing hold of one's mind week after week. And yet the book was never published; it's said, because a breath or two of adverse criticism discouraged the author. Such bleak winds trouble the sensitive tree of literature from time to time. Some lucky readers, perhaps in the next generation, will open that book for the first time.)

*

He was no 'ivory tower' scholar. For thirty years he was one of Kirkwall's most familiar citizens. He was known and liked by everyone. For a time – before Radio Orkney began – he was Orkney's 'radio correspondent' for the Scottish BBC. That job took him into every corner of Orkney with his tape-recorder; he must have rescued hundreds of fireside tales and things vividly remembered by old country folk from falling into oblivion. Many Orcadians, especially the older ones, shy away from a microphone and from all the sleek 'magical' symbols of the twentieth century; Ernest had the gift of putting them at their ease, so that question-and-answer flowed sweetly. In those early days of his BBC work, Ernest went from place to place on a motor scooter; I must say, it was strange to see this scholar on road or street with his crash helmet on, like some man from space; and yet I sat on his pillion in utter trust, many a time.

Later he drove a minicar.

*

Ernest Marwick did not seek out popularity. He had the gift of giving his opinion simply and directly, but never with arrogance. His Liberalism in politics and Anglicanism in religion were held with utter sincerity. His reaction, when there were rumours of possible uranium mining in Orkney, was that he would oppose any such oper-ation, even physically, even to the point of going to prison. And, if necessary, he would have done just that. Under the natural kindness and courtesy and gentleness of the man was a will of iron. (I have seen that will in operation, and admired it; for I do not have such an inner core of strength myself.)

Above everything else, Ernest was a happy person to be with. Westermill was a joyful house. Ernest and Janette looked with charity on all men and women and on the things that happen under the sun; and charity comprises, among other things, gaiety without malice. Entering Westermill, one was aware of an air of happiness and clean-ness and peace that never, with the passing years, turned stale.

And yet life, for Ernest Marwick, was often hard. There are sensi-tive minds which have to endure stresses that most people, thank-fully, know nothing of. No one has expressed those dark difficult regions of mind and spirit more vividly than the poet Gerard Manley Hopkins.

> O the mind, mind has mountains; cliffs of fall
> Frightful, sheer, no-man-fathomed. Hold them cheap
> May who ne'er hung there . . .

That kind of desolation Ernest had to endure at different periods of his life. And always, the strong life-force in him won through, with his heart as generous and intellect as strong as they had ever been; and with an insight that is perhaps the hard-won profit of such peri-lous fated voyaging.

There were one or two things I did not understand; even the person you know best must remain, at last, something of a mystery. For example, Ernest chose in his last years to spend his annual holiday in Stromness during the 'shopping week' in July, when that quiet town is taken over by loud amplified pop music and awash with drink and, in general, a whirling coloured noisy kaleidoscope. What on earth was a quiet ascetic scholar doing in the midst of that wild carnival? One might have thought that a cottage in Birsay or Hoy, with the ripening crops of summer all around, would have been the place for him. But no: to Stromness and its gala on-goings Ernest and Janette returned, year after year. One year, indeed, he was asked to make the official opening speech. He was very proud to be invited to do that; and his speech, as might have been expected, was excellent.

*

With average luck, it seemed that two decades or so were still before his ever-questing mind; years of patient research and study that would have hoarded the granaries of Orkney scholarship with 'full-ripened grain'.

It was not to be. We heard, one Sunday evening in July 1977, that Ernest's car had crashed that afternoon against a farm wall in Rendall, and that he had died of his injuries soon after. And we knew that a great and a good man had gone from this generation of Orcadians; but had left treasures behind still to be estimated, and a most fragrant memory.

23 April 1984

WILLIE FARQUHAR AND THE GOLDEN SLIPPER

I

Willie Farquhar's at Brig-o-Waithe, Stenness, Orkney, was the last of the famous shebeens in Orkney. It operated till midway through the 1960s. It took a long time for the authorities to put the shutters up at Willie Farquhar's.

Willie Farquhar's shebeen stood gable-end on to the Kirkwall–Stromness road, part of a little hamlet. Nearby a stone bridge had, last century, been thrown across a mingling of Clestrain sea water and the fresh water of the Loch of Stenness.

Stone Age Orkneymen, pausing on the verge, might have thought of the crossing between life and death: a mysterious place. Not far away is the megalithic Ring of Brodgar and the burial chamber of Maeshowe, with its daring symbol of resurrection, being so set for the tombs to catch the last light of the midwinter solstice. Other knolls (or knowes) cluster around – there the music-hungry trolls (or trows) wait to lure young fiddlers in, and so bestow on them a timelessness of half a century or so: for they come out apple-cheeked into the dawn, among withered contemporaries.

II

Willie Farquhar seems to have been a cobbler, to begin.

During the Second World War he and his mother began to sell tea and buns to the soldiers who kept the fortress Orkney, all about the naval base of Scapa Flow. The soldiers left, but Willie kept open house for the young men of three or four parishes round about. They went to Willie Farquhar's after a dance or a rural cinema show. Presently they began to desire a stronger stimulant than tea.

Willie set a bottle of whisky in a niche. There were no glasses. There were no measures. Willie poured the whisky straight from the bottle into cups that had tea stains in them, and probably a crack and a chip in bowl and rim.

Nor did a customer pay for his whisky at once. He paid upon quitting the premises and he paid for what he and Willie estimated roughly was the amount he had consumed. You might think that whisky in such a perilous unlicensed situation would be expensive. By no means. The general impression is that Willie made hardly any profit, if at all.

In the end, Willie stocked bottled beer, too. I think by this time the liquor was kept in a chest under his bed. If you purchased a half-dozen bottles of export, Willie wrapped up each bottle in a sheet of newspaper, the way farm women would wrap each egg separately.

III

Willie Farquhar was like a toby jug come alive. He was always smiling out of his rubicund round face.

He wore a cloth cap, and an apron so greasy it shone like a dark mirror. He seemed to be delighted to see everyone, he agreed with everything that was said to him, he was all benignity and good-fellowship. You had the feeling that he wanted to be among happy folk, and he did his utmost to stoke the fire of contentment. The kettle burbled on the hob, for those who might want tea or coffee, or to make a hot grog or toddy.

The interior of Willie's had an earthiness, rather like (I imagine) the knowes the young fiddlers played inside. Spiders and moths and mice found comfort there as well as people. The chilliness of modern hygiene was utterly absent. After the second or third whisky, you might have thought you were being lipped by the waters of timelessness, like the fiddlers. Here was a good earthy place to be, blessed by the hidden sun.

Occasionally, a tea chest of pies was delivered from a baker in Stromness.

Willie's came to be called 'The Golden Slipper'. For a time it was the most celebrated house in Orkney. Tourists were taken there. Respectable townsfolk of Kirkwall and Stromness dropped by, just to see the Golden Slipper and the jovial host.

The law began to cast an eye on this door that was open night and day.

Willie was an elder in Victoria Street Church, Stromness, and cycled there every Sunday: sometimes, in a strong wind, his cap secured with string to the handlebars.

IV

One Saturday evening in March 1940, Willie stood in his doorway in a storm of fire.

A German bomber, flying home from an air raid on Scapa Flow and the warships, glad to escape the intense anti-aircraft shells, jettisoned its bombs over Brig-o-Waithe. A young man, John Isbister, was killed. Willie was hit with flying shrapnel, but not badly. If the hot metal had pierced him mortally, there would have been no legend of the Golden Slipper. We would have lost the only piece of folklore that the twentieth century has presented us with, new minted.

V

The law took an ever-closer interest in this threshold that smelt of whisky but had never submitted any application to the local licensing court (which would, on many counts, have been refused: hadn't the nearby Standing Stones Hotel, a respectable fishing establishment, had its applications turned down year after year throughout the

1930s? Hadn't the nearby town of Stromness been 'dry' since 1922 – Stromness that, in the year 1840, had thirty-eight drinking houses?) Where, moreover, was the hot and cold running water in Willie Farquhar's? Had the Sanitary Inspector put his foot inside the door, ever? Where were the toilets?

The young men of five or six parishes now went, night after night, to the Golden Slipper, and came out sometimes into dawn-light.

The servants of the law turned their faces ever more squarely upon this jovial unlawful door.

One sergeant of police (a newcomer in the islands, a stranger) in guise of a trout fisher, entered the premises. The following dialogue is reported as having taken place.

Willie: [his face a harvest moon of delight] Hello. Fine day. What can I do for you?
Sergeant: Had a long day on the loch. I could do with a refreshment.
Willie: A very good idea. Tea or coffee?
Sergeant: I was thinking of something a bit stronger. [A longish silence ensued.]
Willie: Ah, you must have mistaken this place for the Stenness Hotel. That's a mile further on.

The following Monday Willie went to the cattle mart in Kirkwall. He saw coming down the street the Chief Constable and the sergeant, in their uniforms. Willie seemed to be overjoyed to see them. He stopped right in front of the sergeant and said, 'Aha, aha, I see you're no' fishan the day . . .'

It is said that on another occasion, one Saturday night late when the Golden Slipper was full of music and booze, the police made a coordinated raid. Among the revellers, the Chief Constable's daughter was observed. A whistle blew, the raid was called off.

The revelry went on, louder than ever.

(By this time, old Mrs Farquhar was dead. She had not objected to strong refreshments, but she could never endure strong language. So anyone who said a bad word was shown the door.)

VI

Matters were now perilous in the extreme. Willie's triumphs over the law could not be expected to go on for ever. One day a more efficient raid was organised. A search warrant was flourished. The hoard of booze was laid open to the light: many bottles of whisky.

Willie was summoned to appear in court, at Kirkwall.

Sheriff: Why, Mr Farquhar, do you keep so many bottles of whisky in your house?

Willie: My boy works outside. I would never dream of sending him out on a cold morning without a dram in him.

It is said that, at this point, the sheriff had to cover up his face in documents and papers, to hide his mirth.

In the end, Willie Farquhar was nailed on the technicality of having too much spirituous liquor in his house, it not being a licensed inn. He was fined £15. His stock of whisky was forfeit.

A city hack, reporting the case, had his 'story' headed THE AL CAPONE OF ORKNEY.

VII

It might be thought that after that 'guilty' verdict and fine, Willie would be a broken man.

He was dented a bit, not broken.

He thought it prudent to resign his Kirk eldership. He went on bravely selling tea and pies. But the powers, having tasted blood, were not satisfied.

A restaurant? It was quickly seen that the Golden Slipper did not come up to the necessary standards of hygiene. Willie was prohibited from selling pies and tea. But he went on providing them for hungry young men and women after a dance.

Another court summons was served.

Procurator: Please tell us why, if you don't sell them, you have so many pies on the premises, a tea chest full?
Willie: Me and my boy are mad for pies.

Another fine was imposed.

And so the Golden Slipper, holed fore and aft and the mainmast broken, and the master an old sick man, drifted out of time: but at once into legend, a richer chronicle by far; the man and the shebeen voyage for ever. What I have written about has the light of legend in it already, after only thirty years. The cold tongue of reportage would tell the matter differently, no doubt. But such reportage is a dusty whisper in the joyous song of a people.

26 July 1993

DANNY WATT

Danny Watt was a character through and through. He looked like a character. He spoke like a character. He acted like a character. There was no mistaking him for anybody else. He was unique.

To begin with, for a long time, he was only known inside Orkney, driving his horse and cart through Stromness to bring to the merchants the goods that had just arrived for them on the 'north boat'. He was also a Mercury, a bringer of news. He seemed to know all the extraordinary events that occurred sooner than other folk; and some said almost before they happened. His acquaintance with genealogies was exact and detailed. He knew everybody in the West Mainland, and probably in the East Mainland too, and there were precious few in the isles that he didn't know. On market day (Wednesday) he hailed everyone by the districts they came from: 'Hello Swanney', or 'Hello Tenston'. Quite an astonishing piece of virtuosity, when it is done accurately every day over many years.

During the last war, when Stromness was chock-a-block with soldiers, Danny rose to his greatest heights. Some say there were 60,000 troops in Orkney in those years, a large proportion of them concentrated in and around Stromness. It was impossible for Danny to get to know them all, for there was a constant coming and going. So he inverted the process, and they all came to know him instead. I think I may safely say that Danny Watt was better known to the troops than the General Officer Commanding. It is a well-known fact that soldiers who had served in different parts of Orkney would meet subsequently, nearer the end of the war, in North Africa or Rome or the Rhine and talk for long about Danny Watt, with much appreciative laughter. Probably they still talk about him in quiet taverns in Somerset and the Old Kent Road.

Between 1939 and 1946 the Stromness streets, built for fishermen and farmers and their slow carts and barrows, became a main artery through which roared, night and day, enormous tarpaulined lorries, and staff cars, and furious dispatch riders. They knocked the corners off ancient houses and cracked nearly every flagstone in the town. Stromness became almost overnight a khaki metropolis. There were such swarms of men that the local girls could coolly pick and choose where they liked. Many scores of thousands of pounds rattled across shop counters in that brief season of military madness.

Danny Watt triumphantly asserted the rights of civilian vehicular traffic in those years. His horse and cart dominated the street. The general's car, the huge motorised caravans stuffed with Lewis guns or army blankets, or cursing pioneers, had to stop while Danny patiently manoeuvred his horse and cart up Porteous' Brae or along the narrow chasm of John Street. He was the master, and he knew it, and they knew it. He drove along, his mouth full of wit and chastisement and repartee – a living symbol of the ultimate victory of the pastoral over the industrial, of the man of peace over the men of war.

For long after he retired, he was a familiar daily figure in Wishart's and Nicolson's buses, where he acted as a kind of unofficial conductor: perpetually astounding summer visitors with flashes of pregnant advice or astonishing buffoonery. Into any human specimen of false granderie he pushed his long, shining, deadly point of derision. It could be very delightful to watch. To those travellers who genuinely sought help he was a priceless asset.

Now that this rather small man, with his deep-set brown eyes and his virtuoso tongue is no more, we salute a unique, deeply original personality who will certainly take his place among the shining dead of local legend.

15 July 1958

THE HAPPY FARMER

He was always to be seen in Stromness on a Saturday, toiling along the street with his two 'staffs', or sitting at the pierhead helpless with laughter, or relishing a glass of stout (he always called it 'porter') in the pub, or disappearing into Sandy Tait's for his weekly shave.

For decades 'owld Harvey o' Lea' has been known in the west, but only in recent years did he establish himself securely as a character. There are quite a few characters in Stromness, but he occupied a niche of his own.

Never have I known a happier man. Age had withered him and bent him and racked him with rheumatics, and yet his voice was always tremulous with laughter, and his eyes were crinkled with perpetual delight. Life for him, in his old age, had become a rollicking comedy that eclipsed all pain and disillusion. He was well past the allotted span, driving full on eighty, and I had the feeling that he didn't care how early or late he died. He used, at the pierhead, to chuckle about an aunt of his who died aged 105, and perhaps he wouldn't have minded living himself to that great age, making a long epilogue to the comedy. Certainly he had no fear of death, and the approach of that august majesty only roused his laughter, like everything else in the world.

Handicapped though he was, he enjoyed life as few young people can. He enveloped everyone in his cheerfulness. Sitting at the pierhead, if he saw anyone passing that he knew even remotely, he would shout his unique greeting, 'Hello, you!' And up would go one of the sticks in salutation. Strangers especially were delighted with him. I have heard two old Englishwomen murmur to each other as they passed him, 'What a charming little man!' And indeed, though charm is not a quality one usually associates with Orkney farmers, it brimmed out of old Harvey like bright wine.

Few things disgusted him, but one of them was the quality of post-war whisky. 'Disgusted' is perhaps too strong a word – 'distressed' is more accurate. Shaking his head ruefully, he would say: 'The strength's no in it.' And then his laughter would break out, while he took a long swig at his porter and the ruby drops hung from the ends of his ragged moustache: 'If it was like it used tae be, I would throw away me twa staffs and dance home tae Lea.' Lea is four miles out of Stromness.

For a while – two or three years – a strange craze held him. Every Saturday evening, summer and winter, he toiled up Hellihole to the pictures in the Town Hall. He called them the movies. I don't know what possessed him, but he wouldn't have missed his weekly talkie for anything. Finally he gave it up. Perhaps the hill was too steep for him, and certainly the impetuous youths of the town used to bump into him in their outward rush at the end of the show, often knocking him off his precarious balance. 'Ah'm whet the talkies,' he said a couple of years ago, and never went back. He had a remarkable store of old Orkney expressions and phrases that have passed completely out of use now, except among the very old. It was delightful to hear him referring to the market men as 'play-actors', for example.

I forget when I first became friendly with him. It was a slow growth, for we only met each other casually on Saturday afternoons. To the end we retained a certain half-humorous formality – I called him 'Mr Harvey' and he called me 'Master Brown'. And if, as often happened, I was with my friend, Ian MacInnes, the artist, he would turn to him and say: 'Weel, boy, are thoo been paintan any photos?' And then that spurt of laughter.

When I last saw him in Stromness there was a great change in him. He had suddenly become thin and tired-looking. He stopped to speak but had hardly the breath for utterance. 'Ah, boy,' he managed to say. 'Ah'm been aawful troubled wi' the bronchitis.' But of course there was no self-pity in his voice; his eyes still had a dark gleam of humour, and voiced his unspoken philosophy – 'Life is good, though he's almost finished his game with me.'

He toiled on, on his two sticks, towards the pierhead. I was with Ian MacInnes at the time, and after he had gone we looked at each other, both guessing that perhaps we would never see him again. We never did. Some time later I read he had died in the County Home.

He was not a poor lonely old man, he was not a figure to be pitied. He had an imperturbable gaiety and courage, and the gods bestow no rarer gifts. Shakespeare would have loved him; would have put him in *Twelfth Night* or *As You Like It* or perhaps made him the third gravedigger in *Hamlet*.

21 January 1954

Orkney Legends: The Joyous Song of a People

THE SHIP THAT STRUCK THE MOON

The ship was so huge that when the seamen were loading sheep from North Ronaldsay at the stern, amidships Norwegian pine was being stowed into the holds.

A sailor aloft at topmast dropped his knife accidentally. It was a new knife that he had just bought, with a glittering blade and a bone handle. When the knife struck the deck the blade was brittle red rust; it was recognisable only by the bone. That is how tall the masts of this Mester Ship were.

One day the skipper of the Mester Ship said to a young sailor: 'Go forrad, tell the men there to weigh anchor.' The young man, who was very handsome and blond and blue-eyed, did as he was ordered . . . Who or what was the decrepit old creature who came toiling and hirpling back to the skipper? He was none other than the young sailor, come to report that the master's orders had been carried out. That ought to give some idea of the overall length of this ship of legend.

There was the famous trouble with the moon. Two of the seamen were working on the foretop-gallant mast one night – some say they were mending their sandals – when the ship lurched violently, before a sudden squall. The mast struck against the moon and a piece of it snapped off, carrying the two sailors with it. Look at the moon, very closely, next time it is at the full, and you will see the two castaways on the surface, carrying the piece of mast, and the cross-trees and topgallant sail hanging between.

How such a vast ship managed to manoeuvre on the narrow oceans of this world is a mystery; so are the cargoes and the folk that sailed in her.

One great service for mankind she performed, however – she

destroyed, albeit by accident, the great serpent that girdled the sea. 'Land on the port bow!' shouted a lookout one day, when the Mester Ship was driving on under a full spread of sail. He was immediately echoed by another lookout: 'Land on the starboard bow!'

The skipper drove the ship between the two ugly islands. There was a tremendous crash: the ship quaked in every timber. Then the scores of thousands of sailors on board – for you couldn't work a ship like that with a few hands – saw a terrifying thing. The two islands writhed and plunged. Other islands near and far writhed, thrashed, trembled, sank. Liquid black as midnight poured out of hidden reefs over the sea. The ship had cloven the great sea serpent in two. What the lookouts took to be islands were, in truth, two humps of the monster, which was 700 miles from horn to tail.

In the end the Mester Ship vanished, or was broken up in the ice at the world's end. Her last voyage was to chart the great wall of ice that girdled the earth. Either she smashed her way through, and fell into the void beyond; or the ice held her in its gray claws and frosted the masts, and glassed her over entirely, and her grave and shroud is the white expanse that covers the North Pole.

*

The legend of the Mester Ship was one of the most popular of Orkney fireside stories. They were still telling it when I was a boy.

It is, of course, the purest fantasy; perhaps a kind of compensatory gigantism. The crofters of Orkney lived their lives within narrow bounds. The rigs they tilled were small; their low houses fitted into the green-and-brown swell of the hill; their fishing boats might hold three men and a basket of fish. They saw, from time to time, merchant ships sailing between Scandinavia and America; and occasionally, the dreaded men-o'-war came and took their young men away for years, sometimes for ever. Was the Mester Ship some attempt, by a master storyteller with a comic bent, to describe those huge cleavers of the deep? He would have been listened to with awe and delight. Or was it some ancestral memory of their great past, when their ancestors sailed as far as Vinland and Byzantium?

Or was the communal imagination working allegorically (as individual writers have done since) and saw the whole world as a ship sailing bravely among comets and stars, over many centuries, to some cosmic destination?

1973

YMIR'S SKULL

Orcadians in former centuries, before the days of archaeology and ancient monuments commissions, were intrigued by the standing stones that were everywhere in the islands: mostly single monoliths, but also small groups of two or three, and in the district of Brodgar – between the lochs of Harray and Stenness – a circle of sixty on the wine-dark moor.

What were they? Why were they there? Who set them up?

One strayed reveller on New Year's morning – the time when the Orkney folk still visit each other's houses with bottles and gifts and songs – stumbled at last on the truth. Walking with a merry heart, he saw the great stone on the verge of the Loch of Stenness stir, and uproot itself, and trundle down to the edge of the water. It stooped down and drank into its stiff cold mouth. Then, refreshed, it returned to its place. And the sun rose.

The man walked on homeward, sober and sick at heart. He had heard stories, from different parts of Orkney, of the stone that quenched its thirst on the first morning of the year. Folk had seen the thing happening, and told it in the smithies and the ale-houses; but those witnesses had never lived to see the year out. At seedtime, or peat-cutting time, or harvest, they had dwined and died. Very likely our strayed reveller too was coffined and buried before the next Hogmanay.

What he had seen was a giant, one of those legendary creatures that blunder and rage through the folklore of Scandinavia. A certain tribe of these giants go about their brutish business in the dark. If they are touched by the sun's rays, they are immediately changed to stone. There must have been some marvellous circular dance of giants at Brodgar a very long time ago, so enjoyable that they were still at it when the sun got up. Now, between the two lochs, the stone dance goes on for ever.

But it seems that the Orkney giants liked fighting better than dancing. The most quarrelsome of them was Cubbie Roo who lived mostly in the island of Wyre; he was so huge that he could walk about Orkney in a very short time, using the islands as stepping stones. Once, when he was in the island of Westray, he had a shouting match with another giant who lived in Rousay. Cubbie Roo picked up a huge stone and hurled it across the sound at the Rousay giant. The stone fell short – it is still to be seen on the Rousay shore with Cubbie Roo's finger-marks on it, and it is called the 'finger-steen' to this day. There is another of Cubbie Roo's stones in the parish of Evie, and a third in Stronsay. The Stronsay stone was thrown in friendship, to waken a giant who had slept too long.

Cubbie Roo led his monstrous existence in the island of Wyre. Long after the sun had made a stone of him a Norse chieftain called Kolbein Hruga had his great hall in the same island. This Kolbein Hruga must have been a formidable man as he strode about Wyre, or sailed in his ship between the islands, or made land after a Viking cruise when the fields of Wyre were beginning to turn from green to gold. The peasant children, one imagines, ran in terror from his imperious eyes and fierce beard; so much so, that even after he died and was given a quiet Christian burial, mothers would say to their children, 'Behave, or Kolbein Hruga'll get thee!' The mighty man stalked through their innocent dreams, he was the noise down at the shore, and the thunder over Rousay. In time, the giant and the chieftain began to merge in the popular imagination, and the name Kolbein Hruga was simplified to Cubbie Roo. That is how the Wyre giant – who was probably nameless in the beginning – got his name . . . It is interesting to note, further, that a son of Kolbein Hruga of Wyre was the bishop and poet Bjarni Kolbeinson, who wrote *The Lay of the Jomsvikings*. Wyre must be a good place for poets as well as giants – Edwin Muir was brought up there. Two great poets from one small green island – surely that is unique in the history of literature.

But, to return to our giants.

Stones seem to have been the giants' only weapons. They were inordinately stupid creatures, incapable of imagining arrows or axes. They sometimes tried to build bridges between the islands, but they always failed; usually the stones for the building slipped from their backs into the sea, and that is why there are so many skerries and holms around Orkney.

There was one enormous Scottish giant who wanted to cultivate a kale-yard. He had heard that the soil of Orkney was the best for such a purpose. With three enormous splashing strides he was across the Pentland Firth that separates Scotland from the islands. He scooped up soil and stones from two places in the largest Orkney island; the springs rose up and filled the depressions, and they became the lochs of Stenness and Harray. When he had filled his basket with good Orkney earth he turned for home. As he lurched through the sea, scaring even the whales, the topmost sod fell off his basket and became the green island of Graemsay. Another huge step, and the strap of his basket broke and all the clods and rocks fell out into the sea. That dark tremendous accident is called Hoy to this day.

The Orkney giants, however, were tame and small compared to the giants across the North Sea. They had to be, because essentially the giants were mountain creatures, and in Orkney where there are no mountains to speak of but only gentle rounded hills, they were starved of their true environment. Snows, and pine trees, and mountain tarns, were where the giants had their exultant beginnings. They were the mountain spirits, and had all the attributes of mountains. No wonder the Orkney race of giants, exiled, went into a decline and ultimately became extinct.

That is all that is left of a once mighty race – a few stones on the moor. Brodgar is full of silences and broodings and whisperings. Do the stones remember their heroic ancestors back in Norway, who were as huge as the mountains themselves, and many-headed? Some of these eastern giants had as many as nine heads, but there was one with 900 heads. Their voices were like thunder, and their eyes 'were blank and deep, like mountain tarns'.

Yet even these Norwegian giants – the mighty progenitors of the Orkney giants – were puny compared to their original begetter.

The great god Odin and his brothers came upon the body of a giant called Ymir who must have been as big as a star. The gods brooded upon the vastness and beauty of Ymir for an aeon or two. Then out of Ymir they created the earth we live in. The sea and the lakes are his blood; the earth is his flesh; the rivers are his veins; the forests are his hair. The gods pondered for another century or so over Ymir's skull – to what conceivable use could they put it? At last they made out of it a very beautiful thing. The sky over our heads is Ymir's skull.

6 October 1973

THE TAKING OF ORKNEY

I

Three old people stood on the shore against us.

This was the first of the Whale Islands that we took.

What are the old ones but withered leaves on a tree?

They had burned their houses. The fires warmed us from the snow for an hour. It was a cold long winter afterwards.

The name of our ship was *Swan*.

Ringan is the name of our skipper.

We called the place 'Island of Ringan' – Rinansey.

II

One by one, a month apart, our ships sailed from a populous district in Norway called More.

The home valleys, once so bounteous, could no longer feed so many people.

From fjords north and south, in our fathers' time, ships had sailed out to Iceland and beyond.

We west-voyagers were kin, but some had small liking for their cousins.

We knew about the Islands of the Whale (Orkney). Our fathers had often raided there. 'In Orkney are good tilth and pasture, and fish abound . . .'

Hjal and his brothers and serfs in the ship *Dolphin* sailed against an island with many sand beaches.

The islanders defended themselves well but in the end were chased over the island like dogs, showing the whites of their eyes.

Some of the women were comely, very dark with gray eyes.

Hjal's men put out the flames in the largest house with buckets of sea water. Hjal lived there that year.

The islanders had poisoned a well. Three men died.

Hjal's men suffered much thirst till a new water-hole was dug.

They found many cheeses and smoked fish and ham in a smoke-house.

Most of the sheep and swine and cattle had been driven across to other islands.

They called it 'island of beaches' – Sanday.

III

Our plan of occupation of Orkney in More, Norway, had been that each month a ship would sail west and take a particular island.

In this way we ensured that a storm in mid-ocean would not whelm the westerlings if all sailed together in one fleet, and would prevent any quarrelling about this island or that. The ships were chosen by lots, one to embark at each new moon, for the moon rules the sea and voyagers, and might round out each enterprise to a fullness of fortune.

For a year the caves along our fjord had rung with hammers and rasped with saws, and braziers burned under the tar pots, and the hulls grew.

The ship *Moorcock* that sailed in the month of ploughing ended on a reef in the north Orkneys, and all but one were drowned. Swart the skipper was drowned.

Hosuck swam ashore. He was yoked to a plough and a farmer on that island prodded him over stony acres. 'I did not expect to make such a hard landfall,' said Hosuck.

The island girls spat at him.

Hosuck was given an armful of straw to sleep on, in a byre with the beasts of Stronsay.

IV

Bran in the fine ship *Shark* sailed against the most western island.

The island men – even boys and white-beards – were drawn up with bows and slings on the shore against Bran and his brothers and nephews.

Every man was hewn down on that shore by the men of *Shark*. Women came and grieved over one man. Bran guessed that that man must be the chief, and that he had been much loved or feared.

'The men who have come are better in every way,' said Bran to the keening women.

But one of the women wept the more sorely.

Some of the women of this west island, Westray, ran about burning thatch here and there. Bran's men plucked the torches from their hands.

'We have come to a fertile island,' said Bran, 'with spirited women in it.'

Later, Bran took the woman who had wept so sorely over the chief, to be his wife.

The men of *Shark* honoured the slain islanders with a funeral pyre.

V

At the beginning of summer Sven in his longship *Snowgoose* had a peaceful landfall in an island that seemed to be lived in by a few bald men in long white coats.

Those monks neither welcomed us nor fled from us.

They lived each man in a small beehive hut, and indeed they kept bees, in addition to digging little cabbage plots and going out to fish in curraghs.

In their bede-house they had a bell which was rung often throughout the day. Then each man would leave whatever he was doing and go into the kirk, as they called it, and they sang together in a strange language. Deep voices and sweet voices intermingled.

Sven asked them where the other islanders were. They shook their heads. The oldest monk pointed vaguely south and west.

Sven's brothers and sons were in favour of killing the bald-heads and making use of their lobster boats and gardening gear.

But Sven said the Irish monks knew the soil of the island and the seas round it, and they had much to teach the Norwegians, and perhaps they could live at peace for a while in this island of monks, Papay.

'But there are no women,' said the young men.

'There will come a time to see about that,' said Sven. 'Speaking for myself, I am glad my wife Ragn is at home in More, tending to the pot over the fire, and not here. Orkney is full of beautiful women and they will come to you when they see what good fighters and providers you are.'

'That bell is driving me mad,' said Sven's ill-natured uncle, Bui.

'That bell seems to me to make a peaceful sound, eight times in the day,' said Sven, 'compared to the clacking tongues of Ragn and the women home in More.'

The fleeing islanders of Papay had ploughed and sowed their barley fields. Now there were green patches all over Papay.

The cows yielded good milk.

'But making cheese and butter is not work for men,' said Sven's second son, Arn.

'You'll pluck wool from the sheep and card it too,' said Sven. 'The brothers will show you how to do it, till the women come.'

The bell rang in the bell-tower.

The monks trooped into the kirk, one carrying a weakly lamb.

VI

There was a hilly island with two lochs among the brown hills and good farmland all round the shore.

One of our finest ships, *Skarf*, sailed against that island. The skipper was Rolf Amundson, a good sailor and a wise man in every way.

Rolf had on board, among his crew, a poet called Thord, his cousin, a lazy man.

It seemed that Rolf could take over any island he pleased, without much trouble.

This island was hard to subdue.

The islanders had built a line of stone circular forts above the shore, and there they sheltered, men and women and children, with as many provisions as they could carry inside. They called those little castles 'brochs', and there was a well of good water inside every broch.

Their cattle and sheep they had driven up among the hills. A few herdsmen looked after the beasts there.

Rolf's young men attacked the first castle. The defenders threw down big stones and buckets of ordure. They had good archers in the battlement whose arrows sang like birds and enchanted six of Rolf's men to death, in the course of a week.

'This is a costly siege,' said Rolf. 'Our food and water are running low, too. It's good there are fish to catch in the Sound.'

'But theirs are running lower,' said Rolf's uncle, Sigg. 'Now their only weapons are women's insults.'

Indeed from the broch-tops old women and young women and girls were putting, morning to night, black curses on our ship and voyage.

'Their farms are good,' said Rolf. 'In a week I think we will be bringing their cattle and pigs down from the hills. We will light fires in the hearths.'

There was now no sound from any of the brochs.

'We should storm the first broch now,' said Sigg, an impatient man.

'We will wait for a day or two yet,' said Rolf.

Early on the morning of the tenth day, the little armoured door at the base of the broch was opened from inside and a small boy was thrust out into the sunrise, and the door was shut and barred again.

Rolf went up to the child and the child laughed and pulled his beard.

The women looked on from above, wanly. What would Rolf do with the boy: dash his brains out on the obdurate broch wall?

Rolf gave the child a fish from a bucket of new-caught fish. 'Take that to your mother,' said Rolf. 'Tell your chief, his people can have plenty of fish if they yield us the island.'

The boy kissed Rolf's sea-smelling hand and laughed.

Rolf set him on the steering bench of the ship, to play with shells and coloured stones.

The seamen drew the dark hair of the child through their fingers. Some of them thought of their children back in Norway.

Later that day, the door of the first broch opened and all the people inside came out stooping, and stood in a line on the sea-banks. Some of the old islanders were weak in the legs with hunger and confinement. The women looked sullen.

Rolf took the hand of the chief man. The man wept, considering it a shameful thing to have yielded up his broch after a short siege.

A young woman called to the child sitting in the ship. The boy paid no attention to his mother, he was testing the edge of one of our axes on his finger. There was a blood-bead. The child laughed and sucked his finger clean.

'That child will be a good warrior when he is full-grown,' said old Sigg.

One by one, in the course of that midsummer day, the five brochs surrendered. They yielded all their possessions and land and animals to Rolf. They agreed to become his people and work for him.

From that day the name of the place was 'Rolf's island', Rousay.

Thord made a poem about the taking of Rousay.

> We waited for mighty warriors
> To break from the broch,
> A mingling of island blood with mariners' blood
> Till rockpools were red.
> They have offered one infant.
> A child, a butterfly chaser.

At the same time as he subdued Rousay, the men of four neighbouring islands surrendered to Rolf.

Rolf gave one of the islands to his helmsman Egil, and it was called Egil's island, Egilsay, afterwards.

A little green island shaped like a spearhead Rolf gave to Thord the skald. Because of its shape, men called it Wyre. But Thord said it should be an island of poetry, and he would see to it that Wyre, before long, would be seen to have the shape of a Norwegian mountain harp rather than a spearhead. 'Poetry is for peace,' said Thord, 'and mighty poets will live in this small green island. Look how tall and thick the barley is standing in the fields of Wyre.'

A small neighbouring island with fifty grazing sheep on it Rolf gave to his awkward uncle Sigg. That island was given the name Fara ('sheep island').

There was another small island that divided the tide-race, one foaming torrent on each side. This place too had a monastery with a dozen white-coated brothers on it.

'We will do nothing to harm those peaceful men,' said Rolf.

That summer and for years afterwards, till the time of his death, Rolf often visited this 'island of the saints' (Eynhallow) and had talk with the abbot and monks there.

Rolf was entertained simply there, on fish, honey, bread and ale – the same food that they offered to the wandering beggars.

VII

The large ship *Raven* anchored off the north-west shore of 'the island of horses', Hrossey, and Olaf left the ship with thirty armed men.

Hrossey is by far the largest of the Orkneys, a very fertile island, with trout lochs, streams, good pasture land and tilth, and small strong horses among the hills. Also every little beach had a few fishing curraghs.

Suddenly the dunes erupted with men, and their assault was so fierce and well timed that Olaf and his men were caught with the sea still washing about their knees.

Five men were killed among the shore waves. Then Olaf and the others withdrew, some with wounds and bruises on them. Olaf said, 'Sea water is the best cure for cuts. I did not think, though, that those farmers had such courage.'

Seven of the Hrossey men lay dead on the shore stones.

There was much wailing of women along the sea-banks. Those women wept unashamedly, voice after voice, in a kind of ordered chant, not like our women back home who think shame to voice their feelings of joy and sorrow, but if they exult and grieve, it is in the loneliness of their chambers.

But more and more island men were gathering with spears and arrows. They surged out of the barns and smithies.

'We will try our luck further south,' said Olaf.

Next day, sailing south, they came to a broad sweep of sand with a scatter of houses at either end and good farmland beyond, stretching back to the low fertile hills of the interior.

They waded ashore, a half-dozen of them ('for we cannot afford such a blood-letting as we had on the tide-mark two days ago,' said Olaf) and though they walked openly but cautiously as far as the fields and the first houses, not an arrow sang against them. Not one woman's curse chilled their blood.

The people of all that district had taken to the hills.

A few wild horses came down to greet them.

A dog here and there barked at them, then either fled or nuzzled against them.

The corn was growing tall in the fields.

Before sunset Olaf had taken possession of all that rich country-side.

It was the richest conquest in Orkney up to that time.

Olaf called his territory 'bay of sand' – Sandwick.

VIII

Rolf of Rousay paid another visit to the monastery in Eynhallow, one rainy morning in the eighth month when the monks were labouring among sunbursts and rainbows to get their barley harvest in.

'Olaf, my second cousin,' he said, 'had good luck in Sandwick, after losing those young strong men on the beach at Birsay. Now I hear that a Norwegian ship, the *Sea Eagle*, has been lost in that storm a week ago, trying to make a landfall further south in Hrossey. A wave threw her against a huge black sea-crag and the seamen were drowned, except Grim the skipper and three others. Grim swam to an island. The islanders pulled Grim half-dead out of the seaweed and warmed him back to life with hot ale and honey. "This is my island," said Grim, in a half-drowned delirium. "I call this island Graemsay (Grim's island)."

'The folk in the farm there stood all about Grim and laughed. They thought it better to agree with the stranger. "Yes, it is Grim's island, to be sure," they said. Grim and his three men are still there, as far as I know, working in the hayfield. A dozen bodies have come ashore, on this beach or that skerry in the neighbourhood of the Black Crag. Many seamen will be eaten by salt and lobsters.'

'Grim is a lucky man,' said the abbot. 'A generation ago the people of Graemsay would have cut their throats. We have, I thank God, infused a little light and charity into some of the islanders.'

'What troubles me,' said Rolf, 'is to know how this Norse settlement is to be effected. We are a small tribe back in Norway. It will take more than a few hundred men from the fjords to subdue all the settlements here. We have taken over only a few islands and bays. If the Orkney men organise themselves in their defence, it may go ill with us yet.'

'This will happen, I think,' said the abbot. 'When the tide of fortune goes in their favour, the islanders are capable of great courage and ingenuity. They ebb and flow like the waters of the moon. Let them be tangled in difficulties and small thwartings, they give way quickly to ill thoughts and premonitions and in the end to defeats. But nothing so terrible as your invasion has happened to them up to now. They know well what has befallen the people in the north islands. Already the dark mood is on them.

'They know, with a very ancient wisdom, that time has run out for them, their history is a mere moon cinder now that will soon go out. They will come suddenly and offer you everything. They will come from the islands of the south, from the region of the stone circles and from the island of the blue hills, and they will become your loyal men. This will happen, I think, before the year is out.

'Then you easterners will be the lords of Orkney.

'But you should not crow like morning cocks because of that victory, Rolf.

'The islanders came here as conquerors five or six generations ago, and they took the land from the people who had it then. They put yokes on the strong men, they chose the best women, they swore peace on the sacred stones of the original islanders.

'But there are no original islanders. There never have been. All over the face of the earth, as far back as Eden, the peoples of the earth have been in constant flux and motion. The wild horsemen ride from the steppes and the risen sun. Their horses drink the wind, their curved blades flash in the sun, the cities and settlements fall before them.

'Always the movement of the tribes is westward. In the west, some-where, is the land of heart's desire. In the west is the bourne of earthly happiness. *But follow the sun!*

'Their hooves bend westward. Their ships seek the undiscovered enchanted islands beyond the sunset.

'And the people whose plough land and fishing banks they take over? Those original ones make a token resistance, for a year or a decade, then suddenly they yield everything to the strong strangers. It is as if they know in their bones that their time has come. It is a part of their ancient tragic wisdom. It is a doom on them. "Our recent har-vests, our grapes and wheat, are thin. Our music and stories have lost their relish. We are a sentenced people, the doom will soon fall on us . . ." Then the fierce horsemen ride out of the east. A few of their undiscovered scrolls – their history – lie in caves here and there, hidden.

'My friend from Norway, I would not have you ignorant of this perpetual drift of history. I do not have to remind you of it – it is written in your bones. You will stay here, you and your sons and your sons' sons, for twelve or fifteen generations. Then on your folk, too, the weariness will come, the salt will lose its savour, the doom will lie heavy on you, you will yield up your sovereignty to strangers.

'You think you are kin only to a tribe back in Norway. I tell you you are the same stock and blood as those you are uprooting. All men east and south and west are sons of Adam. You are kin to the horsemen of the steppes and the black men in the forests and rivers of Ethiopia. We cannot hide from the curse of Adam in Iceland or in that island of pure felicity further west, the earthly paradise that Abbot Brendan from Ireland stumbled on with his sailors a hundred years ago. The blessed Brendan was glad at last to let his bones be laid in the green hills of Ireland. We monks think we have found one answer to life's perplexities here, in this little monastery with the crested tides singing their "glorias" on either side of us. Here, surely, is the still centre of history.

'If we do any wandering at all, Rolf, it is a spiritual quest, a far seeking into the mind and heart of God. And that voyage never ends.

'So it seems to us, meantime. But there will come a time – we know it – when we will be uprooted from the quiet sanctuaries, and our psalms and candle flames scattered to the twelve winds.

'Yet the light is endless.

'Other men will relume their clay lamps from the Gloria that girdles time and eternity.

'For our brief time, in Eynhallow or in Papay or in Iona, we plough our small fields, and reap them, and catch fish in the sounds, and take honey from the hives.

'Brother Augustus, put some ale in a cup for Rolf our guest, and mix some of last year's honey into it.

'What, the hayfield is all cut? Our old ox will not go hungry this winter.'

IX

It did not happen exactly as the abbot foretold, at haytime in Eynhallow, to Rolf Amundson, skipper of the ship *Skarf*, lord of Rousay.

Halverd and his forty men in the ship *Ice Maiden* made landfall, just before the time of the barley harvest, at a bay which the sailors called Fjord (Firth). Halverd was an unpopular overbearing man and his crew, including his seven sons, did not think he should have the honour of a settlement named after him.

But anything less like a Norwegian fjord it would be difficult to imagine, for the bay was shallow and girt with low flat corn-lands.

The people of Firth were determined to defend their houses and fields against the bright-bearded easterners. There was a hard battle on the beach, but in the end the men of Firth broke off the engagement. Halverd was glad enough to bind up the *Ice Maiden*'s wounds. Ten of his men lay dead in the seaweed.

It seemed to Halverd and to all of them that the men of Firth had only to press them with another assault of spears and stones, that morning, and the Norwegians would have had to push out and sail away.

Certainly Halverd could endure no more slaughter of his young men. They would be compelled, he thought, to seek and claim a quieter shore than Firth.

But suddenly, for no good reason, it was the Orkneymen who gave in. They shouted to their women-folk on the banks above to drive the herd and the flock up among the hills. And so the folk of Firth left in the course of one golden sun-step down the sky. In the afternoon the shore was empty.

But Halverd and his men were too weary and battle-sore to pursue them.

The natives had taken with them also the ploughs and yokes and sickles, the flails and the harrows.

That night the Norwegians slept in the scattered houses along the shore, and it was the soundest sleep they had had since leaving More.

But afterwards, for a score of nights, they had small peace in the houses of Firth.

In the dark of the moon, men came down from the hills and burned the thatch over their heads, then were gone before sunrise.

One morning they got up to find that their ship *Ice Maiden* had been smashed here and there about the water-line with axes, so that she would not be able for sea for a long time. Also the Orkneymen had unwrapped the well-woven sail and torn it to shreds. Halverd had woken in the night, once, and thought the din down at the shore to be thunder-stones.

Halverd's men were hungry, and they were having to make do with seaweed from the ebb and the tough oily flesh of cormorants.

'I think,' said Halverd, 'we will have to make a few more trench-ings into our good ship *Ice Maiden*, for kindling. It will be a cold winter in this place without logs to warm us.'

Now the barley hung golden heads in the fields round about. There was no way of harvesting the barley.

One cold morning the men of More were plucking bits of seaweed from the ebb to eat when they saw people coming down through the gap in the hills.

The sailors rushed up to the houses for their weapons, for it seemed to them that the people were coming back to attack them and make an end of them.

But then Alt, a young nephew of Halverd, a keen-sighted man, saw that the people were carrying ploughs and yokes, flails and sickles, and they had their few sheep and cows and pigs, and one black ox.

The crew of *Ice Maiden*, armed with axes and daggers, stood above the sea-banks waiting to see what would happen.

An old man and a girl came forward and stood in front of Halverd. The elder pointed to the ripe barley field. He spoke to the girl. The girl took from a fold of her coat a new sickle.

Halverd, a rather stupid man, seemed bewildered. He twirled his axe in his hand, he took sun-flashings from the blade. He ought perhaps to kill the old man and the girl there and then? He looked at his men, seeking advice.

Alt said the people had come to them in peace. They could not bear, obviously, to see their harvest rotting. They had come to offer their services. If they could not eat the bread in winter themselves, let the strangers eat and drink; they would show them their mysteries, then perish in the land that had nourished them for a dozen generations.

The men of *Ice Maiden* agreed with Alt's explanation. They called to the people of Firth to come and meet them.

The people came across the burn and down the meadow slowly.

One of their dogs ran, joyously barking, and put his muzzle into Alt's hand.

Then the people came more urgently, until they stood all about the old man and the sickle-bearing girl.

The old man knelt in front of Halverd. The girl gave Halverd the bright sickle.

Two young men led the ox, a black block, to the strangers, and left it there.

That night the Firth people showed the men of *Ice Maiden* how to burn peat in the hearths – a thing they had not known before.

Next morning the field was full of harvesters, Norsemen and Orkneymen, and the barley fell in bright swathes. The women followed the reapers, stooping and binding sheaves.

Later, when the harvest was gathered into the barns, the old man married his granddaughter, the girl with the sickle, to Alt, Halverd's nephew.

After that there was no more killing or burning in that district.

But it was clearly understood that the easterlings were from then on masters of that hill and shore, and the original people were their serfs and must do their bidding.

It took a long while for Halverd to accept this situation.

'Halverd's skull is thicker than the ox's,' said Alt.

X

Ivor and his men in the longship *Storm Petrel* sailed west at the beginning of winter. They had a stormy crossing from Norway.

They sailed through the northern islands, and saw that every shore there had a Norwegian longship drawn up on it, and stooks in the fields, so they avoided those islands.

They steered south along the coast of the big island, Hrossey, and saw that their kindred had taken Birsay and Marwick and Sandwick. The land was barren south of Sandwick. A line of cliffs confronted the western ocean.

Further south, they saw 'the island of the blue hills' (Hoy) but considered it to be even more barren.

'It seems to me,' said Ivor, 'that the best land has been taken. We will have to take to fishing, lads. We will haul our ship up the first sheltered beach, and we will have a hard winter of it. What we must do is this, we must break up *Storm Petrel* and make a dozen small fishing boats out of her. A great pity, because the shipwright in Norway put much work and skill into the building of her. *Storm Petrel* is a beautiful ship. Her children, a dozen little boats, must reap the ocean here in Orkney.'

Ivor and his crew were very tired after the storms at sea.

They were sailing between the south-west of Hrossey and the little green island, borne swiftly along on the flood. Ivor shaded his eyes with his hand and said, 'I swear I know that man carrying stooks. He is our cousin Grim. He seems to be working hard among the islanders. This is not what Grim came west for, to be a servant. Grim was always a proud boastful man.'

Some of Ivor's sons said that indeed the farm servant in Graemsay looked like Grim.

Then the man lifted his head from the stooks and began to wave his arms wildly at the *Storm Petrel*, that was going past swiftly on the flood tide.

They saw that the master harvester ordered Grim back to his tasks. Grim must have given the overseer a hard answer, because the man struck him on the face, and Grim went back meekly to his labours.

'A great change has come over Grim in this place,' said Ivor. 'We will have to learn to make friends with the land and sea and sky hereabouts. We haven't come all this way to be serfs.'

They found a very sheltered harbour between a granite hill and two small islets. They called the place Hamnavoe.

That winter – a very hard hungry time – they decided indeed to be fishermen. They could see from the flocks of cormorants and seals that there was an abundance of herring and cod and lobsters.

With grief in their hearts – which each man hid from the others – they broke up the beautiful longship *Storm Petrel* that was said to be the most beautiful ship out of Norway in that emigration. They built a dozen small fishing boats. They built stone bothies of granite and clay.

No one in that part of Orkney opposed their landing.

Ivor and a dozen men crossed over to Graemsay to bargain for meat and cheese and ale.

'We will ignore Grim,' said Ivor. 'We don't want a ranter like Grim in our community. He has proved himself a luckless man.'

Ivor and the farmer of Graemsay were bargaining on the shore, agreeably enough, when Grim got wind of their presence and he came running out of the black-house where he stayed with the serving men. 'Ivor! Welcome, dear friend. Save me from those savages! Well done, Ivor. We will rule here in Graemsay together. We will bend them to our yoke, Ivor.'

Ivor and the farmer went on bargaining for pork and bread and a dozen skins of ale.

'This servant of mine seems to know you,' said the farmer.

'But the less I know of him, the better I like it,' said Ivor, and counted out two silver pieces into the farmer's palm.

'I had much trouble breaking him in,' said the farmer.

Then Grim stood by, and wept like a fool.

XI

The ship *Heron*, skippered by Rognvald Limp-leg (he had been wounded in the hamstring in Sweden in his youth) sailed east in the lessening sun.

It was a poor time of the year to make a voyage.

Rognvald steered the *Heron* to the east of Orkney and landed on a large fertile island, which he called Ronaldsay at once.

His men prepared, on the shore of the island, for a hard struggle. Such fields and farms were worth defending.

But no one opposed them.

When Rognvald and his sixty-five men went up cautiously to the sea-banks, each man armed with axe and shield, there was no one there.

By now the sun was down and they could see, here and there, small cruisie-lamps being lit in the houses. The doors stood open. Men and women came and stood in the doors, a group of shadows in every farm.

There was no sound but the barking of dogs here and there.

'I think we should go and warm ourselves at their fires,' said Rognvald. 'It is, after all, our island now. We have every right to eat and drink in our own houses, and sit at our firesides.'

The men of *Heron* thought that would be a foolish thing to do. At midnight the farmers would fall on them when they were asleep on the benches and cut their throats.

But Rognvald chose two men to go with him to a house.

They went up, unarmed, to the open door, under a half-moon, and the farm people ushered the three Norwegians inside. They set them down to porridge and cheese and beer.

There were no words spoken.

The farmer gestured to the straw pallets round the fire. His guests should sleep there, and welcome, after their long winter voyage.

'It is our fire,' said Rognvald, 'and our sleeping-straw, and we will sleep there whenever we feel like it. But tonight we will sleep on shipboard. My sailors are afraid, if they sleep in the houses they'll be a long time wakening up. And young men, such as I have in my crew, like to be up betimes about their business.'

So it happened that all the crew slept on board *Heron* that night.

'But,' said Rognvald, 'I have a feeling that those islanders are anxious to have us as their protectors. The land is good hereabouts. I think we winter-farers will have more luck than some of the ships that came in high summer.'

Again, the next morning, the doors of all the farmhouses stood open, and the people stood outside in the cold sun. They stood there patiently, like people expecting guests.

'They must understand this,' said Rognvald: 'they are not our hosts, they are our servants. So long as they understand that, all will be well between us.'

'The girls are beautiful,' said Bui, Rognvald's son.

'I won't have any kin of mine marrying serfs,' said Rognvald. 'We will fetch our own women from Norway, next spring. We have promised. They are waiting.'

Over the island only a few women moved, going with buckets between the byres where the cattle were stalled for the winter, and the kitchens to make cheese and butter.

The smell of sweet milk on that frosty morning was delicious to the nostrils of the men who had smelt nothing but salt for weeks.

'Now,' said Rognvald, 'we will take possession of our island.'

Not a door was barred against them.

At half a dozen farms round about they were set down silently to a breakfast of fish and barley bread and ale.

The peat fires were stoked up to warm them.

Then the farm people all over Ronaldsay went about their daily tasks. Some of the men went into the barns to thresh oats. Others went out in their curraghs to fish under the crags, or further south into the crested tide-race. The women and girls baked bread over the fires, and prepared pots of broth. An old shepherd wandered away to the hill.

The islanders spoke not a word.

The children came and looked with wide eyes at the strangers who had come among them.

That night, after such hospitality, the Norsemen slept in the houses, with their axes beside them, all but half a dozen whom Rognvald still thought it prudent to stay shore-bound and guard the ship.

In the days and weeks that followed, the men of *Heron* and the farm folk used courtesy towards each other. 'We will not speak their serf language,' said Rognvald. 'They must learn to speak like us.'

The young sailors, weary of idleness, went and threshed corn with the farm workers in the byres.

The small horses came to them and laid friendly heads on the sea-smelling hands.

Rognvald limped down to a lobster boat that was being launched, and offered to take the steering oar. An old fisherman pointed to the rowing bench. This open sea was too dangerous for strangers.

'The sooner I learn the good fishing grounds of my own island, the better,' said Rognvald from the thwart. The three young fishermen nodded, as though they were beginning to understand what the stranger was saying.

A young Norwegian called Finn walked up the hill to look at the hill sheep. His father owned a large herd of goats in More. 'It is time those sheep were folded for the winter,' said Finn.

On the way down, as the first stars were coming out, Finn met the girl whom the sailors agreed was the most winsome in the island, the granddaughter of the old shepherd. They spoke with each other, or rather, they mingled words. It was a good sound, more like music than language.

They agreed to meet each other, on the hill road, the next night.

It was an overcast dark night. A shadow rose out of a ditch and stabbed Finn, but Finn threw his arm across his face and the dagger cut his elbow, so that his hand was gloved in warm blood. Then Finn turned on his attacker and lifted a heavy stone and broke his skull.

It turned out that the young man who had attacked Finn had, all that year, been the sweetheart of the girl Finn was going to tryst with that night.

The girl went wailing along the shore next morning, after the body was found.

'It seems to me that our servants might turn against us now,' said Rognvald. 'That was a foolish thing you did, Finn. You have ruined the peace that was all but established between the ship and the island . . .' He rose from the bench where he was sucking the large bone of a halibut and he struck Finn thrice, so that Finn's head jolted back thrice on his neck. 'You will go and make peace with the father of the young man you killed. You will pay heavy compensation. Learn this now, Finn. Men must treat even their servants with civility.'

When Finn went to the farm where the young man had lived, the door was bolted against him. The people did not appear for a fortnight, except once to gather up the body of their son and bury it under a howe at the end of their house. Nor did they have dealings with any of the Norwegians again.

But the other families in the island continued to have good relations with the ship folk. They did not object when Rognvald insisted that runes be carved on every doorpost: THIS FARM BELONGS TO ROGNVALD INGVISON.

Finn was sentenced by Rognvald to stay on shipboard alone, as further punishment for the man-slaying. His arm wound was slow to heal. One night the girl came to see him with some oil of herbs and she applied it to the wound. She came every day until the wound was healed. Now she knew many words of the shipmen's language.

A week after that, Finn asked leave to marry this girl, whose name was Gaia.

'Remember this,' said Rognvald. 'She is a serf-woman, and you have a young wife and a child back in Norway. When this news gets back to them, they will not exactly be dancing for joy.'

'I do not think I will ever see Norway again,' said Finn.

Life went on in Ronaldsay as it had done. The Norwegians worked as hard as the islanders, at threshing and malting and fishing. They had to work hard, for now there were thirty-five extra mouths to feed in the island.

Rognvald, the lord of the island, caught a wild horse among the hills and, lame as he was, brought it, whinnying mightily and whirling a hoof, down to the main pasture.

At midwinter Rognvald sat in the great chair of the largest farm in Ronaldsay, and the wife of the man who had owned the house formerly came in and set before him a plate of roast pork and new-baked bread.

'Enjoy this, lord,' she said in the Norse tongue.

And her husband said, 'No man likes to see his gear and goods taken from him. But Fate has said it must happen this way.'

He bowed his head, there in the door, like a faithful steward.

*

In addition to the large island, Ronaldsay, there fell under Rognvald Limp-leg's governance in due course the surrounding islands of Burray, Hunda, Swona, Glimps Holm and Stroma.

The farmers there came to Rognvald's farm in Ronaldsay and promised him their labour and rents, as overlord.

But some of the islanders took as many of their people and belongings as they could carry in their small boats, and sailed south to their kin in Scotland.

A few boats were lost in that perilous sea, the Pictland Firth.

A stranger voyage was begun, a dozen small boats setting out westward from the Island of the Dog (Hunda).

The Norsemen wondered where the curraghs could be sailing, for there is no land west of Orkney, only sunset and the roaring waterfall of world's end.

An old islander said that those people were sailing to Tir-Nan-Og, 'the Land of the Young', where there is no want or sickness, or old age or death, but the eagle and the dove sit at peace in the apple-laden trees; nor is there time or chance, and the people live as in the time of their best youth, and desire, forever pure, never fails.

XII

The time of departure from Norway had been fixed by lots, the previous year.

It fell to Osmund's lot, back home in More, to sail east at midwinter. His ship was called *Fulmar*.

There is not much to be said about Osmund's voyage. He ran into strong contrary winds and was driven north-west almost as far as Iceland. Two young sailors, his nephews, were washed from the ship by a great wave.

'I think this will be an unlucky voyage for us,' said Osmund. 'We have set out at the darkest, most dangerous time of the year. It is certain that the best land of Orkney has been taken before now. And I have lost two promising young men, Leif and Valt.'

The wind swung to the north-west, and soon brought them among the Orkneys.

Osmund was told in Rinansey that his brother Rolf Amundson had taken possession of the island Rousay and all the smaller islands round about.

Osmund thought it would be a wise thing to visit Rolf and take advice from him. Rolf was spoken of as one of the most sagacious men in Scandinavia.

'It is true, brother,' said Rolf, 'that most of the best land has been taken. There is a large island in the south called Hoy. None of our people has set foot on Hoy.'

'I have heard,' said Osmund, 'that there is nothing in Hoy but blue barren hills.'

'South of the hills is a large fertile plain,' said Rolf, 'ample enough for you and your people, and I hear that there are good harbours on the east side. You would do well, brother, to attack that part of Hoy at once. They will not expect you in winter. You will have an easier fight than I had here in Rousay, against the stone castles.'

Osmund thanked his elder brother.

The sailors were so weary that they insisted on staying at Rolf's house for a few days.

Rolf was visited at that time by the poet Thord from the island of Wyre. Thord asked to be taken on the *Fulmar* when she sailed in the short days to Hoy. Thord said he had heard of a beautiful thinly cultivated valley in Hoy, that sloped south-west between two crags as red as fire, and the place was called Rackwick on account of the spars and staves and barrels that were washed on to the beach there after a westerly gale. 'But,' said Thord, 'the place is so small the few people there are hard put to it to win a living from earth and sea.'

Much ale was drunk in Rousay that night for the success of Osmund's settlement of Hoy.

Next morning *Fulmar* left Rousay at sunrise and sailed south past the settlements in Birsay and Sandwick.

They saw the two blue hills in the distance.

They sailed between Graemsay and Hamnavoe into Scapa Flow, and on south between small barren islands, till they entered a deep well-sheltered bay in the south of Hoy. There was good land on either side of the bay.

'We will go ashore and take the place before the sun goes down,' said Osmund. 'The name of this harbour is Osmundsvoe, whatever it was called before.'

A dozen men waded ashore from *Fulmar* and were attacked at once with arrows, spears and slings. Four lay wounded among the rock-pools. The others returned to the ship.

Then it was too dark for any more fighting.

In the days that followed, the Norwegians had little success. The weather turned murky, with flakes of snow. There were only a few hours of twilight between dawn and sunset.

They were awaked from their sleeping-sacks one night by a noise of splintering, then it was as if a wave had broken over the ship. They got out of their beds and saw that the islanders had smashed a part of their galley and ruined what was left of their food with buckets of salt water.

They heard much mockery from the shore.

The stars seemed to pierce them with nails of ice, that midnight.

'If we had come here in high summer,' said Osmund, 'we would have known how to deal with those savages. Now there is nothing left for it but that we should return to Rousay and beg leave of my brother Rolf to winter there. The mockery of those savages will be nothing compared to the mockery of our own people. It may be their mockery will maim my reputation for ever.'

At dawn an eagle flew at them and dug a claw into the face of a seaman called Prem, so that he lost an eye. Prem was the helmsman of *Fulmar*.

'I have one eye left,' said Prem, 'to steer our wounded ship back the way we came.'

Thord the poet from Wyre said it would be a pity to leave Hoy without visiting the valley in the west of the island he had spoken to them about, Rackwick.

Osmund said that could do no harm. 'But we will not all go together. That way, a worse defeat might happen to us. A small group of us – say, three – will go secretly over the hills, like tramps. Our battle did us little good in this bay. We will go like peaceful men, with gifts to the Rackwick people.'

Osmund chose, besides himself, Thord the poet and Erik the sail setter, to be his companions.

The ship had a wicker cage of doves amidships that were kept for food. The sailors sometimes got tired of fish and oatcakes on a voyage.

Erik took a dove out of the cage to give to the valley people, if they got that far and were not cut down on the way.

Osmund the skipper took a fine gold ring from his finger and put it in a pouch. 'I hope they will like this better than axes,' he said.

Osmund and Erik and Thord left the ship soon after dawn.

It seemed that no one on the island saw them.

They soon left the farmland behind and walked across a dark moor with little lochs in it. The moor sloped up northwards, and they could hear the crashing of waves far below them. Soon they were walking along the verge of high cliffs. They topped a rise and saw the valley beneath them.

The valley people were taking fish ashore on the wide beach below. They looked up and saw the three strangers against the sunset, high above them.

At once the valley people dropped their lines and fish and ran quickly among the hills on the far side.

And then the winter sun went down – the briefest sun of the year

– and the valley was a tilted bowl of darkness, with the ocean foaming at the rim.

'I think we will do small business here,' said Osmund.

Then they noticed that one of the cottages had a fish-oil lamp burning inside. The door stood open.

'They haven't all gone,' said Erik. 'We will see if we get a welcome in that house.'

As they approached the cottage, they saw that some kind of simple ceremony was going on.

There was a man and a woman carrying a very small child, standing between the fire and the cruisie-lamp.

The Norwegians stood silently in the open door.

There was another person there. Thord recognised one of the brothers from Eynhallow, Columb.

Columb took a silver flask from a fold of his white coat. He signed for the man and girl and child to come to him. Then he opened the vial and poured water over the child's head, three times, speaking Latin words as he did so.

The child cried, more in wonderment than in distress.

Columb put a little salt on the child's tongue. Then he bent and kissed the child on the head.

Osmund thought he had never seen such happiness on the faces of simple people.

The priest of Eynhallow and the little family seemed quite unaware of the visitors in the door, so rapt were they in the ceremony.

Then Osmund put the gold ring on the table.

Erik set the pigeon in a niche of the wall.

Thord recited a poem:

> Beach shineth in blackness,
> After hard voyage a hidden valley,
> Hills for bees to be hived,
> Beasts kept, a cod-hungry boat,
> A comfort of fire in the crofts.
> We furled sail, set firm our feet,
> Stone laid against stone,
> Laboured long till ebb of light,

Hungry men round a half-made hearth.
Dreamed I that darkness
Of horse, harp, a hallowed harvest.

When they turned to leave the house, the snowflakes were falling fast.

The sun was down.

They saw, through the gray drift, that the valley people must have returned. There were lights in the big farm and there was a noise of music and dancing.

The winter solstice was past. The people were rejoicing in the return of the light.

'We should walk quickly to the ship,' said Osmund. 'I don't want to sleep in the snow. There's no awakening from a snow sleep. But that kind of sleep might be better than to awaken to the mockery of our red battles and defeats.'

October/November 1995

THE MILKMAID AND THE WIFE
WITH BUNIONS

On the feast of the Epiphany in the year 1151 Rognvald, Earl of
Orkney and William, Bishop of Orkney were unable to play chess, as
they did every morning after mass, because the chessmen kept sliding
off the board. A heavy sea, between Galicia and the port of Narbonne
in France, was breaking on the beam of the *St Magnus*.

Six of the oarsmen were sick. The bailers were the busiest men on
board. There was nothing to eat but cold bread. It was one of the
dreariest days of the crusade.

The earl and the bishop sat among the routed chessmen and
agreed to exchange stories till the sea moderated, events that had
actually happened to them – 'no ignorant fables', said the bishop, 'and
no second-hand yarns either.'

'This story I'm going to tell,' said Earl Rognvald, 'is a kind of
comedy, though it didn't seem very amusing to us at the time, especially at the beginning.'

Asa the Milkmaid

We sailed from Norway to Shetland three winters ago, twenty seamen
in two small ships *Arrow* and *Help*.

A sudden gale got up in the first darkness and flung the ships
against the east crags of Shetland and smashed them to pieces. We all
got ashore somehow, swimming and floundering to the beach like
seals. We walked to a house with a light in the window, it was a big
farm with a lot of servants. There was a milkmaid there called Asa.
She screamed in the byre door when she saw so many wet blue strang-

205

ers. The women inside blew up the fire. They stood us round the flames. They stripped the clothes from us. Then they rubbed us with rough towels and they put dry clothes on us, anything the ploughmen would give. We were like twenty scarecrows round the fire. Asa laughed at us as she went by with her brimming pails to the kitchen. Then the women gave us bowls of hot ale. Soon we were singing. They kept filling our bowls with strong hot ale and sometimes they would break a honeycomb in it. About midnight the shipwreck seemed like a good thing. We thought we were fine chaps, real heroes. Three of the Norwegians took farm girls on their knees. Suddenly there was a splash and a cry from the darkness outside. We ran to the door. Asa the milkmaid had fallen into the well. They brought her to the fire, her teeth rattling in her skull. Sven dried her in his arms. Then the women opened a new keg of ale.

I think that was the happiest night I ever passed.

*

'Is that the end?' said the bishop. 'The story I'm going to tell is a comedy also, though when you consider it closely there's little to laugh at but a great deal to wonder at. It happened thirty-odd years ago, when I had been bishop in Birsay for ten years or thereabout.'

Gerd's Bunions

Your uncle Earl Magnus of Orkney was killed with an axe in the island of Egilsay that April morning in 1116. He lay in a furrow all night and next morning they buried him in the island. Then they dug him up and ferried him across the firth and carried him over the hills and they buried him in the church at Birsay. At once all the riff-raff of the islands went to Birsay, as if a famous juggler or wrestler was performing there, all the most offensive ignorant kind of people, folk with hare lips and ulcers and a crowd of women not right in the head. They filled the kirkyard and ate cheese off the tombstones and the stink of them drowned the altar incense. It was getting so that respectable people couldn't get near the church. 'Saint Magnus,' the riff-raff kept muttering and howling, 'Saint Magnus, pray for us' . . . It got so I couldn't read my breviary in peace. So in the end I sent them packing home to Yell and Lybster and Tiree (they were beginning to come now from the furthest ends of Scotland). None of that nonsense in my kirk! I herded them down to the beach, I saw them off our holy island.

Well, that same autumn I had to sail to Shetland about some church business. We had a good enough voyage. I finished my talks with the Shetland priests on the Friday. I very much wanted to be home to say mass in Birsay on the Sunday – it was the anniversary of my ordination. But bad weather set in from the south, rain and fog and wind, it drove the birds far inland. And there the wind dug its heels in. It looked set for a long hard blow – hopeless to think of setting out in that weather. There comes to me that old half-drunk seaman Skop, he used to wind ropes in the hold, and he says, 'If I was you, Bishop, I'd pray to Saint Magnus and you'll be home on Sunday morning in time for the opening of the ale-house.' 'You old soak,' I shouted at him, 'what the devil do you know about prayers? And who's Saint Magnus anyway?' 'He's the man they killed in Egilsay,' says Skop, 'and he cured my old woman Gerd of her bunions.' 'Get away, you old selkie,' I said, 'or I'll stop your grog.' So off he went, back to his ropes.

I took a turn round the mast and I said, fingering the crucifix under my shirt, 'Magnus,' I said, 'if you are a saint, I'm wanting to say mass in my cathedral in Birsay on Sunday first' . . . And with that I took another turn along the deck. 'You heard me, Magnus,' I said (though privately I was thinking myself all kinds of a fool for muttering under my breath to a dead man). 'Maybe I'll do something about you,' I said, and with that I took a turn to the stern and back. And when I looked up the birds were being blown out to sea over Sumburgh and the sun was out again and the sailors were raising the anchor and cursing and swearing the way sailors do, unfortunately (and none was cursing and swearing so much as that old Skop whose wife was cured of her bunions). We had this fair wind all the way to Orkney. When we rounded Costa Head the kirk bell was ringing for morning mass on the Brough-of-Birsay.

So then I had to admit that Magnus Erlendson was a great saint after all.

I ordered the body to be dug up. You know what like a corpse is when it's been in the ground a year or two – a festering clod. Nothing like that with Magnus: no stink, no rottenness. The bones were clean as silver. You know the smell of an oatfield that has violets growing up among the oats? Just after corn and violets are cut together there's that one moment of piercing sweetness in the nostrils before the wind blows it all away. Saint Magnus had that smell when we dug him out of Birsay. And it kept brimming out as we carried him over the hills to Kirkwall, to the new cathedral there. The sweetness remained. And remains to this day. And will bide for ever, the odour of saintliness that is utterly unmistakable and, it may be, gives us mortals (so to speak) a foresmell of heaven.

*

The ship was riding the swell easily now. No more spray stung the lips of the storytellers. A long headland stretched to the right, the coast of France. The earl shouted 'Paul!' and a boy came running from the stern; his face was pale and strained; he had obviously been sick.

'Paul,' said Earl Rognvald, 'set up the chessmen for His Grace and myself.'

'And afterwards,' said the bishop kindly, 'bring us a skin of wine. There's a good boy.'

November 1961

The First Football Match

New Year's Day, in the town of Kirkwall in Orkney, that's when the game of football commenced 500 years ago.

There were two powers in the little city, the earl and the bishop, the earl living in his castle, the bishop in his palace. Those two powerful men got on in a cold rather formal way. They had to get on, otherwise Kirkwall would have been a lawless ungovernable town.

The townsfolk were quiet people – seamen and joiners, weavers and blacksmiths and brewers, saddlers and fishermen, and their women. All those good and godly people wanted only to live out their lives in peace. They grumbled about the earl's taxes, and the bishop's taxes. But they did their grumbling in secret, in the ale-houses, beside the fires, in whispers. If one of them had shouted their rage under the earl's window, or at the bishop's gate, that would have been the last shouting he did for a long time.

There were deep dark dungeons for disturbers of the peace.

*

The earl had a bodyguard, a 'household troop' – a score of young men mostly from Scotland, younger sons of the gentry from Lothian and the Mearns.

The bishop had a retinue too, a troop of young men who drifted in and out of his palace and sat drinking in the well-stocked episcopal cellar. Most of the bishop's men were Norwegians, the sons of timber merchants and skippers, whom their fathers had cast out as work-shy and useless.

There was no need for those small private armies at all. The magistrates and their bailiffs kept good order in the town. But the earl thought it owing to his high office to have a bevy of young courtiers about him. And the bishop reasoned that if the earl could show his power and grandeur in this expensive way, so could he. So the Scandinavian merchants sent him their no-good sons.

They had to be accoutred and dressed in fine uniforms, of course. The earl's men wore red coats and black velvet caps. The bishop's men wore blue coats, with yellow leather hats, swan-feathered. The looms of Orkney were never so busy, turning out broadcloth for the earl's men and the bishop's men.

But the townspeople were taxed an extra penny, as from Martinmas, to pay for such grandeur. They grumbled about it, but only in the secrecy of the ale-house and the chimney-neuk.

They dreaded the dungeon, and the stern magistrate, Mr Jeremiah Tulloch, who had the ear both of earl and bishop, and reported regularly as to the state and mood of the commons.

*

To feed earl's men and bishop's men in their separate establishments was far from inexpensive. The courtiers preferred wine to ale. They would have no farmyard hens – not them! – only geese branded and dripping from charcoal spits. They spat out the coarse oat-bread of the town wives. Earl and bishop imported a few extra sacks of fine-ground French flour.

Another penny was added to the islanders' tax, as from Michaelmas. There was no other way: the red-coated retinue and the blue-coated retinue must be stylishly maintained.

The chief magistrate, Mr Tulloch, brought word of unrest among the tradesfolk of Kirkwall. Many claimed that their daughters were being molested, increasingly, by those dandies and drones.

Privately, as winter came on, the earl and the bishop began to have doubts about the courtiers they had gathered about them. Each thought that, after Christmas, they would consult with the other about the disbanding of the luxurious braggarts and brawlers.

But meantime, as the winter sun dwindled, earl's men and bishop's men hung about the castle and the palace, playing at cards, drinking wine, bragging, singing bawdy songs, stuffing themselves on salmon and white French bread.

*

The red-coats and the blue-coats did not mingle with each other. They kept to their own part of the town. The earl's men spoke Scots, the bishop's men spoke Norwegian.

So, there was no way they could speak with each other, even had they wished to. At most, they glowered at each other from opposite ends of the street.

There are, of course, other ways than speech, of communicating.

If ever it chanced that a few of them drifted towards each other on the darkling street, with gathered brows, there was Mr Jeremiah Tulloch, the chief magistrate, standing between them, a warning finger uplifted.

*

Jeremiah Tulloch was a merchant with five ships sailing between the Baltic and Scotland.

So many silver and gold coins ran between his fingers, rilled and rang and richly echoed on the heap of coinage in his iron-bound chest with five padlocks that he kept under his bed, that at the beginning of winter he had opened a hostelry in the centre of the town, for the better class of customer: skippers and lawyers, and farmers come to the mart with a flock of sheep or a dozen bullocks for sale.

Mr Tulloch was a sagacious man. Opening the Crown Tavern that winter, though, was a very foolish thing for him to have done.

The earl's men sniffed the rich aroma of mulled ale on the cold air one Yule noontide.

Lanterns were hung here and there along the street, in the early afternoon. A very bright lantern hung from the lintel of the Crown Tavern. Like moths, the earl's men began to eddy and drift towards that promise of hot spiced ale.

The bishop's men lifted their heads from their archery in the cold Palace yard. What was the enchantment that assailed their nostrils? Ah, it could only be coming from the new tavern – the Crown – that potent mix of malt and nutmeg and brown sugar.

They flung down their bows and set out for the Crown Tavern.

Outside the door, on the very threshold, earl's men and bishop's men melled with each other – clashed with each other – began to hurl abuse at each other.

Soon the Kirkwall street was hideous with the yelling and shouting.

Dogs barked all over the town. The quiet townsfolk hurried home and locked their doors.

Under the lantern of the Crown Tavern, amid the uproar, a dagger flashed here and there.

There was a young courtier called Jamie Geddes from Leith among the earl's men. He had gotten, in his ill-starred travels, a Turkish scimitar that he was very proud of. Now he unsheathed it – it flashed in the winter darkness like a meteor.

At this point Mr Jeremiah Tulloch came out of the hostelry, with all his authority about him, to restore peace. He took two of the gentlemanly ruffians by their scruffs – a red-coat and a blue-coat – and clashed their heads together.

The unseemly brawl might have been broken off then, but Jeremiah Tulloch slapped Jamie Geddes, the loud-mouth, very briskly on the face, first this side, then that.

What proud young blood would have put up with an indignity like that? Not Jamie Geddes, son of a chandler in the port of Leith.

The scimitar flashed like a meteor at Mr Tulloch. And not only at Mr Tulloch, right *through* Mr Tulloch, where his head was joined to his body.

The threshold of the Crown Tavern was starred with sudden splashes of blood. The young swaggerers – the blue-coats and the red-coats – felt the warm blood on their hands and faces.

Mr Tulloch's head bounced on the street, and rolled this way and that. The young braggarts recoiled in horror!

Then, after a few seconds, some kind of primitive urge compelled them to fall on the severed head; get it away; hide it somewhere, as if the burying of the head might somehow cancel the fearful crime, blot it from their memories, make them what they had been ten minutes before: young braves with the clean gale of life blowing through them. Who knows what possesses the minds of men in such a crisis?

But it seemed to the earl's men that the head should be taken by them to the far end of the town and hidden in a field there, and thence smuggled out of the islands into Scotland, a skull; until, at last, time healed the frightful wound that had been inflicted on the whole of Orkney.

Simultaneously, the bishop's men wanted to take the head and bury it fathoms-deep in the sea. They were descendants of Norse seafarers, who had gotten rid of many a victim that way. It was an instinct bred in them.

The sea washes everything clean at last.

Red-coats and blue-coats hurled themselves on Jeremiah Tulloch's sodden head, to take it to some bourne of utter oblivion. Body piled on body, a wild whirl of arms and legs. The battle swayed this way and that, up and down the street. Sometimes towards the field at the edge of the town, sometimes towards the waterfront. A steam arose, like fog, and covered the mêlée, as it shifted a few yards this way and that way, till three hours passed and the sky was sprinkled with stars.

It is not recorded who won this first football match in the western world.

The bishop wondered that his young ruffians were so quiet in their chambers that day. The earl was glad he could listen to his balladsinger in peace, this one night of the year. 'They don't usually play their card games so doucely,' he said.

*

As for the first football match, it might be said to be a draw, in the end.

The fact is, the 'football' got lost.

After three straining grunting heaving mauling raging hours, it occurred to the teams that Mr Tulloch's head had not been seen after the first half-hour. They disentangled themselves, slowly, man by man, until the two score stood, bewildered and separate and guilty and bruised and breathless, under a flaring street torch. Their fine coats hung from them in tatters; they were splashed moreover with blood and slush and dirt.

A few looked furtively here and there for the head. It was nowhere to be seen.

Then a collective panic took hold of them.

The bishop's men made for a ship that was riding at anchor in the bay, a Bergen merchant ship that would be up-anchor and away with the first tide, before midnight. They begged and pleaded for a passage home. The skipper knew most of their well-to-do fathers. He would be paid. He agreed. 'Get below, you scum,' said the skipper, 'and keep quiet . . .'

The earl's men did not stop running and stumbling through the night till they came to Hamnavoe, fifteen miles away, where they knew a Leith-bound merchant ship was due to sail, freighted with whalebone and whale-oil, on the first tide next morning. Gavin Abercrombie the skipper knew their affluent fathers. He would be paid. 'A credit ye are to the good burghers that begot ye!' he said contemptuously to the frightened scarecrows pleading with him. 'Even you can come!' he said to Jamie Geddes. 'You shame and disgrace that you are. You look like a pigsty keeper, man! But you'll hand over that heathenish curved Turkish sword before you step on board this ship.'

*

When the main street of Kirkwall was quiet again, at early evening, the citizens unbarred their doors and ventured out, householder by householder.

There, on the threshold of the Crown Tavern, they came on – hideous sight! – the decapitated body of the chief magistrate, Jeremiah Tulloch.

And there, under the rosebush in her garden, the widow Maggie Spence found the poor sodden head.

Word was brought to the bishop, sitting in his deep chair by the Palace fire with a leg of roasted capon in one hand and a cup of claret in the other. Word was brought to the earl, where he sat playing a game of chess with silver chess-pieces against Mr Balfour, his chief taxman and honorary falconer . . . The blood drained from his wine-purple face.

His Grace the bishop and His Excellency the earl met that night on the kirk green, under a purple sky ringing with stars.

The earl and the bishop had hardly spoken to each other all the preceding year, apart from exchanging formal courtesies on their birthdays, and at Lammas and Martinmas. They were in the habit of speaking disparagingly about one another, behind their hands, with a sly nod and a wink.

Now, with the terror of the day's event vivid in their minds, they fell on each other's necks, like brothers long parted.

No one had ever seen the tear that glittered like crystal in the bishop's eye that night. No one had seen the elegant shoulders of the earl shaken with grief.

But all the townsfolk of Kirkwall witnessed the reconciliation, and they were glad of it; though sorry of course, that peace and charity had to come through the appalling death of the worthy magistrate, Mr Jeremiah Tulloch.

Mr Tulloch's remains were laid reverently in the bishop's private chapel, with lighted candles at head and foot, and two guardsmen keeping watch over it all night until it was buried next day in the kirk-yard of St Magnus.

*

The game of football has come a long way since that first crude blood-splashed beginning, 500 years ago.

And yet the original game is still played twice a year in the streets of Kirkwall in Orkney, on Christmas Day and New Year's Day, a wild chaotic day-long surge and ebb and flow, not all that different from the original struggle between the earl's men and the bishop's men. But now, instead of the chief magistrate's head, the young men play with a well-stitched leather ball stuffed with cork.

*

Students of myth will tell you that the game is much much older, of cosmic origin. It may be the struggle of Winter and Summer, Fire and Ice, for possession of the sun.

December 1995

215

How the Sabistons Came to Orkney

Five years James Seatter of Forss tried to find a man for his only daughter Kathrin, but no crofter or fisherman would have her.

'She's too ugly,' they said.

John of Garth however said to James, 'How much comes with her?'

'A hundred pounds Scots,' said James Seatter of Forss.

The year was 1587.

'It isn't enough,' said John of Garth, and turned his horse's head away.

James thought of the blacksmith, who was recently a widower, a big hard man with a red beard. Shoeing a horse one morning, Sander the blacksmith saw the old man loitering in the smithy door. He knew at once what errand James was on. He made his anvil ring till not a word was heard. He glowered at James through the reek and the clamour, till finally the old man's mouth stopped opening and shutting and he slunk away.

James went home and said to Margit his wife, 'Nobody wants Kathrin.'

Kathrin came through from the byre with a bucket of milk.

'Kathrin,' said James, 'no man wants thee. There's a hundred pounds behind the loose stone in the wall, if ever it's the Lord's will that you should be left alone in this world . . .'

Kathrin poured the milk into the kirn.

That winter Margit died. Now Kathrin was mistress of the house. Her father used her rather more harshly than before. He called her thin and unlucky, an old unwanted maiden at the age of twenty-two.

Kathrin said nothing but carried on with her work.

After New Year James broke his leg stepping out of the boat on to a wet stone. It mended badly. He lay in his bed, a cripple for life, men said.

Now Kathrin went to the fishing, in addition to milking, plough-ing, spinning. All that was thought to be heavy work for a young woman.

James gave her instructions from the bed – 'Yoke the horse this way. Cut the peats that way. Rub thus much salt into the pork, no more. Turn the ale on such a morning. Add an occasional penny to the hundred pounds behind the loose stone in the wall.'

Yet the furrows ran into one another. The pig died on the hill with no knife near its throat. The peats were so wet they put the fire out. Ale ran sour into the horns.

'The work is too much for one lass,' they said in the island.

'It's a pity Kathrin is so ugly,' said Sander the blacksmith.

'A hundred pounds is far too little,' said John of Garth. 'A hundred pounds and Kathrin and the croft and that cursing cripple old man is both too much and too little.'

The unmilked cow boggled in the byre. Seven lobsters came dead out of the creels.

Kathrin sat down on a stone one winter morning and wept.

It was the year 1588.

*

The huge ship went past that afternoon, close to the shore, sailing north. The islanders had never seen such an enormous vessel. Her masts were above the level of the crags. Her great sail with the cross on it was an acre broad.

The ship struck the skerry at a few minutes after four o'clock, and began to sink at once. Bodies came ashore on the flood, towards sunset. Three miles of shore were littered with dead men.

The islanders kept inside, behind barred doors. Morning would be soon enough and safe enough to see what had happened.

Kathrin dragged the cow in by the tail out of all trouble, but she left the door unlatched.

'What's wrong?' cried James from the bed.

'A ship on the rock,' said Kathrin.

That night there was a deep silence over the island.

At midnight the door of Forss opened in the darkness. Kathrin got out of bed and lit the candle. A stranger stood at the wall. His arms and his shut face were streaming with water. He was a man not far from death. That much was plain.

James screamed at him, 'Go out, go out before I shoot you!'

Kathrin knelt beside the stranger and blew up the fire. She took his arm and laid him down beside the blaze. He sighed deeply once or twice, but said nothing.

'That's an old foolish man,' said Kathrin. 'Pay no attention to him.'

She poured ale into a pot and set it over the peat flame. Then gently she drew off the man's shirt and breeches and began to knead his cold body with her knuckles. A long hard shiver went through him.

'You mustn't die on me,' said Kathrin. 'You mustn't die.'

Old James lay in his bed, his useless leg at an angle, and wailed, 'A naked foreign pirate, in my God-fearing house!'

'Be quiet with your foolishness,' said Kathrin. The stranger's eyes opened slowly. Kathrin brought the bowl to his mouth. His throat worked once or twice. She covered him with a gray blanket and laid his head against her breast. 'Drink,' she said softly. 'Drink, man.'

The stranger drank. He put his dark head unaided into the bowl and drank.

'My hundred pounds!' whispered James to the wall.

The stranger looked at Kathrin and smiled. He found her hand. He raised it to his mouth and kissed it.

The girl said, 'They call me Kathrin.'

'The whole island,' said James, 'murdered and ravished in their beds!'

'Kathrin,' said the stranger. He touched himself lightly on the breast. 'Sebastian,' he said, 'Sebastian.'

'Sebastian,' said Kathrin.

She kissed his cheek that was still cold, blew out the lamp, and lay down near the sinking fire, drawing the gray blanket over herself as well as the man from the sea.

Presently they slept.

*

The old man died before Yule, full of curses and complaints.

At Candlemas Kathrin married the Spaniard in the stone kirk at the shore. The year was 1589. The old minister had once been the young priest of the island. '*Dominus vobiscum,*' he said, blessing them, and that seemed to please Sebastian and Kathrin and nearly everyone except a few rancorous fundamentalists.

Soon the furrows ran straight once more at Forss. The ewe had her twins, the sow her dozen. The boat came back every day in summer with a basket of tarnished silver.

When the fairhaired island children went by to the kirk every Sunday, they would stop beside the little swarthy boy in the doorway of Forss. 'Sabiston,' they would say mildly, 'Sabiston' (for they could not pronounce the foreign name properly), 'Sabiston, come . . .' Then together they would drift down the brae towards the shore.

Sabiston is a common name in Orkney now.

Winter 1963

THE CHANGELING

A young woman in the island of Rousay called Katherine gave birth to a child. It was a beautiful infant; it throve and flourished, and gave delight to Katherine and the whole district.

Neighbouring women would linger about the cradle, smiling, and touching now and then the boy's dimpled fist and fine flaxen hair. They knew better than to utter aloud any praise of the child; if they did that they might be overheard by the trows and fairies, who would then never rest until the baby was theirs.

But one young Rousay woman, prompted perhaps by jealousy (for it looked as though she might go to her grave unmarried and childless) whispered aloud over the cradle, 'Thu bonny bairn!' Or it may be that she did it unwittingly, carried away by the rare beauty and innocence of the sleeping one.

The very next day Katherine went to get water from the well, and when she stooped in at the door with her brimming buckets a strange hoarse cry came from the cradle. She looked inside, and cried out with horror. A terrible change had come over her 'douce lamb', her 'bonny peedie buddo'. There it lay in the cradle, a dark ugly twisted little creature. If it was to grow up and flourish, it would be a disgrace to her all her days.

Katherine knew at once what had happened. A trow-woman had stolen her child and left in its place a little troll that had been conceived and born in the darkness under the hills.

How could she ever come to love this twisted creature? She shuddered at the thought of that dark mouth at her breast, drinking the sweet earth milk that comes from sunshine and bread and bright water.

The changeling gave a strange ugly cry. It was beginning to be hungry. Katherine rocked the cradle and whispered to it. She was such a good woman that she hadn't the heart to be cruel to it.

But after the changeling had gone to sleep again, Katherine sat in her stool in the corner and tears welled out of her eyes. There was nothing to be done. This underground creature was thirled to her for the rest of her days.

And her own beautiful boy – what had become of him? She tried not to think of it. But the thought of that sun-kissed one growing up among roots and earth-fires and sources made her cry out with anguish.

It happened that old Sara was passing by her door at that moment.

In every island and in every parish there is an old wise woman who has suffered much and learned much. She has endured everything that can happen to a woman – the agonies and joys of birth and the sorrows of death. A drowned sweetheart or son has been carried from the sea and laid at her door. Then, for a winter or two before her death, this old wise one dispenses the honey of her experience where it is most needed in the island. Some folk call her an interfering old slut, but those in need of comfort know better.

Sara took one look at the cradle, and at the bereaved mother, and she knew at once what had happened. Trow-children had come to the island once or twice in her lifetime; and had grown up, sickly deformed creatures; and were usually dead before they were twenty.

Sara said to Katherine, 'Do you really want to get your bairn back?'

'Of course I do,' said Katherine.

'You'll have to be very brave and very cunning,' said Sara. 'You'll have to enter the kingdom of the trows, a difficult dangerous thing to do. Some who trespass there are never heard of again.'

'I'll do it,' said Katherine, 'to get my darling back again.'

Old Sara sat beside Katherine a whole morning explaining carefully and precisely what she had to do – while the changeling grunted and tossed in the cradle.

There was a hill in the island (said Sara) called Blotchniefiold. At the back of Blotchniefiold was a loch called Muckle Water. The slope above Muckle Water was studded with rocks called the Hammars o' the Sinians. These rocks were the gateways to the underground kingdom where the trolls lived.

'I'll beat on the rocks,' cried Katherine, 'till they open up to me.'

'They won't do that,' said Sara. 'They're not stupid, the trows.

What they have, they keep. But there's one rock that opens into the chamber of the trow-mothers and their bairns.'

Old Sara described in great detail that particular rock – the shape of it, the knuckles and the hollows on it, and exactly where the rust-coloured patches of lichen grew on it. 'Besides,' said Sara, 'there is a great cleft in this rock. You can't mistake it.'

Katherine murmured the particulars over and over again. She hoarded every detail in her memory. The rock throbbed in her imagination.

'You must take with you,' said Sara, 'a wedge of steel and a crucifix. You must climb round the hill to the rocks above the loch. When you come to the rock I've described you must drive the steel wedge into the cleft. When you do that the rock will open. You will see then, sitting inside, a trow-woman nursing your bairn on her knee. You must say nothing to her – not a syllable – in the way of reproach or rage. You must strike her on the head three times with the blessed crucifix. Then you will get your darling back.'

Katherine set off at once with the steel stake and the crucifix. She left old Sara to keep an eye on the trow-child. For Sara was so wise now, a winter away from her death, that she even knew how to keep such unnatural creatures quiet.

Katherine climbed round the shoulder of the hill Blotchniefiold. There in front of her lay the gray water of the loch. The heather round about was studded with rocks. She looked carefully at one after the other till she found the rock that Sara had described. There was indeed a cleft in it. She thrust the steel wedge in. Immediately the rock split silently open. Katherine saw, once her eyes had grown accustomed to the darkness inside, a creature with a shape on its knee. She almost cried out with joy when she saw that the infant the trow-woman was crooning to was her own. But she remembered in time old Sara's warning, and kept silent. She stepped into the darkness of the rock with parted lips.

The trow-woman was soon aware of the intruder; and, simultaneously, of the identity of the intruder.

'Who might you be?' she said. 'You have no right to be here, disturbing my child and me.'

Katherine felt like crying out, 'Your child! How dare you! The child is mine.' Instead she touched the crucifix lightly to the forehead of the rock-dweller.

The woman shuddered. The brow of the infant lost its radiance.

'Get out of here!' she cried. 'I'm warning you. If the trows find you here they'll tear you to pieces. Get out now. Leave me and my baby in peace!'

The cries of the woman were so terrible that Katherine's heart shrank with fear and revulsion. But she raised the crucifix a second time and touched the howling creature with it.

At that the trow-woman stopped raging and began to weep and lament. And the beautiful white arm of the child took a dark twist.

'Have pity on me, woman of the sun,' she cried. 'Here I sit with the only treasure I possess, my heart's joy, my little darling one. I will give you gold and silver to leave us alone. I'll let you drink out of the cup that will keep you alive for ever. Can't you see that this boy is mine and mine alone? I gave birth to him down here in the terrible fruitful darkness. Would you tear him from my heart now!'

At these words Katherine had pity on the creature, and she stopped herself just in time from uttering kind sympathetic words. She touched, for the third time, the crucifix to the weeping mouth in front of her.

There was silence in the chamber then. The troll-woman clutched her infant to her – it was no longer a little creature made of sun and earth and seed and water, but a huddled misshapen monster.

Far inside the earth, Katherine heard the murmur and tread of approaching trows. Rumours of an intruder must have reached them.

Katherine turned and leapt from the rock fissure. She stumbled and ran across the heather. She did not stop running till she arrived at her own cottage, breathless.

Old Sara was still there, raking the fire. 'A fine sweat and bother you've got yourself in,' said the old woman. 'Let me tell you this, there's nothing on this earth worth getting so worked up about. I've hung your water-pot over the fire. I'll put a peat or two on the embers. Then I must be getting home. My few hens, poor things, they'll be hungry.'

When Katherine got her breath back she went over and looked into the cradle. There her little lost Mansie lay. He raised his fists to her; then his cheeks dimpled and his blue eyes lighted with laughter.

He grew up to be the wisest man in Rousay, with knowledge of secret matters that – folk said – he must have learned from his day of trow-fostering under the hill.

1974

BETTY CORRIGALL

In the moorland of the island of Hoy in Orkney, right on the boundary that separates the two parishes of Voes (Walls) and North Hoy, a gravestone and fence have recently been erected by some islanders. Underneath lay, peat-preserved for well over a century, the body of a young woman who had obviously committed suicide. Only her name survives: Betty Corrigall.

'No,' said Betty Corrigall, 'I won't go for a walk with you. Never.'

But at the week's end she walked with the sailor, Willie, as far as the shore of Moness in North Hoy.

'Kiss you!' said Betty Corrigall. 'What way would I kiss you, when I don't like you all that much?'

And they walked one evening as far as the sea valley of Rackwick. A slip of a moon rose over the hill, a silver shaving. All the Rackwick crofters and fishermen and their folk were inside. There were sixteen lighted windows, and one dark window where an old man had died the month before.

At the edge of an oatfield the sailor kissed Betty Corrigall.

'I'll marry you,' said the sailor. 'I'll give up whaling and I'll build a house for us both. I have enough money to rent a field at Crockness. There'll be two cows and twenty sheep and a hundred hens. I'm good with a saw and hammer and nails. There'll be a bed and a table, three chairs and a deep cupboard. I'll make a cradle that rocks. A star will shine on the doorstep.'

Betty said she would like that. And he put a storm of kissings and caressings about her: face and neck and hair.

And Betty Corrigall, she put a dewfall of kisses on his cheek and mouth.

*

Then, about the middle of summer, it happened one morning that Betty Corrigall was sick.

'I think the milk last night was sour,' said her mother.

But in the week that followed, the milk in their porridge at supper-time was sweet and warm from Katie the cow; and every morning Betty was sick.

Her mother put a bitter look on her. Her father said nothing. He went out and looked at the tall green oats beside the house.

'Willie Sinclair, he's wanting to marry me,' said Betty Corrigall. 'He's going to rent a field at Crockness. He'll build a house and make the furniture with his own hands. He's been to the factor to get permission, and to settle about the rent.'

'It's not before time,' said Betty Corrigall's mother. 'He should have made a start months ago. He should be carting the stones now.'

Betty Corrigall's father said it wasn't often a sailor made a good crofter. But still, he had to admit that Willie Sinclair's father had been a hardworking man. 'You could do worse, I suppose,' said her father.

'They've made a bad beginning,' cried Betty Corrigall's mother. 'Let them make sure it doesn't come to a worse end! The way things are, this house is disgraced already. Never till this day did I know my daughter was a slut. The sooner you're out of this house and under that sailor's roof the better it'll be for everybody.'

The father said that if there was no heavy rain, or a gale, between now and August, it would turn out to be a good enough harvest, in his opinion.

Betty Corrigall said that she and Willie Sinclair would have a good life together. She said, so low that her parents could hardly hear her, that she loved him with all her heart.

'The first wooden thing that man had better make,' said Betty's mother, 'is the cradle.'

After the corn began to hang heavy golden heads, Betty did not put her face out of doors; both because she did not want her ripeness to be seen by the Hoy folk, and also because her mother blackly forbade her – not even to the well for water, not even to drive Katie the cow from the unsickled oats.

But her father secretly left the door unbarred at night, a thing he had never done before.

Night after night, Betty Corrigall and her lover mingled dark whispers, moon-touched whispers, wondering silences.

Yes, Willie the sailor assured her, the factor had agreed to lease him the ten acres for a fair rent. Yes, he had already taken three cart-loads of stone from the quarry to the site of the croft. With great labour, for the place was stony, he had laid a foundation. He had bought enough planks and spars to make the door, window frames, table, cupboard, bed. ('Make the cradle first,' said Betty Corrigall. 'Make the crib quickly . . .') The blacksmith had agreed to make him a plough. He was negotiating with the farmer at the Bu farm about the purchase of a young ox.

And he kissed Betty Corrigall on her cold mouth.

And the darkness took him; and Betty crept inside and barred the door and went into her little lamp-splashed room, until she lost herself soon in the sweet darkness of sleep.

*

Betty's mother waited until her husband went out to the barn. Then she said, 'It will have to be done quietly. I have spoken to the minister. There will be the two witnesses, nobody else. I've made a wide gray coat for you to wear. The marriage is to be in the Manse. I suppose that man's mother – the trollop that she is – will have to be there. And there's to be no drinking or dancing or fiddle music afterwards.'

Betty Corrigall thanked her mother for having made the arrangements. She herself wanted no more.

And that night Betty Corrigall waited at the gable-end of the croft. The moon was on the wane.

Willie Sinclair did not come that night. Betty had wanted very much to unfold the marriage arrangements to him; also to know what progress was being made with the new croft.

Nor did he come the next night, under the cold ember of the moon.

Betty Corrigall stood there three more nights, and the last night was an utter blackness without stars. The sailor had not come.

*

'Field? A field at Crockness?' said the factor to Tom Corrigall, Betty's father. 'I know nothing about a ten-acre field at Crockness. There is no land at Crockness available. What did you say the young man's name was? William Sinclair. A sailor. I don't know the man. There's a whaling man who's drunk every other night in this ale-house and that. That must be the man. A great teller of tall stories. A great womaniser. So I'm told. Yes, Sinclair's the name – now I remember. Arabella, poor woman, is his mother. I assure you, Tom, even if there was land available, I wouldn't rent a square yard to a fellow like that. No, no, he hasn't carted a single stone from the quarry – never asked – wouldn't get permission if he did ask.'

Betty Corrigall's father, after leaving the factor's office, stood in need of a drink. He dropped in at the ale-house at North Ness. Casually, over drams, he mentioned the name of Willie Sinclair the sailor to Mark the ale-house keeper.

'Gone,' said Mark. 'Cleared out, four days ago. That Yankee ship in Longhope, they signed him on. Bound for Russia. A cargo of grain and clocks. I'm not sorry to see the back of him. He owes me for two bottles of malt – I'll never see that money. I don't grudge it, so he doesn't come back in a hurry. A liar, Tom. A fighter, troublemaker. Couldn't hold his drink. I hope the bos'n of that Yankee ship is a hard man.'

Tom Corrigall drank too many drams of malt that afternoon. Then he went home and struck his daughter hard across the face. A few words blazed like stars in his mouth – sufficient of them to indicate to the appalled woman and the quiet girl how matters stood with regard to Willie Sinclair the sailor, and Betty, the unborn child, and the house that would be built of wind and sun and rain.

'The door's open,' he shouted to Betty Corrigall at last. 'Go.'

And Betty Corrigall went out into the first silver flakes of winter.

*

Of course the crofter, once he had a good supper of boiled mutton and mashed tatties and neeps in him, was sorry for the things he had done and said, partly out of shock, partly from the fires of whisky he had kindled inside himself; black flames.

He put on his coat, for it was a cold night in early winter, and a few snowflakes drifted like darkling moths athwart the window.

Surely the girl would be at the end of the house, crying perhaps – but quietly, for Betty had never since childhood made wild demonstrations of either grief or joy.

She was not at the gable-end, shawled against the thickening flakeswarm.

She was not in barn or stable or byre, nor over by the well where she loved to linger, listening to the songs of the sweet water deep down, bending to the fugitive gleams and glooms. Betty Corrigall was at no croft or farm in the immediate vicinity. No one had seen her.

The father spent a whole night knocking on angry or blank or anxious doors. He even went to the sailor's mother's house, just at jet-and-russet dawn. 'Here?' said Arabella Sinclair in the cold door. 'No, Betty's not here. I wish she was here. I would have a good daughter at my fire and board. But no, I'm sorry. I haven't seen her for months. Oh, yes, that's true enough, *he* left three or four days ago. It's been a quiet house since. I hope you have good word of Betty, and that soon. I love that girl better than the son I bore, and that's the truth.'

Nor was she at the Manse or the factor's or the schoolhouse: places where sapience might have mended the troubles of a breached household.

The man turned for home, after the last door had closed against him.

As his feet slurred through the melting snow, going on the road that skirts the bay at Lyrawa, he saw two fishermen standing at the shore. He knew them; he waved a tired greeting in their direction. The elder fisherman held up his hand, in such a way that it seemed to be a gesture of beseechment and of denial: 'Keep away!' The younger fisherman half turned and then looked down again at the shape in the ebb. His spread hand hung white as a star over it. The body lay face down in a sea-brimmed cleft. But there was no mistaking that spread of golden hair.

*

Oh, it was unthinkable – a suicide, and a child-burdened suicide at that, to lie among the decent men and women and children in the kirkyard – in God's acre. Neither the kirk session of Voes parish nor the kirk session of Hoy parish would countenance such an intrusion.

A few folk thought it a pitiable business. The girl had gone out of her mind with grief – in such circumstances the word 'suicide' had little meaning. A few others said that, muffled in a snow cloud, she had lost her way and gone over the shallow cliff. And others: she must have gone down to the shore, to see if she could see the American ship dipping between the islands at dawn: and the cold had seized her heart, that was bound to be delicate in her condition; and she had fallen into a rockpool, and was probably dead before the waters closed over her . . .

It availed nothing, such talk. A hole was dug for Betty Corrigall in the moor, exactly on the border of the two parishes. The gravedigger consulted a map of Hoy with a thin line going across, then sank in his spade again. And there the gravedigger and the father let down the sodden body of Betty Corrigall, with her head in Voes parish and her feet in Hoy parish. Then the gravedigger lit his pipe on the windy moor, and the father opened a whisky flask and passed it to him.

And while that generation of islanders withered slowly into death, one after another, and after death rotted more urgently until they achieved the cleanness of skeletons, the deep peat moss kept the body of Betty Corrigall uncorrupted; though stained and darkened with the essences that had preserved it.

Soldiers in the Second World War, digging drains in the moor, came on the body of Betty Corrigall as it lay crosswise with the line of the two parishes. The young men looked with wonderment into a face that had lingered sweet and beautiful from, it seemed, the first springs of time.

1987

Betty Corrigall

The girl buried in the moor

Child
   in the blue scarf of wind
      begin to dance

Girl
   in the yellow coat of sun
      ripeness is here

Woman
   in the gray sheet of water
      steep your griefs

Queen
   lie robed from looms of earth
      Persephone
           August 1984

The Last Trow

This is the story of an interview I had with a trow, or a fairy, or one of the peedie folk, or whatever you like to call these supernatural beings that haunt our hillsides.

I was sitting alone, smoking a pipe over a drowsy fire on one of these long serene nights of June. And I had my eyes closed, the better to meditate. All at once I was aware of a presence in the room; and opening my eyes, I was scarcely surprised to see a weird figure sitting in the chair opposite, hunched up, and blinking bright eyes at me. Whatever the thing was, it was neither human nor animal.

I guessed, quite correctly, that it was a trow. I say I was scarcely surprised to see it, for at midsummer season they love to sally forth, the peedie folk, and speak to human beings.

The question now was – was I to drive him forth into the night, where he belonged, with the prescribed Latin curse, or was I to encourage him to unbosom himself? He blinked his eyes rapidly and pleadingly. I puffed my pipe. 'Hello,' I said.

He erupted into a weird cackle of laughter, clicking his tongue against his palate and squeezing his eyes shut till the tears came. He looked like an incredibly old man of 150, and yet there was an air of childish innocence about him.

'Will I,' he said in an antique voice, 'tell thee a tale?' . . . I signified assent by a drowsy nod of the head.

He cupped his face in his fine slender hands and said: 'Would you believe it, but I'm about the last trow in Orkney?'

I said I did not doubt it. But the others, I said, the mad dancing pagan legions of fairies, were they all dead?

'No,' he said, 'they aren't dead, because they've never been born. They're waiting.' And he looked at me out of the corner of his eye, in a most sinister fashion.

'The trows,' he continued, 'haven't the power they used to have in olden times, nothing like it, because people no longer believe in them. People in Orkney no longer believe in the dark and beautiful powers of the earth. It is pitiful . . .

'Listen,' he continued. 'We live and flourish only because people believe in us. But nowadays there is no belief. And the substance of our living, the food which nourished us, was music and dancing. These things too are dying.'

I hastened to contradict the trow. 'Go to any parish hall,' I said, 'any night, and you'll get dancing and music and singing till your ear-drums are dirling with the din.'

A dark sneer, like a cloud ruffling the lit waters of Scapa Flow, passed over his face. 'That!' he said. 'Don't call such shallow imbe-cility by the high and noble names of music and dancing – such debil-itated balderdash!'

Without doubt the peedie man had a pungent turn of expression. I was relieved to see a merry twinkle return to his eye. 'There's one good sign, one encouraging rebirth in Orkney today,' he said, 'and that's the Strathspey and Reel Society.' He tucked our black poker under his chin and began to saw with his multi-coloured forearm transversely across it, as if he were playing a fiddle. He sawed away, blithely and soundlessly, in a kind of rapt ecstasy.

Suddenly he spoke again. 'But even there,' he said sadly, 'it's all Scotch airs. The grand old Orkney music that we loved dearer than moonlight or the sound of Atlantic breakers on the sand, has gone down into oblivion.' A few round glistening tears coursed down his swarthy cheeks.

'We've seen it coming,' he said, 'for years, for decades, this spir-itual death of Orkney which means our exile, harder for us to bear than death. You know as well as I do what the reason is – it's because Orkney is prosperous, everyone is well off. They think, with their few hundreds in the bank, that they can safely ignore us. Poor fools!'

He stamped his foot, till the ornaments rang on the sideboard. 'Listen,' he said. 'I admit the fairies have done some shameful things in their time; and will again, if they return into their own. But it wasn't because of any evil in their hearts. It was because of stark necessity. They needed music and dancing, and all the leaping joy of life in order to flourish, and sometimes they adopted horrible means to gain their ends.

'For example, they would kill innocent children and use their tiny graceful bodies to dance in at the parish festival. And into their knowes they would lure home-going fiddlers, to make music for them eternally, though their families mourned for them as dead, and went with hungry mouths for a long time.

'Music!' he said, 'and dancing! The whole world of Nature moves to the stately measures of the wind and the waves. Have you heard the great year-long symphonies that the breakers thunder out on Skaill Bay? Have you seen the high graceful dancing of the Aurora as she swishes her long skirts? Have you seen the wind on the cornfields, how it sweeps them to a dance of brighter and darker gold, and how the field laughs lyrically as it dances?'

Such extravagant talk would have been out of place in a human being, but it sounded natural enough out of the trow's mouth. He was jerking his arms excitedly in the air, and his feet beat out a tattoo on the mat. The poker dropped from his lap into the fender with a brazen clang.

'And what are we?' he demanded. 'We, the trows and the fairies? What are we but the embodied spirits of Nature, who reflect faithfully her moods, who can be either kind, or cruel, or ridiculous – but not so kind or so cruel or so ridiculous as men. For they are clumsy and graceless in all their actions, but we perform to an eternal background of music and dancing.'

It was growing darker in the room. I eyed the clock, and saw that the hands stood at precisely two minutes to twelve. Through the open window were wafted all the sounds and scents of June – the fragile odour of buttercups, a dog's drowsy bark, the distant desolate cry of a seagull.

The trow slid off the cushion and stood on his stumpy old man's legs, which seemed singularly ill-suited for dancing. He darted a glance at me that was half a leer and half a look of bright promise.

'You all think perhaps,' he intoned, 'that the trows are vanished for ever, and will never appear in the cheap light of Progress and Security and Prosperity – never again. But you're wrong. For we never die, and we're waiting to appear again on the earth in our surging legions.

234

It may be a hundred years, it may be a thousand, but make no mistake, when men have learned humility and returned to Nature as the source of all being, we'll appear again!'

He ended, as he had begun, with an Orkney phrase, 'Geud be aboot thee!'

The first stroke of twelve had hardly sounded when he leapt with incredible agility through the open window. My pipe had grown cold in my mouth. I watched him till he disappeared from sight, leaping and tumbling across the fields in ecstasy, like a thing possessed. And as he sped dancing away, Orkney's last trow, he sang till the bowl of the dark sky and the furthest horizons brimmed with sweet sound. It was weird piercing music, yet tenderer than any lullaby.

As it died on the midnight, the sounds of the hushed earth returned. The dog barked, the seagull complained. Over the hill the Atlantic rumbled, sleepily. The wild flowers of the ditches poured their scents into the night.

Had I seen him? Or had it been a ridiculous dream? I really didn't care, for, sleeping or awake, I had passed a pleasant half-hour . . . A new day began in the north-east, where the summits of the hills were capped with saffron light, and radiated an infinite promise.

21 June 1954

Shetland:
A Search for Symbols

SOUTH – ALWAYS IT is south, into the sun, at holiday-time.

Then I remembered how ignorant I was of our nearest neighbour, Shetland. There we lie, twin archipelagos in the North Atlantic, Orkney and Shetland: and I know next to nothing about those islands of famous seamen and fiddlers in the north.

Four of us turned our faces Shetland-wards, in the last days of May. It was lucky that one of the four knew Shetland well: Gunnie the photographer. We sailed from Stromness at noon one Sunday on the new P & O ship *St Sunniva*.

The voyage north was not at all auspicious. We were sheathed in a thickening sea-haar all the way; Fair Isle blotted out; Lerwick a blank. A calm sea, though.

Gunnie drove the hired car north to Grobsness, a renovated comfortable house on a steep headland: but so lonely that not another dwelling could be seen from it in the hard light of next morning – only ruins.

It had been the toss of a coin whether I would go to Shetland or not, because all the previous week some lung virus had drained a lot of my energy out.

The thick fog of our journey, and the dregs of the virus, must account for the morbidity of the first prose-poem.

Overnight, a wind got up and blew the sea-haar away, and there was cold sunlight as Gunnie drove us to Eshaness, after we had stopped for supplies at the nearest village, Voe. Gunnie and Kulgin went walking on the Eshaness cliffs. I hadn't the energy for cliff-walking, but I hadn't forgotten my small red notebook and yellow Staedtler pen. So I sat in the car and flushed the fever out of my bones with words.

The Black Ship

There came, through the days and nights of a month, slowly, to the shore of the voe, each one alone, a troop of folk, of all ages (most of them old), and they lingered among the rocks.

Each newcomer seemed not to know the others there before, but turned away, seeking to kindle his own lost breath.

On a sudden uplifting of a face, one shore-farer seemed to recognise another, and he spoke a name; there mingled two muted cries.

They stood then, those two, a little apart from the others and made low prompting and response . . . 'I can't remember' . . . 'I was I think in a fever and in a burning dream, and I woke to coldness and darkness – then I found myself on a sheep-path to this shore' . . . 'It may have been, a wave closed over the boat in the west; what took me then to the track over the hill?'

The company shifted about the edge of this low litany and seemed not to be listening, but a sighing like winter grass went here and there.

Then came down the shore road a golden-haired child. And a man in that company cried with the mouth of an ancient carved bell, 'This is Ingi, she was keeping cows from the cornpatch at Rona's Voe on Tuesday last.'

The child came among them, breathless with hurry. She cried out, 'I lost my way in the marigolds and the wet places, and I could no longer see cows or corn, and then the roots had me caught in a web of wetness. I'm glad to be with you, but I've seen happier faces in my time' . . .

Then her eye lighted on a shadow and she cried, 'Halcro, what are you doing here? You died on Friday last. I saw the women going with candles to the kirk, in the darkling' . . .

Then one or two of those people looked with brief rage at the child, and others with a lingering sorrow looked, but most turned their faces to the sea-wet stones or over to the gray horizon looked.

Then a woman cried out, 'Look, a ship off the headland!'

Then all that company looked at the black sail and the black hull in the bay.

Then those strangers began to converse freely with each other like folk met by chance to sail to the fair at Scalloway.

But still there were a few who said no words and looked nowhere and their breath was like cinders.

While they were waiting, a young woman came among them, she

carried a small burden in a shawl, her face was like a wax-drowned flame.

Then from the ship came a voice across the water, it shivered like a star.

*

Who needs to go south for the sun? After the sun broke the webs of fog on the second day, it shone with hardly a break for the next eleven days of our holiday.

We were only a few days from the summer solstice. The peat-dark islands seemed to be soaked in light, afloat on brimming sun-tides. We had to go to Lerwick, the capital, to the bookshop there, to sign books, and to the bank for money, and to buy a bottle of whisky in case we should be stormbound in Grobsness. (We northerners have learned not to trust the sun entirely.)

Sitting in the car at Lerwick pier, waiting for Gunnie and Kulgin to come back, there was nothing to do but scrawl in the red notebook.

The Lerwick pierhead was thronged with people, from fishing boats and oil ships. Two centuries ago, those sea-thirled men would have stepped more cautiously, with more turnings of the head and lingerings in shadow and close-coign.

In Shetland, as in Orkney, especially during the Napoleonic wars, the young men were hidden away and fed, in caves mostly, when the press-gang were abroad seeking recruits for the men-o'-war. The outwitting of those brutish recruiting men is a recurring theme in the recent folklore of the islands . . .

*

One evening we had a visit at Grobsness from George Peterson, English teacher at Brae school, a few miles over the peat-hills, a native of Papa Stour. Medieval historians continue to throw up fascinating facts and speculations. We Orcadians have long laid exclusive claim to the great earl and saint, Magnus Erlendson. Egilsay in Orkney is the place of his martyrdom, Birsay in Orkney saw the flowering of his miracles, the magnificent red Cathedral of St Magnus the Martyr keeps his relics. But now, more and more, Shetland claims its part in the great song. The wide curve of ocean in Shetland's north-west is St Magnus Bay. George Peterson is sure that his own island of Papa Stour was once St Magnus Isle, and that there Magnus had one of his principal residences. The more one thinks about it, the more the evidence accumulates. The first pilgrims to the tomb of Magnus came from this very part of Shetland, and it is noteworthy that the greatest of all the earls, Magnus' nephew, Earl Rognvald Kolson, was far more at home in Shetland and among Shetlanders, at the time when he was laying claim to the earldom, once more so calamitously divided to the advantage of Norway. Did Shetland bear the mild yoke of Magnus, while Orkney was ruled with vigour and skill by his cousin Earl Hakon? Wasn't it from Shetland that Magnus set out for the tryst with Hakon on Egilsay, on Easter Monday 1117? Was it off Sumburgh on the edge of the great 'roost' there, that the warning wave rose up out of a tranquil sea and broke, drenches of stinging spray, over the prow of Magnus' ship; so that all the sailors urged a return; but Magnus held on south to Orkney, to his death and the coming of peace in a manner not at all looked for by those who imagined they would cut the tight-drawn knot in the wonted way of politicians: a clean swift axe-stroke?

One Shetlander taken to the tomb of Magnus in a kind of medieval strait-jacket was a surly farm worker called Thord Dragonhead who had kept on flailing sheaves in Bergfinn's barn though it was Saint Lucy's Day – a very special time to Bergfinn who had been cured of blindness at the shrine of Magnus in Birsay; and Saint Lucy has a care and keeping of the eyesight. Mildly the farmer called the perverse labourer in to the feast-board; Thord kept on swinging the flail in the lantern-lit barn. The story is told marvellously in the *Orkneyinga Saga* – I paraphrase it here.

The Thresher

In a winter barn, surly Thord
Hung the lantern at a rafter. He swung his flail
    At an oatsheaf. The grains
    Scattered, golden rain, from the straw.

Then the farmer, Finn of the Hill
(That had measured his fields in darkness
   Till Magnus Martyr
   Took from his skull the blind stones

South in Birsay; he joyfully then beheld
Seapink and tern and star
   And fields plough-combed
   And the faces of children)

Came soon to the barn door, calling
'Thord, friend, now is St Magnus Eve.
   Put down that flail,
   No man labours this hallowed time,

Come in to the fire and the ale-cup.'
And Thord, dappled with flame and shadow
   Said, 'Not till today
   Have you thought I laboured too long here.'

And, the shadow of Bergfinn
Gone from the star-crammed door
   Thord struck ripeness on ripeness
   From the bare broken stalks

And his strenuous shadow
Jerked across the granary wall
   Like a mad dancer
   In a place of incense and whispers.

Voices from the farm, 'Thord, Thord,
The Magnus ale is poured for you.
   Come in, Thord, soon, or
   We'll froth our beards from your jug.'

But Thord laboured to the last sheaf.
Then he snuffed the lantern,
   Closed the barn door, went up like a troll
   To the fire and the long bench

And his throat throbbed thankless
With the seethe and the gold of summer.
    Then a madness threshed
    Through Thord like a roost in tempest

And he flung between fire and firkins
And fell, foam-lipped, till ploughmen
    Brought bonds, as a mad bull
    Is chained to a byre wall.

Then Finn of the Hill, farmer,
'Saint Magnus, show mercy
    To Thord my servant, as once
    You implored lucency

On my swart skull sockets.
Then your shrine will be richer
    By half a silver mark, after
    I sail Thord to Orkney

For a three-night vigil, by starlight
And candlelight, soon.'
    The women slewed their heads
    Like birds, all the way, in a storm.

The prayer, a palm-branch, fell on that passion.
Then had Thord the peace
    A glebeman knows, at a glebe edge
    Blessed by pieties of plough and flail.

*

Always it was evening when we got back to Grobsness.

    The rocky ground sloped down to a stony beach, with here and there a ruined croft, and one important ruin, the Ha', from where the laird's man ruled, to where the vanished fishermen of Grobsness and round about brought their catch and paid their rents twice a year.

There was no way of getting out of the laird's toils; he supplied the gear and tackle for the haaf (deep-sea) fishing, and he named his own price for the catch. Doubtless, there were ways out of this impasse: places where oatmeal and fish could be concealed so that not even the sharpest-nosed grieve could smell them out. A life of concealment and toil and grinding poverty; and yet the human spirit has springs that rise always into the light, deep quenchless sources; and I think of women as the true guardians of the wells of life.

Summer Songs

Who but us squeezed the livers of a boatload of fish into twelve
 jars, for lamps in winter?
Who plucked the wool, white and black and brown, from the young
 sheep, that spinning-wheels might turn?
Who spoke pleasant things, sunrise and sunset, to Marigold the cow
 and to Daisy the cow: 'Give us your delightful butter and cheese,
 good creatures'?
Who set up the thousand wet peats on the moor to be friends of sun
 and wind in summer, and brought them over the hill in baskets,
 so flames could toss on the hearth and the fish-pot chuckle and
 the jowls of the old men shine with the fat of fish?
Who washed the sarks in the barn, and beat the salt and sweat out
 with stones, and spread them on the links?
Who rocked the cradles, and clothed a bride in whiteness, and in a
 box-bed closed eyes that were like old butterflies' wings?
Who came stooping after the sicklemen, and had sore hands from
 barbs of barley, and later ground the barley between stone
 wheels, and baked the heavy bread from the barley flour: the
 same that puts strength in at the mouths of men, and ale-joy?
Who but us filled this voe with the laughter of children, and made
 bright their faces and feet for the kirk on Sabbath?

Yet when we seven lingered with our jars at the well this morning,
 early, to greet one another, and give from one mouth to a dozen

ears the honey of news, a seven-stranded web, what have we heard from the Ha' door? – *Idle sluts, squandering sun hours, the rent is to pay. The black cow's in the corn.*

*

Two cats waited for our return to Grobsness, a tawny tom and a delightful little she-cat called Tammy. Tammy wore a coat of many colours. Tammy rolled herself in the dust of the road to welcome us every evening; she knew, for sure, that Kulgin had, in that plastic bag, tins of cat food from the general store at Voe.

Two islands shut us off from the open Atlantic: Muckle Roe ('the big red island') and Vementry. Vementry, when we drove to the beach opposite it one marvellous afternoon – all lyrical light and birdsong and the squill-flowers a blue mist over the fields – for a picnic of meat rolls and lager; Vementry is the kind of island that etches itself deep in the imagination, a steep black island, total bog and heather, to which surely plough had never been laid. Never had I seen a place that more reminded me of that German Expressionist painting *The Isle of the Dead*. There is stark beauty in the desolation, and a strange underscoring of the negative by the two great guns that were dragged up to the top of it during the First World War but their mouths remained cold and silent always.

But, the mind nags always, 'Some tribe, 5,000 years ago or thereby, must have followed the retreating ice as far as Vementry.' At that time all the west of Scotland and Orkney and Shetland too were barren moorland, and the sea-routes were busy with tribes going west and north; and though life was dust and shadows to them, always they sought the clarity and ripeness of the sun; and there was nowhere that they would not beach their frail boats and set down earth-fast the stone of settlement, and strike with their mattocks. Why not Vementry, if their kinsmen had made for themselves glebelands and barns and ox-stalls in Harris and Hoy?

Vementry

. . . And left Alba and the wrathful rocks,
Suffered, between Alba and Orc, sore belabourment of sea.

Every beach along the west
Had its stone house and wattle huts
And young horses
That sieved wind through their manes, on a hill
And a woman at well or rockpool.
On one headland, an arch and a bell.
The last island, that also had its coat of barley patches.

Fish, brief brightnesses in the nets
Sweetened mariners' mouths.
We held our sail, a hollow, under wringings of black cloud.
In Shetland, watcher and watcher on every verge,
Boats furled between crag and crag
Wherever a last wave sang among pebbles.
Then, at sunset, drew to a black rock.

'Vementry, black hill in the sea,
We are to gather stones
For a hall, barn, loft of gray pigeons.
We have not forgotten
Mattocks, and the heavy seed-sack.
We will put nets cunningly woven
Here and there under your cliffs.
Will you set your free hawk on the fist of this boy?
Hide us from the voe dwellers
Until we set our tower of strong stone.
You will not lack for fires next winter.
Your fluent heather
Will make caisies for the women, Vementry.
It may be, next summer,
We will have speech with the men in the next valley,
A bartering of well-cured fish for an ox and goats.

Marigold fields on the far shore,
Blue groundmist of squill,
First seapinks in clefts of rock.
Vementry, we will honour you with beehives.'

The helmsman is putting his mouth to the sand now.
'Waken from your long sleep, island.

In the time of our children's children
You will wear a green coat, Vementry,
A young beautiful isle in the throng of islands.'

*

It was a golden time, our string of twelve days in Shetland. As if to atone for the dark death shadows in the first poem, I wrote one about the mystery and joy of birth. (Is it a poem, or a short story? . . . The prose-poem yearns towards the pure form of poetry, like a jar from wheel and kiln, and at the same time wants to have the free flow of a very brief story or a parable. The prose-poem 'Birth', readers might say, is neither the one nor the other. Think of the prose-poem not as amphora or urn for a drawing-room, but as the crude vessel beaten from earth and fire: the kind our ancestors might have used to hold water or grain.)

Birth

When the boat beached at night, the six fishermen said to Peter, 'The child must be born.'
    There was a lamp in one window. All the other crofts were dark.
    The old man said to Peter, 'You're a father.'
    The youngest man, a boy with a finespun gold beard, laughed.
    Peter said nothing.
    They manhandled the baskets of haddock from yole to beach.
    'Now you'll know what life is,' said a gentle-voiced oarsman.

'We'll wait long for our suppers tonight,' said a fisherman with a heavy black moustache and an eye-patch.

Peter said nothing.

'We'll have to clean the fish ourselves,' said the old skipper. 'Peter, you go on home.'

Peter stood looking at the darkling heave of sea westward.

*

The men gutted the fish in two rockpools, and swilled them clean.

When they looked up again, the men could see that three croft windows were lit. Then a fourth candle glimmered in a window. The women were returning home.

A big lamp burned in Peter's window.

'Peter,' said the old man, 'go up now and see your bairn.'

Peter was no longer on the shore.

His share of the catch lay scattered on the stones. An otter had trenched deeply into one.

*

'Now,' said the priest to the boy in the little kirk, 'is the water in the font?'

'It is,' said the boy.

'This new child,' said the priest, 'is it a boy or a girl?'

'The old women say it's a lass,' said the boy.

'Who are the parents?' said the priest from Voe.

'Peter and Sunniva,' said the boy.

'Well,' said the priest, 'light candles for the godparents to hold. Put salt in the dish.'

Men and women came into the kirk.

At last came Peter and Sunniva, who was carrying the child in a shawl (light white lace of lamb fleece that had flowed from fingers long dust and had folded the brightness of seven generations).

The boy put lighted candles in the hands of the two godparents.

The priest summoned the company to come about the font.

Saint Magnus, pray for the child who will both suffer and rejoice.

Saint Rognvald, pray for this pilgrim at the start of her journey.
Saint Peter, pray for this one who will have (it may be) a care of
fishermen and the children of fishermen.
Our Lady, Star of the Sea, shine ever for this shore lass.
Then the priest turned to the godparents and said, *What name*
is to be given to this child?

*

It will be said, for sure, that these prose-poems have nothing to say
about contemporary Shetland, but are questionable delvings into the
past, like archaeology without the purity of archaeology. It would
have been impossible to attempt an account of Shetland and its
people today without staying in the islands for a considerable time;
and, in any case, to someone like me who sees poetry draining away
remorselessly from even the quiet legendary places of the world, as
'the word' loses its power increasingly to 'the number', the richness
and strength of a people are not in oil terminals and overfishing (the
breaking of the ancient treaty between man and the creatures) and lit-
eracy, but in their inheritance from the past, the riches of music and
lore and imagination. We cannot know what is in store for us – some
sinister symptoms are here already, acid rain, and pollution, and
nuclear poison, and the death of seals and seabirds. It may be that our
grandchildren will have to look even deeper into the past for meanings. We must hope that the inherited skills and knowledge and the
traditional sanctities are not lost in the interim.

*

To go back to roots – except perhaps family trees, where the branchings are bound to become impossibly complicated, and frequently
disconcerting, for we all desire to be descended from Viking-jarls, but
more often than not a tramp or a rogue has come sleazing in to spoil
the act – this sentence is becoming as tangled almost as a family
history; but I was thinking in the opening phrase of a ceremony like
Up-Helly-Aa, which I have never experienced, and so I have no call
to comment on what it has grown into in the past century, from some

original dragging of blazing tar barrels through the streets of Lerwick and other villages, with chants and ale-tubs, to mark the retreat of winter, to salute the sun and help it up the sky: the great golden life-giver.

We must think that the entire northern hemisphere participated in this winter festival: one of a remarkable cluster of celebrations. Bound up with it, perhaps, was natural human death, especially the death of princes. But, though the mortal body, wrapped in flame, was borne on the waters into dawn-light, the kingdom endured, strengthened and purified; because when there is any new beginning there is hope and rejoicing illimitable (though it rarely lasts).

Up-Helly-Aa*

The old woman goes to every croft and bothy in the island.
The king in the east is dead.
And she cries again, *Who'll keep us now from the pirates and the hillmen?*
At the headland, her cracked voice still, *Honour the king with a ship and a fire.*

*

In Bergen in Norway, twelve heralds were blowing horns, black, at every corner of the Great Hall. *The king is dead.*
Horsemen with scrolls and black embossed seals were riding to every corner of Norway.
In the royal shipyard, shipwrights sweated by torchlight and under brief winter snow to get the ship ready before the king became an offence to nose and fingers.
Blizzards blew into the boatyard. Awnings were set up over the growing hull. Well-seasoned oak was cut and planed.
The skald was told to begin work on the elegy.
A goldsmith was summoned.
The men who made torches for the watchman and for the royal

---

* Midwinter Shetland fire festival, held annually in January.

portals and for the interior of the Great Hall made a thousand torches for earls-merchants-warmen to carry in procession to the king's burning.

The old king lay on his catafalque. Air and earth and water began their work of unlacing, to get to the skeleton.

But the king must fare out through the flame-firth, in his ship.

*

The fishermen made their winter boat out of a spar of driftwood and six stretched skins.

At midnight men came up from every croft with a burning peat in the tongs and they walked round the boat chanting a song so old the words were unclear as curdled honey. One by one they threw their fires into the well-greased boat. The boat burned between two rocks.

In the biggest croft the women waited with ale.

King? said the oldest woman to a girl. *What do we know of a dead king in the east? Winter is dead. We are sending out the last smoulders of winter to meet the new wind that will blow up for us honey and corn and children. The young summer king will come down to his new ship on a shore in the east.*

*

Those broke their strength on black Vementry, and hoped always till there were only a few old ones and children in the caves. There were about the same time more fortunate adventurers, who beached their boats in voes where the coarse grass above was sand-sweetened and amenable to mattock and plough. These settlers had to be vigilant always; other small flotillas – likely from the same original tribe – had landed men and women and beasts and gear a generation or two earlier in more favourable sites, and dug foundations and mapped hill and sea for peat and fish. And other cousins out of Scotland and Ireland were on their heels, following the star-wheel, likewise seeking places of settlement. We have to imagine a perpetual vigilance, a perpetual readiness against older settlers and new hungry seekers –

blood and broken skulls on the shoreline, the sheep in winter dragged out of the folds, the strong oxen lamed, torches thrust into thatch. There was this relentless pressure, not only small flotillas seeking west and north anxiously; these were only the shore-waves of a mighty European ocean-thrust of tribes and peoples, some universal star-drawn perturbation in the human race . . .

Somewhere in the north, in Shetland or Orkney or Caithness, an architectural genius was born, a poet in stone, who imagined and scratched on sand or rock the plan of the first broch: two concentric walls of heavy stone, bound inside by a spiral stair; the keep narrowed as it rose against the sun, in order to give little scope to the lobbed stones and torches of besiegers, and with only one small opening at the base that could be easily barred and locked. What confronted the besiegers was a high circular blank wall, that blunted their ardour as day followed day and their hunger grew; and always to encourage them the defenders from time to time threw down unpleasantness of ordure and insult, and – the besiegers themselves hungry and hope-less – they would hear the choruses from inside, and smell savours of cooking fish and mutton. A few cold nights of this, and the land-hungry sea-seekers were glad enough to take to their boats and hold north, for Foula or Unst . . . The genius had so designed the broch that it was built about a well, and water, the most precious necessity, was never lacking. Perhaps, the siege being lifted, the folk of Voe or Skeld came out to scorched dwellings and breached hulls; these things could be built up again; the important thing was, the tribe endured, time after time. We wrong those early tribes to think of them as half-brutish people. Another poet-in-stone imagined the magnificent burial chamber of Maeshowe in Orkney, so set towards the solstice sun of winter that the interior tombs, dark always, take on the few midwinter afternoons a fugitive splash of the sun setting over the Coolag hill of Hoy. There, 5,000 years ago, was architecture that thrills the spirit by the daring of its symbolism; not to speak of the sheer technical skill of the stonework itself . . . The circle – one thinks of the Ring of Brodgar too – fascinated them, with its suggestion of everlastingness, no beginnings or ends. Nowadays, the scope of our minds is linear; we demand ends and beginnings, the dance no longer goes round in a circle with endless variations.

Broch

Gather stones. Dress the stones, you that have skill in shaping stone. Set well the stones, the men that have skill in building. He that was at the building of seven brochs, here and there, let him be listened to well. He is master of the circles, well and tower. He unrolls a drawing on a skin.

We are to build, here, a broch.

Now, before midsummer, a tall broch, friend to the sun.

It is not for my honour or the honour of my children that the new friend of the sun is rooted now in earth, on the headland, and is risen by three courses, well quarried and well set circles of stone, locked, circle on circle.

The broch is for the honour of all this folk, a sure shield, a sun-sign.

Consider how the bee-swarm left their golden town and hung, a dangerous choiring throng, at the fork of the tree. So we have come out and clean away from the settlement southward where our disgusting kinsmen broke sourest bread for us, with insults after the hard labour of fishing. So we, true children of the sun, have come here out of the celled house of winter.

Consider: strangers will come in ships and will not be friends to this coast. Consider: the old king-bee, gaunt from winter and snow, will cross the three voes with his axe-men, to yoke us again to be his hunters and harvesters. Consider: we need a place for honouring of the sun with dance, chorus, sacrifice.

I have great care and keeping of you, my children. The broch stands as high as my throat now. The yard shrieks with sound of chisels and split stone. But hurry, that the last circling stone may be set in the spiral before the solstice, for the watchman to keep watch. I put my hand to the wall, it beats like a powerful angel of the sun, a guardian.

Do not waste my time with news of the women. Let them tear open a new acre from the hill. They must comb rockpools for whelk and mussel. Let them see to fire and broth-pot. Next year the sun will kiss the new acre. Let the girls pluck the lambs, let them draw from the turning wheel the thin hard line of thread.

What is more sweet in the mouth than goat-milk and cheese? They are the daughters of the sun, the chatter goes on and on, the music of this new place is woven into it. Honour the mothers of this sun-folk.

That a stone has fallen and broken the head of a quarry-man is a matter of great beauty. His dust will be sun dust before any others of this folk. He has run into death with the sign of the sun on his neck and shoulder.

Poet, find from his mother the name of the quarry-man with the broken skull.

Poet: begin to consider a proper ordering of words for the lintel of this new broch in Norday. For now, in its surge up to the sun, the broch tilts inwards, like the eagle, the bird of the sun, before it begins its true last circle and sun-surge. Let your incisions be harder than the quarried stone. Consider, poet, a hymn for the pure throats of the boys.

*

One day, in the island of Yell, we spent a pleasant hour with Mary-Ellen Odie and her shepherd husband. At one end of her beautiful garden is the ruin of a broch: one should sleep better, I think, with that guardian between house and sea . . . Another evening Gunnie drove us to the fertile southern end of Shetland, and there on the little island of Mousa is the only broch in an almost pristine state. There was no way to get nearer it that evening; we were beginning to be tired and hungry. At the foot of the steep perilous Grobsness road Tammy the cat would be waiting to greet us; there was the fire to light and supper to be made.

I remembered that a modern genius in stone had been born and brought up near the Broch of Mousa: Adam Christie. In his Shetland youth he showed talent for writing and clear courageous thinking; at the time of our most shameful jingoism, the Boer War, young Adam Christie looked into the heart of the situation and wasn't afraid to speak his mind. Illness – the worst kind of illness, mental – visited him in his prime and never withdrew its talons. Until he died, aged eighty, he was confined in the asylum of Sunnyside outside

Montrose. In biblical times they might have spoken of an angel visiting Adam Christie in his cell. (The very name Adam Christie has religious reverberations.) Adam was handed the gift of making. He began to paint pictures on the blank insides of thrown-away cigarette packets, usually scriptural scenes. On a tea chest, he attempted a heroic scene out of Norse-Irish history, the Battle of Clontarf, using the crudest tools, bits of broken glass and nails. An old bridge spanning the River Esk near the asylum was being removed to make place for a new bridge; the brigstones were of uniform size and their day was done. Adam Christie took a heap of the stones back to the hospital and there he began to carve them into heads of considerable power; they might be the heads of Moses or St Peter, or maybe of his Celtic ancestors who had made the first indomitable furrows of salt and earth round Sumburgh in the south of Shetland. A six-inch nail was Adam's chief tool. There was a well-known sculptor in Montrose at the time, William Lamb. Lamb invited Adam to his studio and offered him some of the proper tools of sculpture. Perhaps Adam tried them; in the end he returned to his six-inch nail. Nobody knows how many heads Adam sculpted from the abandoned stones. Sadly, only a few are left. Once the work on a head was finished, Adam gave it to a doctor or a nurse. They lingered for years in Montrose gardens here and there as rockery decorations, enduring all weathers. It is said that when a new roadway was needed for Sunnyside, many of Adam's sculptured heads were smashed to make metalling. He died, a gentle old man, in 1950. He neither expected nor received recognition. Fortunately, Dr Kenneth Keddie, a psychiatrist who joined the staff of Sunnyside after Adam Christie's death, recognised the marks of genius in this artefact and that; he set to work to save as many of the heads as he could; and in 1984 he published a book about Adam and his history and his art, *The Gentle Shetlander*. It was a tribute well deserved, and a plea against oblivion that was urged not a moment too soon.

Ode to Adam Christie

Dark visitors at your door, in starlight.
They would speak only with you, Adam.
Only you can read the word on the summons.

You are sentenced to stand among flames,
Adam Christie.
'Let him thole his torment life-long in a place of stone' . . .

The iron ship is waiting.
You will not see cornfield or fishing boat more.

You sit under a high barred window,
Adam Christie,
Visited by butterfly, bird, star, rose petal, cloud.
And now your mind is quiet.
You thank God for many beautiful things.

I think, one night an angel came to your cell –
Adam, sing.

You woke, prisoner, your tongue touched with the coal.
You sang your days, and our days
On the blank of a thrown-away cigarette packet
And on a warped tea chest
And on a heap of brigstones, striking with six-inch nail.

Beautiful your script among the scattered trash of time.

Then, Adam Christie, you died,
Aged eighty, far from Cunningsburgh.

Ignorant hammers broke your stone poems.
Moths came with the moon,
Their mouths went here and there at the manuscripts.

Did the angel bend, did he gather and sift the work?
Did the adamant mouth
Cry, *Well done, Adam Christie . . .?*

Adam Christie, we don't know much
Moving in these opacities,
Only that sometimes, after cosmic fires
Lies, clear and shadowless, the crystal.

*

Adam Christie's ancestors may have come to Shetland from Aberdeenshire perhaps in the early seventeenth century to work at the building of Scalloway Castle, one of the Renaissance palaces built in Orkney and Shetland by the Stewart earls, Robert and his son Patrick. (Robert was one of the illegitimate sons of King James V of Scotland.) A sinister reputation clings about the northern Stewarts. They were absolute lords of the islands, and it may be that, aside from the fact that the Stewart family were never conspicuously successful rulers, their unstable standing – being illegitimate – tempted Robert and Patrick to wring the uttermost oozings of oil and honey from the islanders, while their sun was still high. The descendants of Viking settlers, a bold peasantry with their own language and law-book, had this Scottish yoke put on them, and they were hard driven. Nothing more cruel can be done to a people than to force them to endure such an alien yoke and goad. An islander might wake up some morning to find that he was no longer a free farmer but a serf. Poverty had been there always; but to have the roof taken off, and hearth and cupboard open to winter!

Then the only folk who are really free are the earl and the wanderer who is bound to no place or liege-lord.

The northern Stewarts had all the graces of aristocracy without the grace of good governance. They had exquisite taste in architecture; the palaces at Birsay and Kirkwall and Scalloway testify to that, and it is not hard to imagine that they gathered round them the best artists and musicians and poets they could get. Many an elegant pavane, to the sound of lutes and pipes, in the ballroom of Scalloway,

after the silver and crystal had been borne away from the winter ban-
queting tables! The well-woven tapestries trembled in the draught;
Scottish voices and Norn voices mingled compliment and courtesy;
rustling of heavy silk, fragrance of musk as the ladies took the floor
for another dance, curtsying to the gentlemen who advanced on a new
tide of music. But the earl was no longer there; the earl had withdrawn, he must be up betimes, for – being the sheriff and sole inter-
preter of the law in Shetland – he must try a poor vagrant and alleged
sheep thief in the morning.

A Trial in Scalloway

Give your name.
No but I have no proper name but they call me, in this place and
    that, 'vagrant'. The seals call me Simon.

Give this, your place of abode.
The house of the winds.

Well, but you are a vagabond, Simon Windfoot. I will enter your name
    so.
I am as birds are.

Tell the court, Simon Vagrant, what have you done with this sheep?
I know nothing about one single sheep, sir, but I clap hands on the
    hill and the flock scatters, making high and low calls, the lambs
    with the old broken-mouthed ewes. They turn at the stone dyke.
    'It's only Simon,' they cry among themselves, then one might
    come to my hand.

Now, man, it is urged against you, a sheep from the flock at Skeld being
    missing, you were seen with a tin and a twig over a fire at the shore,
    stirring stew. Answer that.
I broil a fish at the rock a many a day.

Consider this well, and answer. There were the twenty sheep, at Skeld,
at sunset on Tuesday last. There slept a tramp behind stone dyke there
that night. There were nineteen sheep on the hill at sunrise. And you,
Mister Windfoot, six miles away, at Voe, gnawing on a bone. Answer.
A crust. I broke a crust at Voe, that I had from a croft-lass. What
croft-lass? I know only hands that offer, and this hand kind and
smelling of marigolds. I know no names.

Simon, listen well. I have no ill-will to you, Simon. Think of me as a
friend. No, I have a pity for you, and think of you on winter nights
in a storm without roof or fire or blanket. Now Simon my friend, but
tell me what came of that sheep, confess openly, and you will be let go
from this court, and given a bowl of porage, and a penny in your
hand, and then it will be between you, Simon, and the farmer at
Skeld, William Olafson, an honest man, as to what recompense you
will render him, on account of this mishap as between you and the
sheep, either to help in his hay harvest or to get sufficient heather for
a thatch to William's roof.
I do not tell lies nor take wages.

Simon, vagrant, do you know the penalty for sheep stealing? Shall I
read it out of the law-book here on this bench?
I must be drawn up to turn in the wind.

Yes, man, you know the law well. And a hundred mockers will be under
the tree to mock your dancing in the wind, Mister Windfoot. And
there will be fiddles and a feast, man. Only with you, when the reel
goes round at midnight, there will be a stillness.
I was always a lonely dancer.

You are a poor obstinate creature, lacking all reason.
Sir, I have to laugh. What would a wanderer want with a sheep's
carcass? Can I spin wool for stockings? What would I do, hauling
a sack of rotten bones hither and thither through Shetland on my
back? Have I a rafter to smoke mutton? I get small mouthfuls in
passing, an egg or a fish, and a throb or two of cold water from a
burn.

Then, Simon Vagrant, I have to pass sentence upon you . . .

*

When they came, the tree being set up in front of the castle, and the black bell clanged once, and a crowd from three parishes foregathered, to fetch Simon from the cell beneath, they found no one there.

    Simon was next seen, in the month of July, in Yell, going on thence to Unst and (as he said) Norway, or, it might be, Iceland.

*

A cragsman found a ewe on a crag ledge, the true mark in the ear, the lost one, in the time of the taking of eggs in Voar.

*

Men must always be seeking and searching for larger meanings, beyond the narrow circle of their own immediate wants and desires. It is hard to say how long religion has been in decline; certainly in my own lifetime there has been a marked falling away from traditional pieties. But the hunger remains, to find a meaning beyond oneself that is valid for the whole human race. Into the breaches in Christianity come exotic Eastern variants, or spiritualism, or Marxism, or a mindless genuflection to Progress-without-end. For most educated people, perhaps, reverence for culture takes the place of the Bible in the window-seat or the crucifix on the wall. The Greek triad of goodness–truth–beauty has served great spirits in the past well enough, for example Keats. That goodness, truth and beauty do not always belong together is exemplified by the Stewarts of Orkney and Shetland, who were cultured aristocrats and doubtless charming people in themselves, and filled their palaces with beautiful things and high courtesy; and left only a legend of evil behind them.

*

Concealments, vanishings: much of the history of the north is taken up with such things. Did Simon Windfoot truly vanish, or was the whole affair a dream that Earl Patrick Stewart had in his Scalloway castle, after an evening of rich food, wine and music? There would come a day for Patrick when he would have been glad to melt into the elements like Simon Windfoot; but no, for him there was no escape, he had to walk on to a scaffold in Edinburgh to atone for his bad governance, and there the headsman was waiting, and there Patrick may have run his finger along the axe's edge to test that it was sharp enough, like his later kinsman Charles I. The Stewarts did not lack courage.

What helped to ruin Patrick, and his father before him and his son after him, was that they had no true understanding of the land and the people they were set over. Such alien minglings of dust end frequently in evil. But when a family has lived for many generations in one place, their strength and cunning are given to the soil, and the virtues of the earth pass into them and become one with them. More than the melancholy of kirkyards by the sea are the beauty and fittingness of them: that the dust which nourished the living in their seventy years should take back to itself the worn-out dust, for new cornstalks to grow. So the story of a parish is written on the heavy stone pages beside the kirk.

One era of violent uprooting fell during the eighteenth-century wars, when young islanders were conscripted by force to be sailors in the king's men-o'-war. The island lairds were expected to provide a quota of young men when the officers of the press-gang presented themselves at their gates. Such an orderly 'call-up' of men, as if they were sheep, was beyond the laird's power. Word of the officers' approach went round parish or island like wind, and the young men were bundled into cave or hill-hatch by the women-folk until such time as the laird and minister, shaking their heads in sorrow at this lack of patriotism, waved farewell from the beach when the longboat of the press-gang pushed out; and then the young men could go whistling down the wind again, on beach and hillside, till the next rumour of a landing of strangers by night . . . Of course many young men were taken unawares, following the ox and plough or miles out at sea fishing. What more violent disturbance of his dust and salt for a

Shetland lad than the strange manifold lingo of his shipmates, the brutish discipline at sea, red-mouthed cannon and broken webs of rigging?

Later generations of Shetland sailors covered all the ocean-routes of the world. The founder of the P & O Line, Arthur Anderson, was a Shetlander. Shetlanders are among the greatest seamen of the past two centuries.

Writing this story that is half-way to folk-tale and poetry, I tried to celebrate the one dust that is a parish and the people of a parish, living and dead and unborn.

Press-gang

The men from the king's ship said to the girl on the hill, *Where are the men hidden?*

The girl said nothing.

One struck her. Still the girl said nothing.

One said, *She's a deaf-mute. No use talking to her.*

One said, *I heard her singing among the sheep this morning, taking them one by one to the shearer.*

One said, *The shepherd called her Margaret.*

One said, *A shepherd Lowrie is on the list here.*

One said, *Listen, Margaret, if you tell us where the conscripts are, we'll spare Lowrie.*

So the girl led them to a cave where five young men sat among shadows.

The king's men took the five islanders and Lowrie the shepherd too. They were rowed out to the king's ship.

The girl came back to a cold croft.

*

No end to the wars, said the man from the king's ships.

It goes on, the battle, from the beginning to the end of time, said the patched woman, the beggar on the road.

263

We need a dozen men from this island, said the sergeant-at-arms. *Their names are on this list. We can't find one of them, in croft or cave or bothy.*

I wouldn't wonder, said the woman that smelt of ditchfires. *Every bird likes his own shore best.*

Now, said the man with crested buttons on his blue serge coat, taking a sovereign out of his purse, *I don't suppose you know what this is.*

It looks like a piece of the sun, said the tinker wife.

This gold, said the man, *will buy you a croft and a cow. That is, when you tell us where the cowards are that won't serve the king on his ship. You travellers know everybody in every hole and corner.*

Do you see that island with nothing on it – not even a sheep – only rocks and heather? I saw them rowing out to the dark shore at dawn- light. Every lad went and hid him behind a rock. You see the twelve rocks. She said that, the woman of the roads. *There's nowhere they can run to.*

So the sergeant put a coin on the withered palm – only it was a moon splinter, a shilling.

When the king's men rowed out to the bleak black island, the twelve young men had melted into the rock.

Madge went to the fair in Scalloway and she bought oranges and gave fairings to the bairns and told fortunes to girls and she danced in a circle of fishermen and she was drunk every day till the bellman went round shaking his bell, *The fair's over! The fair's over!*

Dust of men and dust of their land are one dust. Who shall sep- arate the minglings?

But the wars go on and on.

*

The tyranny of age and office . . . Old age, increase of years, hoarded wisdom and lore, the *pietas* belonging to elders: all these have been honoured always and everywhere, in the tribe and the community. The element of selfishness comes into it: 'Some day I too will be old and a boy will guide me.' Oedipus the outcast king went on his daughter's arm on mountain paths to the place of his change. But there is another thrust in the human spirit: impatience that one's young powers and imaginings are being thwarted always by the out-moded settled tyranny of age. The Renaissance was the great time of those young adventurers. Pirates, bandits, mercenaries, revolutionaries have broken out of the narrow confines of their society, where the old and the hallowed cling to office. That hot impatient arrogance thrust Lear out into the storm and set the heel on Gloucester's precious stones, his eyes. The young eager upstarts, as Edwin Muir argued in an essay, always appeal to 'nature' in such a situation: political hierarchies become outworn, the primal powers of nature must be invoked for the health of society; but nature, unleashed, has the ferocity and the cunning of the beasts, without that innocence that held till the sixth day of creation: 'On the sixth day we came.'

This tension between the restless energy of youth and the vener-ableness of eld is not confined to palaces; it is a constant throughout the generations, at all levels of society, in croft and council house too. No doubt of it, in past generations hundreds of young Shetlanders and Orkneymen must have been glad to sign on as sailors and whale-men, especially in the nineteenth century when the population bur-geoned everywhere.

And yet it has always been a moving thing, to experience the harmony of poor families in their crofts: the tenderness between grandparents and children, the joy at a birth, the sorrow at a wearing-out and a death. (Death of young men at sea was another matter, and evoked in most societies primitive lamentation; but here the Norse tradition of fatalism forbade such communal choruses of grief as are described in Synge's *The Aran Islands*: in the cold north the terrible grief was vented privately, while the mute chorus of women stood silent, in this door, at that gable-end.)

Having written poems of death and birth, there ought, I consid-ered, to be a love poem. The love poem, that I wrote hurriedly one Saturday afternoon in my bedroom at Grobsness, words and phrases and images fairly tumbling into the open red notebook – while the others drove away to the cliffs of the north-west Mainland; this poem is not the rose I had hoped for: it is overshadowed by that grim castle at Scalloway and the roofless Ha' above the Grobsness beach, where a man like Thomas Leisk might have lived. Here the frame of the generations is wrenched. Age in itself is venerable; age with a smitchkin of power might be cause of fear or joy (depending on the old man, and what manner of silver age has put on him); age united with power and pride is a canker in the community.

Thomas Leisk, Factor, at his Ledger in the Haa of Grobsness

Item: 3 score geese in sacks for Scallowa market . . .
I am old, beard lost its blackness.
I dream this, a poor lass may be lady at my Haa.
I have power to part her Peter from his yole.

Item: 12 sacks barley to his lordship, the rent . . .
Cometh not wisdom with silver hairs?
Their love, a bird-cry on the waters, lost.
Would not his salt eat into the apple of her?

Item: A heifer for 2 kegs Hollands . . .
A many a lass clustered my youth.
I know, a sea lantern spans the hill.
Yea, but my sovereigns are surer glitterers.

Item: 5 baulks timber for a new barn . . .
Full harvest it is for me now.
May she not lift the silver cup to my mouth?
Salt covers the mouth of many a fisherman.

Item: Eviction of a father from his holding . . .
I am frown and fist to his lordship, here.
The lass turned from me at sheaf-binding.
The boy makes mock of me at ale bothies.

Item: Order a stone from Lowrie, stonecutter.
Man knoweth not the day or the hour.
She has stood at the kirk door in white?
Yea, and cometh the white coat to all, at last.

*

Continually, especially here on the verge of St Magnus Bay, the mind returns to that man whose life and martyrdom light the history of the north – no local saint either; the bishop's church in Faroe was dedicated to him, and thanks to T.S. Eliot the literate world knows of the 'walls of Magnus Martyr' in London that 'hold inexplicable splendour of Ionian white and gold'.*

In times of prosperity such sanctities are forgotten. Readers of the *Sun* and book-club novels, film-goers and connoisseurs of pop music, have other values; but so too do cultured and humane people, lovers of Bach and Yeats. Shetlanders up to the time of the Reformation and beyond, we must think, listened to the story that was more than a story, it had moved into the intensity of sacred song. Even in the gray light of today, Magnus is a very common name in Shetland. The candle burns low. The flame-bead waits for another wind.

We oughtn't to think of medieval Shetland as a place of hard bitter unrelenting work, the hands ingrained with salt and loam. The calendar – as all over Europe – was starred with feasts and festivals. There was dancing, music, running and wrestling, cakes and ale in a field near the church. And still people crowded in, singly or in groups, by road and sea. And perhaps there was a dull cleric with a ledger at a turnstile to enter and approve their offerings.

April the Sixteenth

Folk came in, in small flocks, by sea and land, burdened, to the Feast of Magnus. A man with cowl and quill challenged them at the gate. They answered, naming cargoes. The scribe wrote at his table, then beckoned them to go through.

* T.S. Eliot, 'The Fire Sermon', lines 263–5, *The Waste Land* (1922).

Yell

A boat-load of peats from Yell, the heaviest blackest peats, dug
between the sun and the fire at the heart of the earth.

Unst

Eight fleeces, all black but one, to hang at Manskirk wall, to keep
the wind from the sanctuary in winter.

Sullom

This rock the sea washed up, a rock from the roots of ocean. It
oozed heavy black drops, that the seals drank from and died.
We drowned that rock, and come with clean sea stones for the
new apse. And we come with questions to the saint. The drops
fall through our dreams still, like black pearls.

Whalsay

A caisie of herring, moon-gleam on the scales, to leave in the kirk
porch. This boy will keep gulls off, and the priest's cat, till the
last psalm. Who can fish like we men from east? A poet will
celebrate our spangled nets.

Lerwick

We come with mud on our feet from the few stone houses above
the ebb. The grass is heavy with April rain. We will brighten
our hands too with rain, for the kirk. Our palms are bright
with coins from sheltering Dutchmen.

Papa Stour

We're going with seven swords for a dance. From the forge of the
dance the swords are beaten, with chants and music, to a star
of peace.

Grobsness

No, I was going to launch the boat. I didn't know it was Magnus
Day, here in the loneliest place in all Shetland. I'll put on a
new gray bonnet, and gather the bairns, and we'll walk to the
mass, each with a peat or a fish for the priest's fire.

Foula
What from the far island of birds but creatures of air and crag?
The birds are quick at Mansmas. Here's a hawk on the
helmsman's fist. The boy that bails has a basket of doves.
Coming to the bay of the kirk, we furl sail and oars. The bell
cries now like a bird of blessing upon the waters.

*

The day we went to Yell and Unst, we had to drive past the oil
complex at Sullom Voe, where most of the North Sea oil is off-loaded
into tankers. Four tall flares burn off the excess gas; even at noon, on
that bright day near midsummer, the flames burned eerily high up in
the zenith, torches of immense perilous power, yet frail too athwart
the midsummer sun. Nearby are the peat-cuttings in the moor where
Shetlanders have dug their fires for thousands of years, and will still
be digging them when the oilfields in the North Sea are dry.
Everywhere in Shetland we passed the peat-cutters at their work of
digging and stacking. The Orkney peatbanks are shallow and scant in
comparison. But it means that those great rich peat areas in Shetland
are inarable. In Orkney you are rarely out of sight of farm and steading, cattle and pasture and tilth. In Shetland it is possible to traverse
miles of bleakness, except that sheep are everywhere, and wild birds,
'infinite wings'. The young lambs were white and black and dun and
particoloured.

Shetland is world famous for fiddle music: Ali Bain, Tom
Anderson, and there are young talents like Debbie Scott. There is a
mystery here; there are and there must always have been Shetland
poets and storytellers, but I think they have never quite had the
artistry and scope of Orkney bards and tellers of tales. Conversely,
Orkney has good fiddle music, but has never poured out such torrents
of song as the Shetlanders. I can offer no solution to this mystery. The
music gift goes far back into legend. There is a Shetland version of
the Orpheus legend, but only a few enchanting fragments survive;
the original ballad must have been current when Norn was the language of the Shetlanders, and the chorus is still in the original
tongue. *Scowan ürla grün . . . Whar giorten han grün oarlac* ('Early

greens the wood . . . Where the hart goes yearly' – perhaps the refrain means that.) The Shetland Orfeo went with his pipes to win back the lost bride. His music 'drew iron tears down Pluto's cheek', and the story ended happily, unlike the Grecian myth, for no conditions were set.

> He's taen his lady an he's gaen hame
> An noo he's King ower a' his ain.

I have been intrigued for long by this ballad, and how it strayed into the lore of Shetland; by way perhaps of some royal palace in Norway, where the laureate had tasted first heady sips of Greek legend. It points to an origin for music and for all the arts that has nothing to do with concert halls, art galleries, and salons set about with tapestries and jars. I have said already in this essay that modern culture for many people is perhaps a substitute for something rooted deep in human nature – the instinct and the impulse to reverence the unknowable, perhaps to placate 'whatever gods may be' – a primitive atavistic urge – but all the same to unite ourselves with the power that moves the stars, by the offering of our best skills and gifts, so that we may share and celebrate what providence has to give in the way of food, clothing, fire, as well as the loveliness we are dowered with from birth to death. It is a mutual courtesy of giving and taking. The mysteries of suffering, evil, loss, though never here to be understood, take on a pathos and a grandeur when artist, poet, craftsman, pattern-maker, dancer, weaver, musician, potter, bring their works to the set-apart place, the place of offering . . . A blight on much modern art is an all-pervading snobbery and elitism, and the cult of personality – 'the famous poet'; 'the world-renowned sculptor'. We should think rather of art as being, in Thomas Mann's words, 'anonymous and communal': a whole community contributes to the making of a poem, the poet is only the person who first utters the dance of words through a mask. So the ballad-men wandered through the towns and villages of Scotland, uttering their great stories, and no one in the enraptured crowd wanted to know their names, but all knew that they themselves were part of the poem while the poem lasted. They recognised themselves and their neighbours and the passions and exchanges that bound them together in a community. The poem was the expression of their highest thoughts and of their deepest joys and sufferings.

To see the symbol in the common objects of daily life is to know a depth and enrichment. This way of looking at things is almost over now. I think, until fairly recently, when a Shetlander said 'fish' or 'bread', he meant something other than the silver-gray shape on his hook, or the crust he broke at the table. A richness of association and experience inhered: a whole way of life stretching back for generations, of keel-laying, line-baiting, drowning, salt, moon-drawn waters, hunger, sea harvest, debts and dues; and of the symbols of agriculture, plough and harrows and scarecrow and scythe and flail and millstones and oven and ale-kirn . . . The hungerer, the food, the provider: each in the triad was beholden and necessary to the others.

It is the task of poets, perhaps, to keep the symbols in their purity and power. In former times it was no empty occupation, the letting out and drawing in of lines – it was no barren stance, the women waiting anxiously at the shore for the sixareens to come out of the storm, with the flock of gulls behind that signified a good catch . . . This sweet compulsion of art, the pattern, must have operated from very ancient times. Christianity, when it came, enriched the symbols immeasurably, and the Celtic monks had eagerness to put beauty and splendour upon the lives of humble people. A later philosopher, looking at our existence with an eye devoid of poetry, thought of it as brief, nasty and brutish.

I tried, more than once in our twelve Shetland days, to flesh out the few beautiful scattered bones of the Orfeo story; and each time I retired bruised and beaten.

All I could manage as a tribute to Shetland music was a prose-poem.

Fiddle Music

I

The fish are in their fortresses, they sit in sea castles gathering
their strength to assault us and our boats suddenly, they buckle
on glittering armour, they will come against us with power and
swiftness in the upwellings of dawn, they will blunt our hooks,
their legion will pour in over thwarts and hull till the boat
Bonny Lass is overset and sunk, they will scatter the fishermen
here and there upon the salt barrenness, they will exult in a
mighty silent chorus over the drowned hands and faces, then
all will flock in (bidden) to the banquet, birds of the blue and
of the gray and golden winds, and lobsters out of their broken
tents of weed in the rock fissures, deep, and creatures too small
to see will sip at the light in the eyes of the boy Lowrie till
there be but two bone hollows.

*

No: we renew again, as every morning, we offer to herring and
haddock and cod, the ancient treaty between fish and men,
made and sealed when the first hand seized a grayling in
anxious joy from an opening under a rock: that fish will come
in a great host to be our guests at Grobsness, the fishermen
have good mysteries to show them beyond sea-salt and their
endless death-seeking moon-drawn circuits out there in the
bleak kingdom of ocean where sun seeks down to them
fractured and cold, we would amaze them with matters of the
true sun: beckoning hook and hand, the basket (blond straw
weavings), the flashing knife, the fire, the pot beaten from
veins of a southern mountain, the sun-kissed oats to stuff their
jaws to bursting, and the iron lamps that for love of us they
will fill from their livers with oil-of-the-moon, so old Norna
will see to knit stockings on a winter night and the ill-paid
fiddler (summoned) see to ply his bow for their reels: come,
fish, sit at our tables, in the pot at the very centre of the table,

precious and particular friends rescued from fluxes and
refluxes of the witching moon, broken (and willingly so) by
the sunbright hands and the sun-praising mouths of the voe
folk: who have too few oat-sacks to see them beyond the black
solstice.

2

'The fishing boat *Bonny Lass* of Grobsness in Delting was
whelmed in heavy seas beyond Vementry last Tuesday.
Fortunately six fishermen were rescued from the scene of
disaster by two other boats in the close vicinity, but one young
fisherman Lawrence Williamson could not be found. The laird
will be put to much expense to either buy or have built a
replacement for *Bonny Lass*, not to speak of the loss of the
plentiful catch in the vessel on that day. Going to press, we
learn that a body has been found on Muckle Flugga, which
could be identified as that of Lawrence Williamson by the
stockings of a pattern characteristic of the knitting of the boy's
grandmother.'

'One hundred and three barrels of best herring in brine were
sold at the pier of Lerwick on Friday last to a Dutch skipper
by the laird of Nesting, at a modest profit. "This means," said
the laird, "that my tenants will be able to pay the rents of their
holdings, boats, and gear this Martinmas, and they will have
an overplus of fish to see them well through the winter, if they
do not squander their substance in barn and bothy dances, and
suchlike vain cavortings, as they are wont to do in good
times".'

'*Magnus Troll* – The above-mentioned person was found to be
living by the inspector in a state of extreme penury in the croft
of Dale for which no rent has been paid since the decease of
his mother ten years ago. The laird has generously agreed to

relieve the said croft of rent for the duration of the lifetime of the said Troll, notwithstanding the man is of good constitution and intelligence and capable of earning his keep by sea-labour or field-labour. It was agreed, the parochial board should pay the said Troll an allowance of one shilling and sixpence per month, to relieve him of the extreme of indigence. However, Troll refused this offer with some heat, saying he could exist well enough on the fish and oatcakes he earned by the playing of his fiddle at reels, weddings, wakes, fairs, sea bounties, harvest homes and Up-Helly-Aas.'

*

In early winter, in Orkney, I took up the scarred 'Orfeo' manuscript once more and unwove and wove, and ended with a kind of masque that, if music and design were put upon it, might keep some of its ancient power.

Orfeo: A Masque

I

Orfeo and the boat *Dayspring*
  And six fishermen off Foula.

The uncoiled line, baited, wandering deep.
Orfeo and the fiddle and empty fathoms.
    Play a reel, man.

The hauled lines, burgeoning hooks,
Twenty score cod,
    Bare barb, a red bead on the fiddler's finger.

Row home, fishermen, flushed with sunset.
Your women wait
    With knives and plates on the shore.

274

No smoke from one chimney. Orfeo,
   He of the winged blithe wooden bird,
Brideless and bairnless, unbeholden, bides alone.

He slimes a flagstone with seven fish.
Glance of a gray-eyed girl through the door.
New flame in the hearth, a fish in the pot,
   The board set with butter and salt.

The lass goes away, unthanked, under a star.

Orfeo dreams of cornfields, a hill of sheep,
The fiddle folded forever at a farm wall,
   A corn bride.

II
Orfeo at the farm door, with a string of fish.
    'A sea gift, for Maurya your lass . . .'

'She's summoned to tend the lady in the Hall of Scalloway,
With silver combs, and silks,
   And servings on a silver plate . . .'

The gray-eyed lass in the lee of the barn
   She listens, lingers.
Orfeo under a net of stars, silent,
   Shut out from fire and farm.

His house is not dark. A girl's hand
Has put the fish-oil lowe in his lamp in the window.

III
Dayspring, the fishermen, the lines let down,
Long lingering furlongs, black, off Unst,
   An empty sea.

The sun bleeds like a whale in the west.
  A rage of women at the shore,
  Sullenness of men.

Orfeo's been all day among fields with his fiddle,
Aware of the lift
  And long liltings of a laverock.
He listens to the green corn growing.

He goes home.
  A gift of new bread is on his board, smoking:
The neighbour lass
  Has not lingered, the gray-eyed one.

IV

Orfeo at the door of the Hall, with an oyster,
A glimmer, cloistered,
  In two storm-gray valves.

He beats. The door
  Is oak, iron-studded.
  His knuckles bleed.

'A gift for Maurya, servant to the lady here,
A sea pearl.'

Dance of laird and ladies,
  A thin cold chime of virginals.

Storm rattles the shutters. Honeyed bread
Is brought, and wine, to a long table.
  Ladies flow through mirrors,
In lamplight, lissom and lovely.

Maurya draws a silver comb
  Through the long hair of the laird's lady.

A hound howls in the kennel.
  A thief! A spy! Pirates!

V

Orfeo in the ale-house: lamp and barrel:
  The luckless crew,
Beards of fishermen, barley-foam fleeced.

Orfeo thrusts the fiddle in his bright beard.
      At midnight
  The heavy feet begin to dance.
Questing, flashing, the bow upon snarling strings.
Shawls at the star-filled door, shrieking!

Gray eyes under a carved lintel,
At Scalloway Castle, alone,
  She weeps, that watcher.

Sixern and ale-sodden six, in the east,
  In swart snarling sea,
And the lift like layers and foldings of lead.

A sudden reef, a knife
  In the boat's long belly,
Six cries, a scatter, soon salted and sunk and silent.

VI

Orfeo on the shore at sunset,
He wanders and watches still
  Under the broken net of stars,
And the fiddle a folded bird at the bothy wall.

The lass at the rockpool, with hot aquavit in a cup.
  The clay grows cold,
Clay and spirit grow cold on the rock.

Clay by clay, a scatter of six, sunk fifty fathoms
And the blood
    Cold and silent as shells soon.

VII

What is the white shape laid
    By gardener and groom
At the pillared gate of the Hall?
It is Maurya consumed to cinders and shadows.

The corpse is taken by four crofters,
    It is borne over the moor to the barn.

It is borne, soon, by six brothers to the kirkyard.
    It is drowned in earth, in a wave of clay.

The gravedigger's spade is bright when the last clod
    Is turned and tramped on.

VIII

Who stands in the ale-house, with tinker
And smuggler and poacher
    And gangrel and beachcomber,
Till ale flushes faces and feet
    And they shout for music?

Orfeo.

    But Orfeo is sick of that fiddle
And the thousand wrongs it has wrought,
The scattered sea dead,
The snowcold folded hands under the mort-cloth.

Who stands at the door of the inn in a black coat?
    A horseman, with news.

Who stands between the corn, throat-high,
 And the fisherless shore,
And waits till the ale-house empties
And the kirkyard brims with shadows?

Guardian. Giver. The gray-eyed sea girl.

IX

Midnight. The dim of summer.
 The unfurled fiddle, a song at the rock:

'Let her go. Let her bend to the scattered corn stalks.
Let her hand
 Shine along knife and fish at the rockpools.
She is beautiful among the daughters of Voe.
 The time is short.'

The rock opens. The fiddle
 Flies in at the fissure.
It sings to the Dark King
With the gold cup in his hand.

The fiddle pleads. The Dark King listens.
The daughter of music
 Death-maiden, Maurya, covers her ears.
The fiddle urges. It wheels,
 A death dance, seven circles.

The Dark King says:

'You man, out there,
Set your face homeward now,
 Maurya will follow.

'You will see her bent and sour and ugly, going graveward
 In a slow broken dance.
 So be it.

Now turn your feet, go home.
She will come
   With marigold, squill, first wild roses.'

X

Maurya stirs – kindled wax and wick –
   A glimmer now
From the clot of shadows at the heart of the rock,
   Death bride.

Orfeo prepares his mouth
   For a surge of kisses (no song),
As many as the drops from a splintering wave,
As grains from the flail,
   A golden shower.

The fiddle flies out into dawn–light.
It lies, trembling, on Orfeo's shoulder,
   In the light and lift of his hand.
Orfeo throws it down, the bird of dancing,
   His dower and delight.

Orfeo turns to take the corn-bride.

She wanes, frail flame,
   Drowned in torrents of noon.
The doors of the rock roll shut
   With a stammer like thunder.

XI

Orfeo sits on the rock, in winter, in snow.
A fell of white hair
   Flows from his face.

A lass finds him, a breaker of ice at the well.
The girl leads the stranger
   Out of their legend

To a house with clock and calendar,
An almanac, births and deaths
   On the blank page of a bible.

Orfeo sits in the poorhouse with twisted hands,
   A nuisance to the strict nurses.

'See what it's brought you to, all that dancing and ale-mugs!'

'Shift your feet, I must sweep the hearth . . .'

'What fiddle? We broke an old fiddle in winter to
   Light a fire . . .'

'What lass, Maurya?
Never a woman of that name in this parish,
We've searched blank stones in the kirkyard . . .'

'Have you pennies put by for a coffin?
Well, there's parish and poor fund. You must lie
   With the paupers.'

He is torn to death, slowly,
By the tongues of the women of Voe.

XII

At last Orfeo was a length of clay on trestles.

A girl came to cover his face,
   Last look of the leal gray eyes.

The girl kissed him. The dead mouth
   Smelt of marigold, primrose, squill.

XIII

THORFINN RAGNARSON − FIDDLER
   Chirped chisel on stone.

The stone sang among silent choirs,
  The dead in the kirkyard of Voe.

It sang through a thousand suns and snowfalls.
  After three hundred summers
The stone was a blank page in the book of the dead.

*

How many skippers and ships have called at Shetland, for shelter, plunder, settlement, provisioning, between the fated landfall at Vementry 4,000 years ago and now? They have come from every nation almost in the northern hemisphere. Nowadays, great fish factory ships from Russia and the eastern European countries lie berthed beside oil ships and Shetland fishing boats at Lerwick. The Second World War saw many feats of derring-do on the black moonless sea between Norway and Shetland, when small Norwegian fishing boats launched out westwards, eluding the German patrols. Not all of them reached safety. In a Yell kirkyard, we stopped briefly at the memorial to some 'who ended their voyage in the sea's jaws', and made the coldest landfall in this austere beautiful island. The sons of the Vikings have been peaceable people for centuries: an example to the angry smoulderings otherwhere on earth. These still go on the world over: the viciousness, cruelty, vaunting, greed that were a counterbalance to the questing, courage and light-heartedness of the medieval sagas; and the 'bad-Viking' spirit had a terrible flowering in Nazism, which darkened all Europe (including Norway) with organised ruthlessness and the refinements of what Winston Churchill called 'a perverted science' so that men longed, beyond any privation or danger, to breathe the free air again.

I thought of other ships and skippers who had sailed into St Magnus Bay.

In Orkney there is a tradition that, in the First World War, a German submarine off one of the north islands sent a rubber boat ashore, and up to the village shop stepped two or three handsome young sailors, one of whom requested, in good English, eggs butter cheese milk sugar bread, and laid down good English money on the counter. What was the general merchant to know about submarines, or distinctions in naval uniform? The horn of plenty overbrimmed. Courteously the exchange was made. The sailors, with loaded sacks, went down to the shore, the perilous dinghy, and the submerged shark. It may not be an isolated interlude; did something like it take place in Shetland too?

Skippers

A skipper came to shore. *Take a few sheep. Let them look on the magic of a bronze edge. They dry fish in the wind. Let that old man tell us where the silver is.*

A skipper came to shore. *This that I am carrying is a crook. This is a cross. The spirit has its winter and its harvest time. Order the scattered stones. Let the faces of this folk shine with the light of our words. Now, boy, set the beeswax candle on a well-dressed stone. My name is Ninian, out of Whithorn of Alba in the south.*

A skipper came to shore. *Hall and barn will have to be built with lumps of stone, there are no trees. The folk are in a stone keep. This place will be called Voe. We will uproot the keep. The folk will wear our yoke. We will leave our bones in Voe.*

A skipper came to shore. *Here is a letter from the king in Norway. That you will pay him rent and taxes. My treasurer will ride from door to door. King Olaf is your father and keeper. My name is Sigurd, earl. I have a business to do out in Ireland.*

A skipper came to shore. *I bring you a great sorrow. The Orkneymen have killed our earl, Magnus. Bergfinn, why do you weep? Blind men should have no tears. The grief of Bergfinn for Magnus, saint, put brightness back into his eyes, after his blundering voyage, with candles and a piece of silver, to the grave of Magnus in Birsay. I, the skipper, saw this with the cold seeing stones in my skull.*

A skipper came to shore. A ship and a skipper and twelve men came to shore and made a scattering from Eshaness to Scalloway. Here and there were brief burials, and ministers with books. No words are reported from the mouth of that Dutch skipper. The timbers are oak. Send word to the consul of the Low Countries in Edinburgh.

A skipper came to shore. *Verlauge Butter, Käse, soviele Eier als sie geben können. Biete die sieben Münzen. Ludwig, sprich höflich in deinem Oxford Englisch . . .* * With such earth-food, the submariners rowed back to their steel shark with its lipperings, off Foula, of black sea.

*

There was one lone voyager who sailed the other way, and expected every hour – poor cripple Betty Mouat – to make a dark broken last landfall. She set out from the southern end of Shetland on the cutter *Columbine* with a basket of woollen knitwear to sell in Lerwick. It was a stormy morning in January 1886 but the *Columbine* (owned by the laird, John Bruce of Sumburgh) was manned by three knowledgeable sailors, and Betty had made the journey before. The sea-way, even in winter, was more comfortable then than the broken road going north. The skipper James Jamieson was swept to his death; his mates, turning to help him, were taken by the sea too, but they got ashore alive. The watchers on the shore saw the masterless *Columbine* driven into the smother and whelm of the North Sea, and poor Betty Mouat coffined (soon, surely) inside.

But Betty survived to become for a day or two the most famous woman in Britain, after Queen Victoria and Florence Nightingale.

* Ask for butter, cheese, as many eggs as they can give. Offer the seven gold coins. Ludwig, ask courteously in your Oxford English.

The Ballad of Betty Mouat

Old kind Betty Mouat
Setting out to Lerwick, to the shop there
With knitted shawls, stockings, bonnets.

Patient Betty with the crippled foot
In the *Columbine*'s cabin,
Wind and seamen shouting above.

Wondering Betty,
In the creaking boat, in the up-and-down sea
Under a broken mast.

Benighted Betty, in a sea cell,
With a biscuit to chew,
With a text or two for comfort.

Betty, a ghost holds the wheel now.
The skipper,
He is one with starfish and spindrift.
Women wail from sea-banks far back.

Brave Betty Mouat, she remembers
Other voyages, God-charted,
Noah with the raven and the dove,
Jonah in the whale's belly.

Ships search in wide circles, they batter
Ramsheads into the tempest.
Nothing – a gray waste, with cold fringes.

Betty wets her mouth with milk.
She thinks of New Jerusalem, no more sea.
'I aye liked tidemark and rockpools.'

Betty dreams. Ocean is a cloth
Sewn with whale, herring, lobster, jellyfish, sailor,
                    whitemaa, limpet, star
Hung on a wall in New Jerusalem,
Just like the tapestry
On Mr Bruce's hall in Sumburgh,
An undulant splendour, mothless immortal fabric.

Beautiful scriptured old woman, Betty Mouat,
Not a ghost kept the helm,
An angel herded *Columbine* through those wolf packs of ocean.
Norwegian fjord-folk
Find you, fold and fire and feed you, you with the basket
                    Clover-sweet still.

*

Always the lairds dominate from their halls, especially after Orkney
and Shetland were pawned to Scotland in 1471, in place of a dowry,
when a Danish princess married James III of Scotland. They exerted
their power more ruthlessly and arrogantly in Shetland than in
Orkney, being so much further from Edinburgh. The Stewart earls
stood closer to the throne, and their cutting down to size was a literal
thing, the axe and the block. The lesser tyrants were too petty to
touch. But for 200 years or so the islands were occupied territory,
under foreign domination. Apart from some summertime shooting
and fishing, the lairds lived much of the time in Edinburgh or
London. They wore fashionable clothes and spoke the language of
public schools. The soil of Shetland was not grained into them, and
they did not have the sea in their blood. They must have felt themselves strangers in a strange land, every bit as much as the German
overlords in Poland and Czechoslovakia; menace and peril were
everywhere, not from the mild biddable islanders, but the elements
of land and sea cried against the strangers. It is sad, reading Sir
Walter Scott's journal of his tour to the northern isles in 1814, on the
lighthouse yacht *Pharos*, in company of men of his own class who
could quote Horace and relished the bouquet of a good claret: the

contemptuous way he speaks of the islanders, as if they were a lesser breed. (Scott's novel of Orkney and Shetland, *The Pirate*, is hardly readable. His Captain Cleveland is a poor shadow of the real Stromness pirate, John Gow.) As if the upstart lairds knew that their time was limited, through their factors they wrung as much profit and rent out of the Shetlanders as they could, while their sun was high. The corn was gold but not for the Shetlanders, nor were the baskets of fish silver for the island fishermen: those coins rang in the strong-boxes in the Hall . . .

How cold and grasping the overlordship of those men was compared with the care and keeping of the Norse earls. There is one beautiful story in the *Orkneyinga Saga* that describes the plight of a poor Sumburgh fisherman who couldn't launch his boat because his mate hadn't turned up. The fisherman was just about to go home through the hungry morning when a stranger in a hood came slithering over the rocks; he offered to take the oars while the fisherman set and hauled his lines. They pushed off, but instead of skirting the strong tides of Sumburgh roost, the stranger guided the boat deeper and deeper towards the heart of the turbulence, until the fisherman, though he drew in better and stronger fish there, feared for his life. At last they made land, with a big haul of fish, and there on the beach as always were the Sumburgh women. They had wrung their hands in grief as the little boat whirled and tossed in the maelstrom; now it was a glad greedy wringing of hands over the heap of sea-treasure on the beach. The hooded stranger left them his share of the catch. Leaving them, he stumbled in the seaweed, and the women laughed. As he got to his feet he gave them an impromptu poem. (What I have written is only a remote paraphrase of the original.)

Earl Rognvald at Sumburgh

You chorus of Sumburgh women, home with you now.
Get back to your gutting and salting.
Less of this mockery.
Is this the way you treat a stranger?

Think, if this beachcomber
Hadn't strayed to this shore by chance
Your dinner tables
Would be a strewment of rattling whelkshells today.

Scornful women, never set staff or dog or hard word
On the tramp who stands at your door.
It might be an angel

Though here, with the Sumburgh querns grinding salt out there,
It was only a man in love with the sea,
Her beauty, her rages, her bounty.

– One who knows that, all masks being off,
In heaven's eye
Earl is no different from a pool-dredging eater of winkles.

They knew then, or soon afterwards, that the reckless benefactor was Earl Rognvald Kolson (nephew of Saint Magnus), one of the rarest most radiant characters in Norse history. A fragrance and a brightness linger about all Rognvald's recorded doings and sayings, as if the long sun of northern summers had been kneaded into him. He could toil at forge and anvil with the best of the blacksmiths. Few better stories have come out of the Middle Ages than Earl Rognvald's pilgrimage with fifteen ships to Jerusalem and Rome in the mid-twelfth century. At every station of the voyage – the siege of the castle in Spain after Christmas, his love lyrics to the Countess Ermengarde in Narbonne, the assault on the Moslem merchant ship and the courtesy between Moor and Norseman after the hidden gold poured like honey through the hull of the burning ship, the devout procession with palm branches in Jerusalem – the earl shows a new rich facet of himself. The sea and soil of Shetland were worked into him, bone and being.

*

The arrogant later lairds were men and they suffered and enjoyed too. I try to imagine one on his deathbed, in the great cold Hall, when

even his children are strangers to him. Sunset and evening star shine
through a tall window, and the ship waits to take the dark flood.

Will and Testament

Has come and gone again, all false smiles
Mr Milln, physician, Edinburgh.
'Your honour will yet see many a summer.'

Winter fell sudden on my strong right arm,
Whereby I could lift not tankard
Nor haul the *Merle* up the beach
Nor take John the grieve a blow across the mouth.

Yea, it was a passing frost,
The limb was a pliant branch next day.
Then I, riding among those hills
To Voe, with silver, to buy a Vementry hawk,
At summer-end, Lammas tide,
I fell, ruining, from the horse,
Knew naught till I woke in the Hall bed,
The ten eyes about me, the heirs
Considering the ghost in its barque of bone,
Their wrecked full-freighted father.

Fourteen nights, and a flood tide
Floated me free again.
I smoked my pipe, ate a hare at supper
With cups of claret, with Mr Mackie,
Went roaring about steading and boat shed,
Censured, smiled on, the six,
And folded, by candlelight, a sealed paper
To Andrew Kaye, W.S., esquire, Edinburgh.

To John, my eldest, but with small hope, this small hope, this
   Hall and all lands adjacent: may the masonry and oak not fall

too soon upon ruin, with his gamblings and wenchings. It must be, by law and custom, however fallen upon folly, the first-born inherit the Hall.

To James, second-born, my two ships *Swan* and *Wildgoose*: earnestly advising that now he look west to America for cargoes rather than to the Baltic; but (I fear me) that while his skills in navigation and calculation of limited bills of lading and ordering of seamen are well enough, his skull is too thick for wider horizons and the changing drifts of trading and commerce, and reading of compass and sea-chart necessary for such gold-seekings westward.

To Jacob, third-born: that all may be well with him, let his innocency be served and solaced and kept from scathe by Mildred and Jessie-Ann and Meg of the Shore, those good women, that have been leal and true friends to him since his first perilous coming among those rocks and quicksands at the time of his birth. And they are to have twenty gold crowns each and my gratitude should they undertake to continue faithful, as I doubt not they will, till the time of the folding of Jacob's hands: the which, Mr Milln assures me, cannot be long delayed.

To Jessica, my only daughter, who can neither spin like the shore women nor make cheeses like the hill women but plinks upon the pianoforte and turns pages from the bookshops of Edinburgh – rhymings and romances – I bequeath dowry of one thousand sovereigns, to whatever suitor first utters sweet breath under her window, in way of matrimony, for if she cannot sew sarks for him he must needs put up with sonnets and sonatas: to console him against sourness and sereness with those thousand gold shadows in the vault.

To Jason, fifth-born: the commission I have purchased for him by delicate dealings with my lords of Admiralty, upon his coming of age. For midshipmen have been known to ripen to petty lieutenants, and petty lieutenants to starred lieutenants; but further than that for my Jason I dare not look, he being dim in the uptake beyond belief: unless the deluge come again and he be set by Admiral Noah to tend the cages of raven and doo. May a good star shine for the boy, that his fond mother cherished beyond the others.

To Jeremiah, the sixth-born, I leave and bequeath the sum of one shilling sterling.

To Joshua, the last born: what gold does a man need who, I hear tell, has lately come from the seminary in Valladolid, a popish priest, and goes in secret by sea-fog and starlight among the straths and isles of the west with chalice and candlesticks in his cloak kept, where men yet speak Irish and plot against our German sovereign in their draughty keeps and castles: it is well for such a son if he gets periwinkle and prawn in his dish upon this or that shore, and he needs nothing from my treasury of rust and moth-nibbled tracery. Yet it may be that he will say a prayer for one who, having put sign and seal to this paper, is become most poor and most pitiful, and must soon set out, a pilgrim soul, upon the moor of thorns.

*

Angels: I see, to my disquiet – for nowadays I will be blamed for it – that angels have come into three of the poems ('Adam Christie', 'Betty Mouat', 'Earl Rognvald'). The word is enough to make twentieth-century readers put a book back on the shelf quickly; for we have moved far along the road of knowledge and progress, and the winged messengers in long gowns are decorations in medieval Books of Hours and in stained glass, no longer pertinent. But I am thinking about powers and presences that we are all aware of, from time to time, still; they 'disturb us with the joy of elevated thoughts', they give us 'the sense sublime of something far more deeply interfused'. I think they may be present at the making of all good poetry and music and art, compelling pure form out of the passions of dust.

Since there is no other name for those supernatural essences that exist beyond the five-gated house of the senses (though they enter and leave at will), it might be as well to write the scriptural hieroglyph 'angel'. Philosophy and science and psychology have their own names for those disturbers of the dust.

Beyond the angelic annunciations to Isaiah, Dante and Beethoven – and perhaps to Galileo, Newton, Darwin and Marx too, since all inventions and laws of physics and science and economics must exist already before they are 'discovered' – were the simple beliefs of ordinary men and women. Heaven was so thronged and tumultuous and resounding with *Glorias*, that to every soul in the brief time between birth and death an angel was appointed guardian. That sword and shield, that urging and preventing and leading on, just beyond the reach of ear and eye; the morning and evening petition carried from shore and hearth-fire to 'an house not made with hands, eternal in the heavens', open and welcoming still to their children's children when the laird's hard door would be rust and rottenness – such simple images of the essential dignity of Everyman would, I think, have been greater daily comfort than, say, reading the zodiacal prophecy in today's newspaper between the breakfast marmalade and the office computer.

*

One bleak day in May 1988 – just a month before we went to Shetland – I turned the pages of a book that almost froze the heart. Two whaling ships in the late autumn of 1836 – venturing too far after the whales (for the whale-masters must have their profits, and the skippers their bounty) – were caught in the ice, winter closed the gates upon them with groanings and clangours. The whalers' long agony began, with increasing scurvy and black depressions, lost for months. Almost daily, another body was lowered into an ice fissure, to the sun's eye. Two ships, thinly crewed by skeletal sailors, who had managed to keep the thread of breath unbroken, just, till the sun's loom kept faith with them in the south, limped into Stromness in Orkney. Earlier whaling men had been recruited in Shetland, and it may be that the same ordeal by ice was endured by them. (Betty

Mouat's father had joined a whaler; after leaving Shetland it was never seen again.)

Whalers

3 April: Their rigs ploughed, over-many hands for the fishing boats, an empty summer before them, six young men came from Delting and Yell in Shetland to the whaling boats in Scalloway, and I giving them hand-wrung greetings under the ancient ruin there, persuaded them for whale-men aboard *North Star* and they made their marks in the ledger, John Robinson, mate, witnessing the same.

5 May: This day we crossed the Arctic Circle, in very fair weather, all the crew being in good heart, the Shetlanders mingling well with English and Scotch and Irish, but for their speech, and I amid much laughter interpret. The wind fair. One Shetlander has a fiddle, the Hull-man, Smith, has a pack of cards. A Highlander, MacAdam, thumbs the pages of a small bible apart. A white mountain, Greenland, ahead.

23 June: We have touched the first slack ice. No whales sighted. The whalers *Bon Accord* of Aberdeen and *Drake* of Hull near. We hail them. Our stomachs much refreshed from cod caught by three Shetlanders from a small-boat, the biscuits and beef and cheese are become hard and tasteless. The fish a cleanness in the mouth. A Shetlander Alexander Williamson unleashes a fiddle at midnight, the disc of the sun in the north still. The men dance on a great solid floe, every cry shivers on to the horizon and breaks there in silver echoes. On this night, says another Shetlander between reel and reel, there is much rejoicing, with feasting and fires, on Shetland braes, for Johnsmas.

8 July: The first whale taken, a creature of immense displacement, a giant of bone and blubber, in shape like a drop

of rich oil. The crew work beyond midnight to mine the
monster, thirty barrels crammed with blubber, a rich stack of
whalebone. I rejoiced inwardly with a great rejoicing, I did a
small jig in the privacy of my cabin, but the whale-men sleep
exhausted in their bunks, and the fiddle is folded in a Shetland
sea-chest. I record now with regret that George Sullivan of
Sligo in Ireland and James Isbister of Voe in Shetland were
lost in the battle with the whale, the boat they were in being
overset and ice almost at once stilling their hearts, neither
being able to swim, Mr Frobisher physician confirming there
was little water in the lungs of either. They lie folded in the
coffins Walter Cairns, carpenter, has made.

1 August: Hearing that the whaler *Albion* is about to return to
Hull, I have written letters such as I had not thought to write
until this day. Firstly to my whaling-masters in Hull,
announcing with joy the red whirls and maelstroms we have
made in this sea, as whale after whale was struck and taken and
hollowed out for the gold and glory within, which will
redound to the profit of all. Second, to the mother of Jas.
Isbister in Shetland with news of her son's drowning: but she
will have recompense, more silver than ever lay on her croft
table before. Third, to my dear Susanna in Plymouth, who has
caused such grief and made such bruises on my heart, by
gentle urging on one day and cold refusals the next, so that I
cannot well know where I stand with her, but tidings of those
triumphs in this dreadful place where only heroes can trespass,
surely that must touch the quick of her in some fashion.

18 August: Capt. Angus Somerville of *Beagle* crossed two miles
over the ice to me this morning. The *Beagle* (said he) and four
other ships would return, the ice continuing to thicken and
crack and threaten, and now stars coming in clusters,
heralding winter, and many men on those ships sick with sore
gums and bleedings, he and the other skippers now consider it
wise to return before the north closes gray gates against us.
Now we are alone, but for the ship broken in the ice-jaws,

Leviathan, that yet tilts a prow, a frail line athwart the stars, five miles to north. I sense, there is a herd of whales browsing near Melville isle, and I rejoice in the departure of those faint-hearts. I have good knowledge of boreal portents and promises, my instinct has ever swung needle-true upon Arctic drifts and eddyings. The men have made a fire on the ice and they warm themselves playing at football. The fiddle is silent, the fiddler is sick with bleeding at the gums, but a month more will take us to cabbage stalls in Dundee, and to ale and oranges. Gold cures all in the end. There will be girls and dances aplenty along wharves in Hull and Gravesend, and silver splurgings, and magistrates' reprimands for midnight-merry whale-men in the gray of morning.

*

The Norse Shetlanders had no notion of tragedy. There was only Fate, which was implacable and had to be endured. The human spirit reached its height in the confrontation with Fate; it was a good thing to go into the last darkness with a few witty words that would be repeated, with wonderment and laughter, beside the winter fires for generations afterwards. A great saga character seemed to carve his own epitaph with his last breath. The women waited with stone mouths at the headlands. Not from them the wild Gaelic keenings of Irishwomen over a sea-death. More than likely some of them had taunted their men from the ale-bench to the Viking ship after seedtime. What blanched the cheeks of those adventurers was the prospect of a 'straw-death', wheezing out a few last years in a fireside chair, repeating stories of old sieges and shipwrecks that perhaps never occurred; a burden to women and grandsons. The heroes sat in Valhalla, after the timely sword had gone through them, or after they were choked with salt; and in the Hall of Death they were young and half-drunk and storied men for ever. The hunger for immortality is very ancient. The corpse of the old chief was set in a ship and the torches thrown in it; through the flame-firth he broke into timelessness.

But they had no notion of the hubris that is the essence of classical tragedy.

Perversities and misunderstandings: those threads forever intrude into the stuff of life. A signal fire is lit at the wrong time; a sheep falls over a cliff and there are black whispers about a foreign ship; two Unst girls, centuries before Betty Mouat, disappear from a holm of milk and butter into the east.

Pirates and Hollanders

Have each man a rock of hiding.

The pirates are set upon the taking of our sheep soon.

Have each man a piece of rock in the fist.

A boy heard the slow surge of the keel.

Have each man a sickle or horseshoe or flail, to greet Hollander pirates, this night black as tar with no stars.

They will take Willa and Betsy and Norna, our best yowes, they will sink their fists deep in the full fleeces and fling them into the boat. 'The men of Voe will hear no sheep flutters, wind and sea being loud along the shore.'

The men of Voe will give good welcome to the sea shepherds. Have each man a knife sharp from the whetstone.

Two days now, said the boy, that Dutch ship hidden off Vaila.

The Hollanders are to stain timbers with the blood of twenty sheep. Then the fires blown, and cleaver on carcass laid, and in the pot wine and leaves and spices. The fire-red foreign faces at midnight!

Be silent as otters, Voe men. Voe men, be watchful. The jaws of the otter sink in till a bone cracks.

The jowls and knuckles of the Hollanders are to shine with fat of mutton. They will crack bones and suck the marrow. They will wash the fragments from their teeth with gin.

But let the women keep to the lamps and fires. There will be silence, no screechings or skirlings, till I give the word. Then will be brief kissings of stone with skull.

They are to roll the fleeces up for their fat Dutch wives. They will up-anchor, full fed, before dawn.

Those that are left will up-anchor after dawn. Hungry, with a rump crew, they'll shake out sail in terror from the west cliffs of Vaila. We will lay man-moulds of Holland in a Shetland mound.

When keel scrapes shingle, I will stand and say the word 'sheepfold', we will be about them, a circle of barbed blood broaching shadows.

Very stylish their sluts would troop to the market, in our Shetland shawls and stockings.

Listen. Slow beat of oars, the song of the keel, quiet. A widow or two will howl along the quays of Antwerp when a Shetland-broken sailor comes among them.

*

Men of Voe, why is your shore dark?
Why no lamp in your windows?
Men of Voe,
Here is your friend Van Reim of Amsterdam, skipper.
I have this wonder, a telescope,

So you can see gulls over hidden shoals, very far out. It is a gift.
Women of Voe, we men of salt
Have much longing
For your cheese and oatcakes and buttermilk.
It is cold, off Hirta and Rockall.
The ganseys you knitted
Are worn out with three winters' wear.
I have doubloons in my purse.
See, the silver shines in the light of this wave.
The laird will be ignorant of this business.
Men of Voe,
I have here, in the stern, two kegs of gin.
Will you not light fires on the shore?
Will you not get out fiddles?
Men of Voe, likewise I have tobacco for your pipes,
Cones sealed with tarred twine.
Men of Voe,
What is this silence along your shore?
Has the skeleton with the scythe
Walked from house to house here, before harvest?
Their windows are dark.
May it be well with you, men of Voe,
Barn and boat and sheepfold.

*

Lives caught on a narrow grid of time and chance; Fate bequeathed a certain dignity; the Christianity brought by the Celtic fathers infused a sweetness into the generations. As late as two centuries ago the Shetlanders' calendar, especially round about the darkest time of the year, Yule, was starred with ceremonies of great beauty: the baking of little sun-cakes – Yule brunnies – on the hearth; the crofter's visit to the byre-fast beast carrying an ox skull with a lighted candle in a hollow of it; the straw crosses over the lintels of barn and byre; the hands withheld from work at quernstones, oar, spinning-wheel, from Thomasmas (the solstice day) to the end of Christmas; 'so holy and so blessed is the time'; the dropping of three live embers into a basin of water, in which all the family would wash and afterwards put on clean clothes (the dwelling-house had been swept and garnished already); the children with their candles at the breakfast table on Christmas morning, a feast of light, and the whisky bowl brought from mouth to mouth by the man of the house (even the children had to put their lips to the essence of summer) . . . That beautiful winter masque was still going on three centuries after the Reformation. The minister up in his cold manse, powerful as he was, turning the pages of a concordance, could do little about it . . . Most extraordinary of all, the Mother of God was still, after so long a banishment, a living lovely presence in the crofts. For the grandmother, on Helya's Night (20 December) went among the sleeping children softly chanting: 'Mary Midder, haad de haund / Ower aboot for sleeping-baund, / Haad da lass and haad da wife, / Haad da bairn a' its life. / Mary Midder, haad de haund / Roond da infants o' oor land.'

Foolishness, to try to echo even such a perfection of prayer and poetry. After our return from Shetland, I attempted a variation. I ought to have known better. Instead of the seamless purity of the original, I was left with a few tatters, after a morning of sweat over the writing pad in Rackwick, Hoy. (Rackwick is a place where inspiration comes, if it is to come at all.) But I brought the fragments back to Stromness, and after a session or two of invisible mending, a poem of sorts emerged.

Yule Candle

'Mary Mother, we women of Voe
Bring one small flame from many peat-flames to a long
    Gray column of beeswax
For you, this Yule night.'

The children stand about that light in the sill,
    A winter petal, pure-mouthed.

A lass kneels in the lantern-dappled byre.

The bride of last winter sits by a cradle.
The boatman's boy hangs on a wave of sleep, the candle
   His mast-lamp.

A widow's sun-cakes lie on the hearthstone.
Her hands are folded
Except to shore up wax in the weeping candle.

An old one says, 'This heart-fire
Will be cinders soon.'
The blessing laves her, bone and winter breath.

Then all those women:
Star of the Sea, shine for the fishermen of Voe.

*

The story of a place must have a beginning somewhere. 'Very deep is the well of time', wrote Thomas Mann; and the searcher for a sure origin must go deeper and deeper, and the one stone of foundation forever eludes him. We know that there were Shetlanders before the Norsemen, but little is known for sure, for they left no writings, only buried and scattered stones, at Clickimin and Jarlshof. Fragments of their stories, of their gods and demons, lingered long in the folklore of Shetland. But folklore withered fast in the airs of Calvinism and compulsory education, and though there is much ransacking nowadays for every fragment of story, it is certain (I think) that most of the treasure is lost. We will never know, either, how the very early Shetlanders spoke; whether their rhythms and intonations were like 'the song' of modern Shetland speech. It is probable that they were close to each other. 'The song' takes small account of time or space. Listening to Norwegian fishermen in a Stromness pub, they might be men from Papay or Hoy, though a thousand years and hundreds of miles sunder them. Tongue and mouth attune themselves to the same boreal winds and seas, the same music is woven across all the lan-

guages of the north. I think modern Shetlanders must speak very like
the women who laughed at Earl Rognvald on the slippery sea-path,
and very like the builders of Jarlshof. It is a beautiful unique way of
speaking; and it is still there, though education and radio, television,
pop singers and American films assault it ceaselessly. Was ever such
nonsense as 'accepted English'? Only a shallow snobbery and a
shamefaced desire to conform would try to ape that curt and ugly
speech.

Somewhere this essay must begin; somewhere end. Words written
on parchment, in Bergen, Norway – we could make an arbitrary
beginning there. Norway in, say, the tenth century, is full of young
restless men. Sailing among the hundreds of small islands that fringe
the eastern seaboard of Norway, they have over generations become
acquainted with sail and oar. Now they have laid in their yards the
ocean vertebrae, the keel; they can go striding into the deeper ocean,
they become acquainted with vaster sea rhythms, they can read the
stars. Westwards: that magic spell has haunted the tribes of earth for
ever, it seems. In the west, far in the west there are richness and fer-
tility undreamed of. The first seekers falter out, out and under the
horizon; many ships are never heard of again, the storm has swallowed them, or the sea-dragon, or they have gone over the roaring
cataracts at the world's end. But most come back; they have made
landfall in Faroe, in Shetland, Orkney, Caithness, Iceland – fertile
shore fringes, peaceable folk in stone houses with sheep and cows,
bald-heads who ring a bell eight times a day in their community bede-
houses . . . A man might set a steethe-stone there, and plough and
take a wife at last. But first the harrying, the breaking and plunder-
ing, after the swift descent out of dawn-light; then back to the longships, with a pig for the roasting, with bits of silver and tapestry for
the skipper's hoard, with a chant to the cold-eyed gods, with an
urgent homesickness for fjords and mountains. But always, the
memory of fertile hills (Orkney) and deep rich fishing-grounds
(Shetland): they should not be forgotten, if the homestead in
Trondheim, say, or Hardanger, had too many heirs after a deathbed.
So they sailed home, with a new saga for winter nights, and a promise
to brighten the eyes of boys too young for sea.

The settlers came, wrenching what land they wanted from a folk grown mild with peace. Very late in the time of settlement came Hold Bergfinn, having answered more or less satisfactorily the questions of the king's scribe in Bergen.

A Scroll in Bergen

Of what allegiance art thou?
Norway and Harald with the long golden hair: king. I am his man.

And what seekest in this ante-chamber of the king's hall in Bergen?
Land in the west: a title.

Of what extent and kind and quality is this land in the sea westward?
Sufficient for a strong man and his wife and three sons, two of them children that play with shells and reed-boats, but the eldest has strong arms for oar and fish-line and plough, and three servants, and a hawk and a young horse.

Hast thou heard of this land in Shetland from the mouth of a seaman (many of them weave imaginings from the loom of the mouth), or has a skipper drawn for thee chart and sea-route?
I have sailed to and from the place, and measured a sufficient bound with eyes and feet, and left the blood of a Celtic farmer on a threshold there.

This place, Voe in Shetland, is it fruitful? Will a large barn be necessary, or a mill? Can it harbour the strength of two oxen? Will a girl draw combs from the hive there, and butter and cheese from a docile herd?
There is but barren hill, a pasturage for sheep and diggings of dark winter fire. The household will not blow into blue fists in winter.

Wert thou not better, Hold Bergfinn, to bide at home with thy fifth of

*the inheritance up in Espeland? – For the strength of thy people is
drawn from that rock and cloud and corn-nurture, many generations
now?*

   I would be free of the four hard brothers and the sharp tongue
   of the mother. My sons are not to starve on three sour stony
   patches.

Will there not be many a hungry day in the east?

   A voe, blue tongue of sea, has sung to me among those hills:
   beyond a black isle Vementry and a red island, there are
   courses of fish that fail not, cod and haddock, at all seasons. In
   that voe my small boats will not lack for caulk or clinker. My
   three sons cried out with the sharp joy of those waters.

There are greener places in Shetland than Voe, that place, surely?

   The farmlands in the south: the boundary stones have been set
   by strong farmers, a generation ago.

*Hold Bergfinn, what rent will you pay for that bleakness and danger
at Voe and Vementry?*

   What is fair and true, no more. The taxman, twice a year, will
   have a good seat at board and fire. The name of the king will
   not lack for honour. We will hold the voe mouth against
   Vikings and Irishmen.

1988

Shetland Diary

28 May 1988

Wake to clogged bronchial tubes. The cold worse.

Shetland: unlikely.

Simon Chirgwin is due for last day of filming; a short profile to go along with a recital of my verse at St Magnus Festival, midsummer.

A pity, a lovely day outside. Phone Simon Chirgwin: 'not up to filming' . . . Filming was to have been among Folk Festival fiddlers at the Braes Hotel, and at the book launch for Fiona MacInnes' book of poems, *To Step Among Wrack*, at the Pier Arts Centre, Stromness.

Phone surgery. Dr Johnstone comes, prescribes oxytetracycline – that drug has been a good friend often in the past. We agree it might be best to forget about Shetland. But tomorrow morning will tell.

Also, I wanted very much to hear Professor W. Gillies (Celtic Studies, Edinburgh University) talking about Jacobite songs – an item in the Folk Festival.

Irene Worth – visiting Orkney for the first time, with Kulgin Duval and Colin Hamilton – gave me after supper at Tam and Gunnie's house last night a copy of Primo Levi's *The Periodic Table*. This cold isn't good for reading either, but I enjoy a few pages of this writer who's new to me.

Elizabeth Bevan comes with a cluster of primroses.

Visitors in the evening: (1) Valerie Gillies, poet, wife of Professor Gillies, with a box of biscuits (parkins) she's baked herself. Delightful company; (2) Kulgin Duval, to see how it is with me – I was due to sail to Shetland with Kulgin and Gunnie tomorrow, Sunday; (3) Renée Simm.

I make tea, but every mouthful brings out a gush of sweat . . .

Take yellow 'oxytet' tablets religiously – one, two, three, four – at four-hour intervals.

A first parcel of *Portrait of Orkney* comes by post. Why do my own new-published books depress me so much when I'm off colour?

Before early bed – 10.30 – throw a few things, without conviction, into two cases.

A broken sleep.

29 May

My father used to say, 'If you can eat and smoke, there's not that much wrong with you . . .' I can't any more apply the tobacco test, but I put down an egg and a roll for breakfast. And truly, I feel better.

Dr J. comes early, sees no reason why I shouldn't go.

I have a feeling this indisposition, like so many of my ailments, is psychosomatic: there is a deep-rooted aversion to do anything new or go anywhere among strangers. It's dangerous to have feet and wings and be a voyager. So, all my recent poetry has been about voyaging. Strange.

Tam drives us to the pier.

Gunnie sees to the purchase of tickets, etc.

The huge bulk of the *St Sunniva* at the pier. (Well, she's twice as big as our little Pentland Firth ferryboat, *St Ola*.)

A thin gray tissue of sea-haar.

The boat leaves at noon.

Gunnie, Kulgin and I find a sheltered coign with a view over the sea. Tourists everywhere; what more exasperating than the trivia of tourist-talk? We move to a quieter corner.

No wonder folk feeling poorly sought the sea air in the nineteenth century and earlier – it was a great discovery, two centuries ago. I feel better already.

The fog thickens imperceptibly. The sea is calm. The ship throbs on steadily northwards. The island of Westray slips by like a ghost.

The sea has put a thin crust of salt on our lips. In a corner of the bar we cure that with cans of export. A black-bearded Shetlander, Charlie Johnston, joins us for an hour. In Shetland, he says, the red cans of McEwan's Export are called 'Shetland roses'. Once, a few years ago, says C. J., we met in Stromness, at my nephew Erlend's house, when C. J. was in a visiting Scalloway football team. C. J. returns to his table of friends in the far corner of the lounge.

We get hungry, all three, at the same time; twice; and enjoy lunch (ham) and, later, supper (steak pie) in the diner. The stewards cheerful and obliging, white-jacketed; the Aberdeen accent predominant. The food not expensive.

The *Sunniva* pulses on northwards, steadily, into thickening fog. We've missed Fair Isle.

Time at sea, as T.S. Eliot noted, is altogether different from the time of clock-makers, clerks and computers. The mind is caught up in a lulling swooning rhythm, it measures by horizons rather than hours or miles, it seems adrift on the brim of eternity. (All Orkney churchyards are beside the sea, where time encroaches on everlastingness.) It seemed to me we still had a long way to go. Gunnie said, 'We're there.' We couldn't see Lerwick, it was lost in such a thick gout of fog: only the pier and a woman waiting beside a red car.

This was our hired car. Gunnie had arranged everything. The car-hirer said no planes had landed at Shetland airport that day, on account of the fog.

Gunnie drove us north through the blindfold island. A stream of cars passed, headlights probing the fog, going towards Lerwick. 'Workers from Sullom Voe,' said Gunnie. (Sullom Voe is the oil terminal at the northern tip of the island.)

We turned left down a side road. 'Wrong road,' said Gunnie, who's been this way before. 'It's the fog' . . . The next road, with rocks and lochans beside it, was the right road. The car went down, slowly. Kulgin got out and opened a sheep gate. 'We're being met, that's good,' said Gunnie. A car sat outside the cottage we had rented.

Our hosts, John and Liz Somerville, gave us a good welcome. They live in Brae village, where J. S. is janitor at the school and Liz teaches music there. I knocked back a glass of schnapps, that had a chthonic palaeolithic taste to it, but sent warmth branching everywhere along the veins.

John Somerville showed me my bedroom, a pleasant airy room. He showed me how to work the many electrical appliances, including one that would wake me in the morning and make a cup of tea. He might as well have tried to teach me the elements of Chinese or the higher mathematics . . .

The journey was over. 'The achieve of the thing!' . . . Last night,

I didn't think it would be possible . . . One-two-three-four oxytetra-cyclines; the infection and the cure met and melled in battle, silently and interiorly.

30 May

Kulgin has been up since 7.30 a.m., lighting the range, fetching coal, collecting eggs from the hens.

We have fresh free-range eggs for breakfast, each egg in a little quilt, and nestled in a basket.

The oxytetracycline; devoutly observe the discipline of the cure. One yellow tablet with the breakfast tea.

There are many things we must buy. Gunnie drives us to the little village of Voe, three or four miles away. That hill road to Grobsness, that we drove down last night! – I'm slightly awed by the steepness of it, and the sheer drop on one side, now that the wind has blown the mist away. Mr Adie's little shop and post office in Voe sells every-thing. All I need this morning are two writing pads and stamps. Gunnie and Kulgin stock up with groceries, then climb the stair to look at a range of Shetland tweeds, woven in Voe. I sit in the car and begin to write a dark prose-poem. (That bronchial shadow is still shivering through blood and bone.)

On past the village of Brae, littered with modern bungalows deposited there by the golden wash of oil. A beautiful sea loch. The island is thrust through, from the Atlantic on one side and the North Sea on the other, by those gleaming voes.

There is one isthmus, just beyond Brae, so narrow that you can stand on the road and throw a stone into the North Sea on one side and into the Atlantic on the other.

Gunnie and Kulgin walk along the cliffs in a cold wind. I sit in the car, muffled in that long gray scarf an anonymous Norwegian woman sent me a dozen years ago, and work on the prose-poem. No good – the images petered out in a marsh.

They are interesting, those fragments of failed writing. They are rarely lost beyond recall. They have taken one wrong turning in the labyrinth of the imagination. It may be a day, a month, a year, before they find the skein that takes them to the open sun-smitten door. The worst thing a writer can do is lose patience, get into a panic, drive the image from blank wall to dead end; at last cancel the whole delicate seeking with a stroke of the pen . . . The poem knows its own way, and will find it out. Let it have its delicate pilgrimage. I think this must apply to all writing and all writers: more than one isolate individual is at work; an ancient chorus urges, warns, celebrates, all the poets through the centuries who have worked in the tradition. Of course there are poems and stories that get lost beyond hope, but the marks of loss were on them from the beginning, and no bandagings or crutches, proddings, urgings or cajolings will see them through. The chorus has turned away. This is my experience.

All I knew was, this cold afternoon in the middle of a black moor, my prose-poem had got bogged down.

We have tea and scones in Hillswick Hotel. Kulgin delights in people and situations. Almost at once he is at home with strangers, treasuring every word they speak, weaving speculations about them for hours and days afterwards. Whereas I sit, half turned away, indifferent really, but touched to a faint warmth if someone actually speaks to me.

The energy of Kulgin and Gunnie! They've walked along the Eshaness crags all afternoon in the cold wind; now they go to explore the beach below Grobsness.

Grobsness is littered with ruined crofts. One big roofless house, the Haa, where – they say – the laird's man lived.

The luxury of stretching out in this comfortable bed, with *The Periodic Table*, in the long light of a summer evening.

Hunger: sign of returning health. We eat mince patties and potatoes and fried bananas, with cans of lager.

Today we've seen the bones of the landscape.

31 May

Sun.

I write my weekly short column for the *Orcadian*: about sailing to Shetland, of course. Also my weekly letter to Gypsy the cat in Deerness, Orkney.

Scan yesterday's prose-poem again: only a shadow moves, here and there.

The greatest joy for a poet is when his poem comes off first time: it must be one of the supreme delights.

We must go to Lerwick of course, the centre and capital.

The town looks prosperous and handsome in the sun: compared to tranquil Stromness, that has drifted out of the stream of history and commerce.

Such a kind welcome we get in the *Shetland Times* bookshop, from Mrs Sandison, the manageress. There we meet Bobby Tulloch, naturalist, whose book *Bobby Tulloch's Shetland* has just been published, and with him a good-looking young woman from Macmillan the publishers. That makes three of us with new books: *Bobby Tulloch's Shetland*, Gunnie's *The Shetland Story* (with Liv Schei), and my *Portrait of Orkney*.

Jonathan Wills, editor of the *Shetland Times*, sends down a photographer, Dennis Coutts, and we three pose in a group for a newspaper picture, each holding his/her book. (I feel foolish in those circumstances.)

But everyone so pleasant.

Kulgin has been out buying a bottle of Grouse whisky, for our night-caps. He wanders into the bookshop, asks Gunnie for 20p, having been that much short in the licensed grocer's – then hesitates – returns – and thinks he might require another 10p . . . We introduce him to Mrs Sandison. He is, he tells her, a 'second-hand bookseller', and I have an image of a down-at-heel selling bundles of old Penguins from a barrow at a city street corner . . . The fact is, Kulgin deals in rare limited editions: university libraries from all over the world – Japan and America – ask Kulgin and Colin to obtain the almost unobtainable for them in the way of old precious books.

We twirl the postcard stand. I buy ten.

I'm still too tired to trek about the shops of Lerwick. While Gunnie and Kulgin get the errands, I sit in the car at the pierhead and write in my red notebook. This new prose-poem is about the ima-gined beginnings of Up-Helly-Aa, the great Shetland fire festival that takes place at the end of January.

It comes easily. It seems OK – it won't be possible to say for sure for a month or so.

Home via Scalloway and Weisdale Voe – sweeps of haar and sun – loveliness beyond compare; lambs, masses of marigolds, spring greet-ing summer . . . Late meal at Grobsness: pickled herring and tatties, bread and cheese and beer. The two cats. Bed early, tired, 10.30.

1 June

Gunnie and Kulgin go to Sumburgh airport at the south tip of Shetland to meet Colin Hamilton, who has had to go home to Loch Tummel from Orkney, before joining us today in Shetland.

How the memory tricks you! I had thought eleven days of unbro-ken sun followed that first fog-laden day. I see, re-reading my diary,* that today was overcast. 'Late evening, the sky lifts a little, but no sun.'

Alone by the big fire Gunnie has lit, write eight postcards and a third Shetland prose-poem, about the press-gang – it seems OK.

Gunnie brings news: George Peterson, English teacher at Brae, wants to visit for a half-hour this evening. G. P. duly turns up with John and Liz Somerville. He is a native of Papa Stour, and has a theory that St Magnus lived in that island. He has brought a hand-written manuscript for me to read, a twelfth-century story of Papa Stour and its Norse inhabitants, his own work. Of course I'll read it; but I don't like to tell G. P. that partly I've come to Shetland to get away from manuscripts, books, writers. G. P. a very pleasant man. All seven of us sit round the big fire and sip glasses of whisky and talk

---

* George kept a private diary for his last twenty-five to thirty years. He seems not to have neglected it during the Shetland sojourn, though the entries would have been much shorter than those in the 'public' Shetland diary.

three hours away; we almost send the sun down the sky. G. P. invites us to attend a performance of the famous Papa Stour sword dance at Brae school on Friday.

I should have said that this is no primitive island house. There are books and tapes everywhere, musical instruments, wall posters, heaters, electric gadgets, hot and cold water, radio and TV.

The rocky promontory, sea and sky, the islands on the horizon, are what they have always been: eternal presences.

There must be a feeling of flux, instability, even in a deep-founded house.

A northern hunger is on us, not having eaten since noon or thereabout. We stay the hunger with bacon, eggs, cauliflower, good white tatties, beer.

2 June

Gunnie drives us to a broken coastline teeming with ewes and lambs, mostly black. How many photographs? A hundred? I should think, more. She goes into a long trance-like dance of picture-taking, on the rocky hill among the lambs that seem to be mostly black.

On the road to Walls, we meet old friends of Gunnie, Sandy and Mary Fraser, farmers, of Culswick. Introductions. 'Yes,' they tell Gunnie, 'Henry's expecting you!' There, soon, at a little jetty, Henry Anderton and his metal boat. We pile in. Again, memory is a liar, it's a cold day, and the sea is cold, and the big Victorian pile on the little steep island of Vaila, built by a Victorian ancestor of Henry, is cold. But Henry piles coal on the stove and pours us generous whisky. (I for one never needed a whisky more, for the ghost inside me is quaking in its cage of bones.) The others go with Henry to visit the crags of Vaila, and I crouch over the stove and in the whisky glow think it a pleasant and an easy thing to let another prose-poem flow out. Bacchus and Apollo are not really friends. What I wanted to write was a lilting lyrical piece about the first fiddle in Shetland, that land of fiddlers. Nothing came right: the images tangled with one another and, tugged this way and that, became hard knots.

At last, voices in the hall. The walkers were back, having spanned the small steep island and been suitably impressed with cliffs and horizons and wild birds.

The big house on Vaila is an extraordinary Gothic place, with a great high dining hall hung with ancestral portraits and a minstrels' gallery above. Henry says he might sell it soon. He might go to live in a house nearby, on the main island.

At present, he is a salmon farmer – that new industry has grown very quickly all over the west and north of Scotland recently. One can't help but wonder how, in time, the quality of farmed salmon will be affected, now that their mysterious seven-year circuit from the hatching home river out among the salt cold North Atlantic streams, then back inerrably to the same fresh source that bred them, to spawn and die there, is cut out. The salmon peregrination must be akin, somehow, to the force that drives the blood through the veins and keeps the stars in their courses.

There was nothing insipid about the large salmon Henry Anderton set on a salver on his broad kitchen table. We ate it, hunger honed by sea air, with salad and white wine. I forgot about my second ruined poem.

Then Henry boated us back, not the short crossing, but right round Vaila, through a natural rock arch of primitive and awesome savagery such as you find nowhere in tame Orkney. I feel, as the metal boat champs the sea, spume-snorting, and a cold Atlantic wind comes at us, and we go in under the shadow of the black cliffs of Vaila, the way an average eighteenth-century man felt about mountains, crags and torrents: that a town street with folk coming and going, a house and a decent garden of herbs and roses, a fire and book and viol – these were the gifts that society had wrested from the mindless ageless savagery of Nature, a precious perilous heritage. (Wordsworth then was still in his cradle.)

As Henry's boat turned the last cliff buttress, though, a small wild bird was beginning to cry in the spirit.

Foula, the most remote of the Shetlands, was in the north-west distance. (An uncle of mine that I never knew was once the resident missionary there.)

Back at Grobsness, John Somerville arrived with a gift of four trout he'd just caught.

It was too late to light the fire.

I thought I would sleep at once, after such a day. Instead, in my bedroom, I wrestled with 'The First Fiddle' for two hours. I convinced myself I was winning, I would win, I *must* win. Strange, the relationship of poet and poem. The poet is not really the master at all. The poem is the real shaper; it will not stand being coerced or driven. In the end it says, coldly, *Destroy me, don't let me go through to the market-place misshapen and hirpling.* And the poet who has spent so much blood and tears pleads, *Truly you are beautiful, you will be beautiful soon.* If he's wise, he does what the poem wants: tears it up and gives it to the wind, burns it. A poem exists in its purity, as the perfect statue is hidden in the rock. Silence is best: poetry is forever striving for the unattainable perfection of silence.

3 June

The fine new school in the village of Brae. There, at noon, seven boys perform the Papa Stour sword dance, in white shirts and dark trousers, each holding a sword. George Peterson, their English teacher, fiddles. The dancers make intricate patterns, crossing and interweaving in a masque of combat. They are the seven champions of Christendom – St George of England, St James of Spain, St Denis of France, St David of Wales, St Patrick of Ireland, St Anthony of Italy, St Andrew of Scotland. St George of England chants the verse, the other saints enact a ballet of vaunt and battle. In the end, the embattled swords form a star of peace, and the music ends.

The very strange thing is that this ancient exotic ballet should have been performed in a remote Shetland island, Papa Stour, and there alone. It is surely not indigenous, it bears all the marks of an English seasonal market-place dance from the Middle Ages. St George of England is the leader of the dance, the other dancers seem to do his bidding. What was its origin: a stylised crusade? If so, the Shrovetide dancers made it a secular masque, with the star of Venus ending the story. (The crusaders flocked back to their sweethearts and wives all over Europe.)

> Mars does rule, he bends his brows
> He makes us all aghast,
> After the few hours that we may stay here,
> Venus will rule at last.
> Farewell, farewell, brave gentles all
> That herein do remain.
> I wish you health and happiness
> Till we return again.

Sir Walter Scott prints one version of the text in his Notes to *The Pirate*. He quotes Olaus Magnus: 'moreover, the northern Goths and Swedes had another sport to exercise youth withall, that they will dance and skip among naked swords and dangerous weapons . . . And this play is showed especially about Shrovetide . . .' So obviously the dance, with trivial variations, must have been known all over Europe. And if the dance was brought to Shetland from Scandinavia, it must have been at some time anglicised, considering the style of the verse – both awkward and pliable, as is the way of popular ballads and plays – and in the primacy accorded to St George of England. We might hazard a guess: some English-educated laird put his stamp upon a medieval European masque. And there, in a lonely North Atlantic island, it survived for generations, for centuries.

And George Peterson is still blowing the embers into flame.

They looked after us well in the school at Brae. We sat down to a lunch of beef olives and pudding and coffee, with the voices and faces of pupils coming and going, casting sidelong glances at us, like shy seabirds.

Then north we drove to the oil terminal at Sullom Voe, and the high quadruple flames.

Then Lerwick again. I still have no energy to go shopping, but sit in the car and write another prose-poem 'Birth'. It flows from start to finish without a break. A delight. To the writer, anyway.

Jonathan Wills, editor of the *Shetland Times* (and forby broadcaster, socialist, doctor of philosophy, one-time student-rector at Edinburgh University, author and illustrator of delightful children's books like *The Travels of Magnus Pole* and *Linda and the Lighthouse*) has invited us to visit him in Bressay just across the sound from Lerwick. The ferry takes five minutes to cross. Jonathan meets us in a yellow van that has seen better days. We get driven to his house, a converted Manse beside the sea, its yard strewn with wrack. We don't see J.'s wife and two younger children; they've sailed to Papa Stour for the day. His eldest, Magnus (twelve years old) is there, with a report card from the Senior School in Lerwick, which Jonathan scans and finds satisfactory, in the midst of cooking for us a very delicious meal of monkfish chowder. (Fishermen are dragging ever more exotic fish from the depths – until a decade ago it was only cod and haddock and herring, occasionally skate and halibut.) I have a great thirst; maybe I put too much salt on the beef olives at Brae – maybe the oxytetracycline tablets – maybe the recurrence, on vacation, of old alcoholic smoulders. Anyway, I find myself drinking Jonathan's white wine like lager, strenuous-throated . . . Jonathan drives us, with some pride, round this beautiful island: the place is quick with summer birds. Noss: the bird sanctuary, a steep bastion, bird-fretted. Gunnie and Colin have a date with that place, later in the week.

There's still too much lead in my bones even to walk the mile to the ruined pre-Reformation chapel of St Mary's. It would have been a good penance, the effort. I sit in the car and write four postcards. Gray clouds pile up in the west: will the weather break soon?

We return on the 10.15 p.m. ferry. (The ferries come and go continually, at short intervals: a good cheap service.) A young man is stretched out in the cabin below, tranced with Barleycorn. Who will dare wake him at Lerwick? We see him later at the pier, on his feet, a bit dazed still, talking to two policemen. He is quiet and 'on the hoof', as the old Orkney whisky-drinking farmers used to say. So the policemen leave him to find his way.

We are all very tired, back in Grobsness.

The wrecked poem about the first fiddler: why can't I let it rest in peace? Note in diary: 'May yet save yesterday's prose-poem' . . .

4 June

It is beyond saving, that piece about the first Shetland fiddle. But a new keel may be laid, and a poem tremble and vibrate with life.

When Gunnie, Kulgin and Colin have driven north-west to the crags and wild places, I remain behind at Grobsness with the cats and set about laying the new keel. At once everything goes wrong, falls apart, is approximately pieced together and nailed. The shape is wrong, there are too many knots and cross-grains, the boards are not fluent enough, there are flaws and creakings and strains in the poem. In vain you try to convince yourself, 'One phrase may come – will come – is certain to come; then the whole poem will cluster about it, exact and singing' . . . The magic doesn't happen. I must face it – the work is radically wrong. The muse of the Shetland fiddle is doing nothing to help me.

I work away till the middle of the afternoon; then have a bath and go to bed in the lonely house. I finish Primo Levi's *The Periodic Table*: 'brilliant writing', I note in my diary, '– my own little myths seem so unreal and faded' . . .

Suddenly there comes another hybrid (prose-poem? story?). I rush to get it down in the red notebook, the words come so fast I can hardly control the impetus and urgency, I herd them on to the page, helter-skelter: an old man of some authority under the earl in Scalloway would marry a Voe maiden . . . Into the midst of this torrent – the torrent has emerged not out of inspiration but out of a kind of rage at my earlier incompetence – the wanderers return, at 8 p.m.

'Now,' says Gunnie, 'get ready, we're invited to a ceilidh at Skeld' . . .

To Skeld we drive, to the Smoke-house there where Dave and Debbie Hammond greet us well. Most of the other guests are there already. There's an enchanting little two-year-old girl, Gabi. The table is spread with seafood. 'Oh,' says Debbie to me, 'maybe this is the wrong food for an Orcadian – you must be tired of fish' . . . Who could tire of the smoked salmon that comes from the Hammonds' own Smoke-house? And even if fish happened not to be to your taste that night, there was Foula lamb, very succulent, a flavour unique on earth. And whisky and wine and beer. (Having suffered the threefold ravages of whisky–wine–beer in my youth, many a time, I study moderation tonight.) One of the guests, Cluny, gave out constant streams of Lowland Scots wit and laughter that seemed to me to be far better than some celebrated TV stars in the same genre. Music and song and laughter; Dave on the fiddle, Cluny on the guitar, a shy visiting girl in Shetland on an archaeology 'dig', on a pipe. They urge me to sing, but I can't sing the Edwardian ballads under a certain level of tipsiness; so I only make a limping contribution with a few half-remembered verses. Cluny improvises with impromptu words. Henry Anderton of Vaila turns up and Ted who is painting the walls of the big house of Vaila. Wilma is there, an ex-art student. And Sandy and Mary Fraser turn up, farmers from nearby, and Emma and Osla their young daughters. Wilma urges me to visit Greece. Ted tells me that once he wrote a poem.

'The nicht drave on wi' sangs and clatter / And aye the ale was growan better' . . . We left that merry hospitable house at 2.30. The dawn was coming up, a morning like the first morning of time, the early light on the voes.

Kulgin retains the essence of an evening like this, and gives it back for days to come, like stored honey. Already, in the car going back to Grobsness, the first combs are filling up . . . Remembered laughter; breath-taking beauty at every new corner of the road.

The diary: 'Broad morning, climbing into bed 3.30 a.m.'

5 June

A quiet day, Sunday, mostly alone.

Gunnie, Kulgin and Colin go to Noss in Bressay, to see the birds on the cliffs.

Grobsness caught in a loop of sun.

I write four letters and a postcard to Gypsy the cat in Deerness (I write to Gypsy every week).

Lunch alone – cheese, a biscuit, a bannock, an apple, a can of Tennent's lager.

In bed some of the afternoon. It seems to me the door opens and someone comes in and walks along the corridor. 'They're back' . . .

But they don't come back till mid-evening. Everyone is tired. James Galway and his flute on a compact disc. Not much point in lighting the fire. We kindle to a dram, instead.

All in bed before midnight.

6 June

Sun morning to night, unclouded: and a cool wind that seems to go about in a wheel. When the wind gets too cool, I go inside and write another metreless rhymeless poem, a kind of chorus of Shetland women: it comes in a single flush. (Not the Shetland women of today, of course: 'timeless' voices.)

Kulgin and Colin walk over the steep hill to Voe. Gunnie drives me. We all forgather at the shop in Voe village.

Then west in the car to a little rock-sheltered coign on the shore opposite Vementry island. The wind cool, still; we shelter behind a rock for our picnic. The grass covered with squill, a fret of sweet blue flowers. An oyster-catcher protests, again and again. It is a most enchanting place. Our picnic is ham and cheese rolls and cans of lager. A loveliness beyond compare again – even Orkney has nothing to show like it. The wind has blown the sea into little formal waves, blue white-crested like in Botticelli: a dancing heraldry. 'I could die in a place like this,' I tell Gunnie as we walk together back to the car.

Miles on, the car stops at a farm. We get a good welcome from Sandy and Mary Fraser and young Osla. They've been busy all day and are tired, and still there's Buttercup the cow to milk; but guests, in the fine northern tradition, must have a fair greeting, and drinks are poured for us. Kulgin is delighted with his – a 'rusty nail' (Drambuie and ordinary whisky mixed). Mary and merriment go together. Gunnie remembers being a guest at the nearby Methodist chapel when Mary's sister was married there in October last. So we drive there. Like many Nonconformist chapels, it is an ugly building. Beauty has always been suspect to those austere beliefs – beauty of ceremony and architecture, of ritual and image – perhaps because they distract the mind from contemplation of the purity of the word. Osla and Mary play a few hymn tunes on the harmonium. I think, 'What a loss rural and seagirt Shetland is to the Catholics!' For Catholic ceremonies enrich the lives of people who get their livelihood from the elements. The beauty of ritual must have been torn from the people by the Scottish incomers of the late sixteenth century. But here and there fragments of the old faith lingered, and there is still a residual courtesy and beauty in the lives of those who

live from the land and the sea. Will another generation of technology
and television see the brashness and uniformity of the Global Village
informing all our lives, Shetland with Shanghai and San Francisco
and the Sahara? The signs are not promising.

There is a wet depression on the floor of the valley at Culswick
where once there was a little loch, with reeds and swans and ducks.
A wave breached the thin barrier, one storm generations ago, and the
sweet loch water flowed out into the Atlantic. A woman had gone visiting from a loch-side cottage, and came home a few days later to find
a seeping desolation: it must have been like a death to her, or worse.
The places of one's childhood become a part of one, the forms and
textures are ingrained. For the people of that district it must have
seemed that a kindly guardian, the loch, had been taken from them.
The swan had lost its home, a mirror had fallen from the hand of the
firmament and broken.

'You must come in, for coffee,' says kind Mary on the way back
from the Methodist chapel.

But we are tired, again, after such a good day. We must be getting
home.

Another rapturous welcome we get from Tammy the little many-
coloured cat! She rolls in the dust. She follows us in.

The air has been on the move all day, in its circuits. Maybe this
wind is keeping the rain away.

7 June

To the northernmost islands, Yell and Unst.

Light on waters glittering; the ferry.

The general merchant's at Yell pier. In a lovely archaic accent, the
shop woman tells us directions.

We drive to the Old Haa, seat of the former lairds, the Mowat
family. A generous welcome from the custodian Mrs Garioch, a
retired schoolteacher; they are making a local museum out of the
laird's home. Mrs Garioch mentions that she has read my books, in
such a way that the mind's gray ember glows.

On then, briefly, to visit Mary-Ellen Odie (Bobby Tulloch's sister) and her shepherd husband: a highly intelligent couple. Mary-Ellen guards her beloved garden from year-long storms. There, at the end of the yard, is a more ancient stone guardian, a Celtic broch. Two collies frisk around in the sun, the older one seems to like me, which is strange.

From Yell to Unst, another ferry, a brief crossing among sea-glitters.

The very names of the islands seem end-of-the-world names.

Yell had seemed to be a dark peat-hill on residual rock.

Unst is greener, unexpectedly.

Another picnic on the beach at Lund: rolls with ham and cheese, apples, beer out of cans. Thinking the sea air might be cold, we had had a whisky to begin with – a mistake, for the fires of whisky deaden the delicate taste-buds.

The twelfth-century roofless church at one end of Lund bay: with gravestones of Dutch and German merchants – we visit that, maybe linger it out too long; for there's a last-minute dash to catch the ferry, and even then Gunnie sees places and creatures and scapes that *must* be photographed . . . The high road skirts the verge of a cliff. Here, as on the Grobsness road, are the kind of sheer falls one negotiates in nightmare.

But we're just in time for the ferry. There's a lorry on board with a cargo of crabs. The driver gives us a few crabs for our supper.

Another short sea-trip from Yell. We enter a stream of cars – oil workers – coming south from Sullom Voe to Lerwick.

The first summer burnish is on us. All four of us keep saying how lucky we are with the weather.

There's only one barb in my mind. Not one lyrical line has been attempted all day. Nor will there be, I'm too tired and sun-soaked.

Kulgin lights the fire. Colin puts on four crabs to boil. Gunnie goes swimming in the bay below.

We listen to a Beethoven quartet on the record-player, sipping a glass of whisky. Whisky, though magic on occasion – when you come in out of a storm, or have to meet disagreeable people, or have done a good day's work – can actually blunt enjoyment; this is the second time today it has happened. It works against natural contentment –

its power and glory should arm one against a temporary darkness or difficulty, or garland a victory, and then only to a limited extent; alcoholism comes of putting too much trust in it; then the dark destructive earth-strength enters which flesh cannot endure; not as should be, the joy of the sun-burnished wind-bent barley . . .

Supper was crab-claws and bread and Guinness.

Midnight was a slow gathering of moth-shadows and dewfall shadows, between early dawn and late sunset.

I realise, with a pang of reassurance, that man can live without radio or TV or newspapers. We have been happy without them for ten days.

8 June

Gunnie I think must know nearly everyone in Shetland, after a few visits while she and Liv Schei collaborated on *The Shetland Story*. That's the way it is with Gunnie; people tend towards the brightness of her nature. (I'm sure that, after a decade, she knows more people in Orkney than I, who have lived there all my life.) It's the difference between the open air and the cloister.

This morning Gunnie drove us to a garden kept by Rosa, a German lady. Not an ordinary garden either, but one presided over by the spirits of Linnaeus and Andrew Marvell. Colin was in his element in this museum of Flora, blessed by sun and wind, he being a highly talented gardener himself on the shore of Loch Tummel in Perthshire. He and Rosa exchanged Latin names, moving from plot to plot, while Kulgin and I sat in the stone garden seat sipping dry sherry, ignorant and contented. It is a garden of cats, and one cat is blind. Customers drove up from time to time to buy roots.

We had to get money from the bank in Lerwick. Colin remarked, while we wrote cheques at the counter, that it might be a good idea to buy fish for our supper. A small dark-haired girl, aged seven or eight, piped up in the most enchanting Shetlandic, 'Dere a fish-and-ship alang da street' . . . The few words put a delight into the entire day. I still smile to think of that small kind girl.

In the sun, against a wall near the harbour, lay a dozen young men and women with beer-cans . . .

We had rolls in a café, one white roll soft and tasteless as blotting paper, the bran roll with corned beef in it more substantial and toothsome.

The sherry, drunk too early, has gummed my thoughts. (Will I end my days preaching temperance?) But Lerwick, that seemed such a throbbing beehive on our last visit, is torpid today. I meet Brian Smith the local archivist on the street, who tells me the Grobsness district is haunted. My friends look into this shop window and that. I would like to hear more about the ghosts, but I have to follow them, fearful of losing myself in a strange town.

The green part of Shetland is in the south, towards Sumburgh. We see Mousa Broch in the distance, near where Adam Christie, the brave talented solitary sculptor, spent his early years before the asylum walls closed upon him, in Montrose.

A company of young folk are on a dig, directed by Beverley Smith, archaeologist, who lives near Stromness. They are camping in a Guide hall. I think we've chosen the wrong time to visit; they are beginning to eat their supper, a dozen or a score of them, after a hard cheerful day's rooting among the stones of pre-history. We get a courteous greeting, all the same, and white wine from Beverley . . . I learn later that one of the girls on the dig is wanting to meet me, and talk about books no doubt; to meet her is one of the reasons why we're here. But she was so shy she didn't come near, and other diggers were talking to us anyway . . . I wish, for others, that they wouldn't be so shy, but I am afflicted with the same trouble. Is it an affliction or a blessing? For shy people guard a mysterious 'might have been', and poetry is always latent. Others rush into the light too soon, and bring with them, like enough, frosts and gray airs. Life has always been a matter of instinct and most delicate judgement.

There was a little islet in a lochan. 'I'd get a wonderful picture,' says Gunnie, 'if the sun strikes the marigolds in the islet.' But the sun teased us, lingering, splashing briefly this field and that hillside, and leaving the marigolds to their own shadowed glory . . . We had more luck with a group of Shetland ponies.

It was another day soaked in light and happiness. A healthy hunger pleaded and cajoled and was at last stayed with fish soup and some curious but satisfying vegetable fry-up: Gunnie and Colin know what they're up to in the kitchen.

Another poemless day. Bees must forage before the honey is made: that's a small consolation. You can't always be sitting by the fire with a red notebook.

9 June

Joy, after breakfast: another prose-poem comes, 'Seven Skippers', straight on to the page.

This morning we go to the district of West Burra. Gunnie's mind is a card-index file of lovely houses and settings. Here at a place called Skarraness, is a house on a narrow isthmus, with a beach on either side. It seems to me, coming on it suddenly, there can be no more beautiful place in all the world. Kulgin and Colin think so too; they long to find out more about it, whether it might be for sale, etc.

We have our picnic on the bank above a little blue voe. Sun and wind have set a star of needling brilliance in every wandering wavelet below us. Fish soup from a flask, cheese rolls, ginger cake. 'Pure poetry' is what I find tritely written in my diary. How can a land-and-seascape be poetry; poetry is made of words; and I haven't the word-craft for a place like this. Forster, Lawrence, could do it. Best for lesser writers to keep silence . . .

'Look at that lamb!' The small creature on the bleak hill beside its mother, later that morning, was black with white feet and white tail and a white mask with two black eye-holes in the mask. But by the time the car stopped and reversed and Gunnie armed herself with a camera, the small harlequin and its mother had wandered off into a fold of the hills. The sun had gone behind a cloud, so that the lochan lost its light. Frustrating for Gunnie – the animals won't wait, like humanity, to pose.

Colin names plants in another lochan, then his eye catches a nest of oyster-catcher chicks, camouflaged. We stoop over them. Even with my new glasses, that have gifted me with pristine sight, I can't see the oyster-catcher chicks, Nature has protected them so well. We leave them to their solicitous circling scolding mother. The light teases the camera. Miles on, Gunnie wants to return to get pictures of the lamb and the lochan in golden sun-loops, but the sun is here and there, a sovereign spillage, everywhere but in the right place. 'I'll come back,' says Gunnie, 'once the sun gets up' . . . That will be in four or five hours' time only.

At the house, our landlords the Somervilles are cutting the grass. Their dog Woodhouse is with them. Tammy the cat rolls with joy in the dust of the road. Kulgin lights the fire and we worry the map to find the places we've visited today.

Little Tammy, Liz Somerville tells us, is twelve years old. She followed, long ago, the big shaggy marmalade cat (who sometimes appears) down from the hill, thin and starved. And here at Grobsness she has been ever since, and her big protector comes and goes . . . We got fonder and fonder of Tammy.

This Shetland air whets the hunger: mince patties, potatoes, carrots for supper, late.

Gunnie can't get that lochan and that hill with the lamb out of her mind: the challenge can't be avoided. She drives off in the pre-dawn, the camera in the car. Again, it was a disappointment in a way, for the dawn was scarfed in cloud. But, light or shadow, what Shetlanders call 'the simmer dim' is enchanting always.

This is our last night in Shetland.

10 June

Up 8 a.m.

A quick packing (breathless).

Egg and marmalade and thick oatcakes and tea.

Nagged by doubt – is my red notebook with the drafts of the poems in it lost? I don't remember packing it.

Wanted to say goodbye to Tammy the cat. But Tammy isn't there.

In Lerwick, Gunnie and Colin go to wool-shops. Kulgin and I have no relish for wool or shop windows. We go to Solotti's restaurant, where the waitresses wear milkmaid's caps, for coffee. Sun shines outside. The open-air drinkers with their beer-cans sit at the sun-bright wall above the pier.

What a drama our coffee-drinking causes! The wool-hunters somehow think K. and I have gone on a farewell-to-Shetland binge. They have searched the waterfront bars for us. And here we sit coffee-sober, while the waitresses in milkmaid hats come and go. They *are* relieved, our friends.

Say goodbye to Kulgin and Colin; they'll fly on to Inverness, then drive to the west coast; while we drift down the curve of gray water between Shetland and Orkney.

The nice woman car-hirer drives us to the *Sunniva*. Gunnie humps both our cases up thirty-six clanging metal steps of the gangway . . . Just to drag my old bones and breath is enough.

Bressay Sound breaks the sun into glittering galaxies.

At noon the *Sunniva* casts off.

After Sumburgh and Fitful Head, a freshening wind blows thin sea-haar about us.

Gunnie and I lunch in the cafeteria. I play safe as always and have fish. Gunnie has mince-in-pasta. (I forget the name; everyone eats it nowadays; it was unheard of in my childhood, when there was 'mince and tatties' only. So I'm only too willing to forget the name of Italian and Greek dishes . . . It might be 'pyella'?)

Another Orkney photographer, Charles Tait, has been on a quick expedition to Shetland with his cameras: the North Mainland, Yell, Unst. We have a drink together and don't notice Fair Isle slipping past on the port side. That's twice we've missed it.

Another of Gunnie's myriad acquaintances joins us, Chrissie – a New Zealander – whose husband is a composer in Yell.

You can buy the *Orcadian* on board. I skim through it. I've been contributing a series of short impressionistic articles on Shetland.

How the sea air hones appetites! Gunnie asks what I want to eat. 'A cheeseburger, maybe' . . . I think, in my innocence, it will be grilled cheese in a hot roll. No, there's a hamburger in addition – the roll so thick I can hardly get my jaws clamped round it.

Now there's no land to be seen. We're on the curve of water between the archipelagos, the old Viking route.

An accident – the thick new left lens jumps out of my glasses; a tiny screw has worked loose. Five minutes earlier, and the lens would be trundling about on the ocean floor between the Atlantic and the North Sea. We'd been leaning over the rail watching the sea.

And there, to the south-east, dimly (because of distance, haar, and my bereaved vision), Westray, the first of the Orkneys.

Gunnie comes to say, Captain Duncan has invited us up to the bridge – a spacious area walled with glass, fitted with radar and all the latest navigational aids, which Captain Duncan explains to us. But my untechnological mind can't take much of it in.

But now, headland by headland, Orkney steps out to meet us: Brough of Birsay (the isle where St Magnus was buried and from where his grandfather, Earl Thorfinn, 'ruled nine earldoms' in Scotland) – Marwick Head – Yesnaby.

Gunnie points: 'The Black Craig!' Beyond, the tawny curve of Warbeth beach. Like guardians on the opposite shore, the Kame of Hoy and Graemsay of the two lighthouses.

They unfold like a fan; Houton, Scapa Flow, Flotta the oil island with its flame-tipped column (hardly visible in the summer light) and the southern islands – as the *St Sunniva* edges through Hoy Sound and turns left.

We have made good time. It is 7.30 on an early summer evening, with the solstice only eleven days off.

On the pier at Stromness, a dog whines and runs here and there and barks in wildest excitement, and can hardly contain himself. It is Nuff, Gunnie's dog. He has heard her voice from the ship's rail. At the gangway's foot, he leaps at her with delight!

A drift of letters in my lobby. Margaret and Renée have scoured the threefold window-panes to glittering grids, in my living-room.

Look in the case. Yes, the red notebook with the poems is there, among shirts and socks and bottles of medicinal tablets and books. All's well.

A house never looks so happy as when you've been out of it for a few days – as if it was glad to see you.

Stromness 1988

The First Wash of
Spring:
April 1996

THIS MORNING – AS I write – is 3 April, and the first wash of Spring has gone over the earth.

It is such a beautiful word – April – that even to utter it lightens the heart. It is a little poem in itself. It is full of delightful images. It has its own music – trembling lamb-cries at the end of a field. The first daring lark lost in light. You feel, in April, that you have come through another winter, a little bruised maybe, but unbowed.

Those chalices of light, the daffodils, having been sorely battered by the March storms, are shedding, one by one, their green covers and opening their vernal tapers. Soon all of Orkney will be stitched by golden threads of daffodils, a lovely spread garment for Primavera. (Goodness, I seem to have got my images all confused there – chalices, tapers, coats – but one may be allowed a little exuberance, tasting now the first wine of Spring. Wine! There's another image to add to the heap!)

So we ought to relish each one of the thirty days of April, the month that tastes of childhood. Easter, too, often falls in April, and 16 April is that wonderful day in the Orkney calendar, the martyrdom of St Magnus in Egilsay.

Most of the months in the calendar have their own beautiful names. May is when the cuithes have their first drink of the floods, and come swarming in to keep their ancient tryst with men (and of course with women, too, I hasten to add, for you can't be too careful nowadays, with all those militant ladies around, and what about the children? – they have their own rites and secrets that are lost to us adults). But still with a word like mankind – who in their senses would want to use personkind?

I have digressed a long way.

The word 'June' is beautiful too, of course, but like May it has a curtness that lacks the lyricism of 'April'. In midsummer there is perhaps too much – what month-name devised by man could hope to contain the light and multitudinous beauties of the season? Best to be simple and brief, to hold the word to the nostrils like a plucked wild clover . . . Such enchantment, under the light that never leaves the

333

sky – not at midnight even. But, of course, in the name of progress and 'enlightenment' we have sacrificed the ancient ceremonies of midsummer, the fires on every hilltop in every parish and island. (There is a price to be paid for Progress; already the 'tabs' are being shown us, one after the other. But let that be, meantime.)

I had hoped to cut a swathe through all the month-names in the year. But alas I have run out of space – and besides, I'm sure we have been that way before; and if there is one thing a writer must beware of, it is to offer second-hand goods to his readers.

11 April 1996[*]

[*] 'The First Wash of Spring' is the last piece that George Mackay Brown wrote before his death.

GLOSSARY

BEDE-HOUSE: prayer-house.

BERE BANNOCKS: scones made with bere (a form of barley).

BLACK-HOUSE: a primitive house in the Highlands and Islands, built of stone.

BOGIE: cylindrical iron stove, common during the Second World War.

BROCH: a circular dry-stone tower.

BUCKLE'S TOWER: A Finstown folly.

CAISIE: a basket of woven straw or heather.

CLEG: a horsefly.

CLOSE-COIGN: a dark alley.

CRUISIE-LAMP: oil lamp.

CUITHE: an older coal-fish.

DARG: a day's work.

DOO: dove or pigeon.

DWINE: to waste or pine away.

FORBY: besides; in addition to.

GRIMLINGS: gloaming; twilight.

GROTTIE: cowrie shell.

HAAR: a cold sea mist or fog off the North Sea.

HANSEL: a gift for good luck at the beginning of a new year.

HIRPLING: limping.

HOWFF: a haunt, especially a public house.

KIRN: a churn.

LAVEROCK: skylark.

LOWE: flame.

MAKAR: a creative artist, especially a poet.

MELL: to mingle or mix.

MELLIFICATION: (lit.) honey-making.

MUIRBURN: burning off old growth on a heather moor to encourage new growth for grazing.

NEUK: nook.

NOUST: sheltered inlet for small boats.

ORKAHOWE: Viking name for Maeshowe.

PADDOCK-SHAPED: shaped like a toad.

PEEDIE FOLK: fairies.

Glossary

ROOST: a powerful current caused by conflicting tides around the Orkney and Shetland islands.
SHELTER: a wartime air-raid shelter.
SILLOCK: a young coal-fish, at a certain stage of its first year.
SIXAREEN: a six-oared boat.
SIXERN: as above.
SKALLOWIRT: segment of sky between the Ward hill of Hoy and the Coolags, as seen from Stromness. A local weather gauge.
SNELL: biting, bitter, sharp.
SOOAN SCONES: scones made from fermented oatmeal.
STEETHE-STONE: foundation stone.
TEEACK: lapwing.
THIRL: to enslave or bind.
THOLE: to put up with, bear; to suffer.
THRID: past participle of thread.
TOOM: empty.
TROW: fairy, troll.
UGSOME: horrible, loathsome.
WARD: highest hill in a parish.
WHET: finished with; quit.
WHITEMAA: seagull.
YOLE: Orkney variant of 'yawl', a small fishing boat.